EPIC TRAILS

– Endless Tracks Across Centuries

– Endless Tracks Across Centuries

EPIC TRAILS -ENDLESS TRACKS ACROSS CENTURIES

BY

CONRAD L. (CONNIE) COX

AND

DR. JIM SCOTT

PHOTOGRAPHY BY

CAL SORENSON

INTRODUCTION BY

CONRAD BURNS
UNITED STATES SENATOR, MONTANA

COVER PAINTING BY

BRIAN MORGER

PUBLISHED BY

SILVER SAGE IMPRESSIONS
193 GERBER ROAD – P.O. BOX 6370
GREAT FALLS, MONTANA 59406

SILVER SAGE IMPRESSIONS
193 Gerber Road – P.O. Box 6370
Great Falls, Montana 59406

Limited Edition Printing - 1991
ISBN 1-879228-00-9
First Printing Hard Cover - 1991
ISBN 1-879228-01-7
First Printing Perfect Bound - 1991
ISBN 1-879228-02-5

Book Design by The Bar Two Outfit

Published by Silver Sage Impressions

Printed in Bozeman, Montana, by Color World Printers

Manufactured in the United States of America
By Montanans

ABOUT THE AUTHORS, PHOTOGRAPHER AND ARTIST

CONRAD "CONNIE" COX

A lifetime of ranching and rodeoing in Montana and a profound respect for the land and its creatures make Connie Cox uniquely qualified to share the experiences and reflections related in *EPIC TRAILS - Endless Tracks Across Centuries,* a brief glimpse through a window between centuries. His free spirited outlook gives the reader an opportunity to feel a reverence for epics past. At the same time one can experience with this man of simplicity and sincerity the challenge of bright horizons ahead.

DR. JIM SCOTT

A broad acquaintance with ranching and cattle people through his practice of food animal veterinary medicine has encouraged Dr. Scott to try sizing up many of the issues facing animal agriculture today. The honesty of mind and freedom from pretense he has seen in many of the people he is fortunate to work with is exemplified by the character and spirit of people like Connie Cox. He prefers rational informed activism to blind misinformed reactionaryism. The thought processes of the mind that ultimately flow through the fingertips must be incisive, regardless of whether the instrument delivering those processes may be a pen, scalpel or brush. Though not always possible, ideally, the impressions resulting should be crisp and clear cut.

Photography by
CAL SORENSON

Following years of working in the Los Angeles film community and doing commercial advertising photography, Cal Sorenson moved a few years ago to Montana to work on a photographic portrayal of the Myths and Legends of the Plains Indians. Cal skillfully combines photography and artistry. He is intrigued by the vast reaches encompassed in the mind and in the region by these myths and legends. He is also taken by the inroads made into this vastness by the arduous treks of 19th Century cowboys and cattle as they criss-crossed Western America and Canada to mingle with those earlier trails which made up a part of those myths and legends.

Cover Painting by
BRIAN MORGER

Noted Montana artist, Brian Morger has a fascination for nostalgia, history and architecture. Brian has always been concerned with the "mood" he conveys in his art. He wants all five senses affected by his paintings, not just sight. The temperature, humidity, wind, aroma and sounds are equally important for his audience to experience. With his painted rendering of *EPIC TRAILS – Endless Tracks Across Centuries,* Brian has also managed to capture a sense of time separation and extension, placing events of aeons into a fleeting moment.

NOTES TO ADDITIONAL CREDITS

As it was not possible for any one person to be at every location one might have liked to have been during the Great Montana Centennial Cattle Drive, and because a portion of the content of *EPIC TRAILS – Endless Tracks Across Centuries* has to do with earlier years and events in the life of Connie Cox, certain photographs appearing in this book were not taken by our feature photographer, Cal Sorenson. Credits for these additional photographs which include some earlier scenes of Connie and his family rodeoing, and certain additional Cattle Drive photographs, appear appropriately adjacent to the given photograph at its location in the book.

All other photographs, not so credited, were taken expressly by Cal Sorenson for use in *EPIC TRAILS – Endless Tracks Across Centuries*. These include many beautiful scenes which Mr. Sorenson made a special extra effort to capture for *EPIC TRAILS* besides those he took while trailing with the Cattle Drive. We are especially indebted to him for such additional scenes as those he photographed of cattle swimming across the Bow River as they were moved from summer to winter range by Neil McKinnon and Bob Hale and their crew, and those he took over a wide area of Montana to illustrate the great contrast this beautiful state has between its "mountainous regions" and the vast panoramas of the immensity of the Missouri Plateau. We feel the eye of Cal's camera has been able to capture the essence of *Endless Tracks Across Centuries* in a way that allows the reader/viewer to bridge the expanse of time through which the various trails made their impressions upon the land.

Pen and ink line illustrations appearing in *EPIC TRAILS* were drawn by author, Dr. Jim Scott, were used to illustrate various Annual Legends of Rodeo Programs published by the Montana Legends of Rodeo Association, are copyrighted by Dr. Scott and The Bar Two Outfit, and reprinted here with their permission.

The poems, "Didn't He Know. . . .?" and "The Misfit" were written expressly for Connie Cox by his friend, Buster Barbee, of Winnett, Montana, and are published here for the first time with the permission of Mr. Barbee.

The poems, "An Old Time Cordial (A Toast To Friendship)," "A Night Watch Prayer," And "Cactus, Yuccas and Rocks" were written by Dr. Jim Scott, are copyrighted by Dr. Scott and The Bar Two Outfit, and reprinted here with their permission.

"An Old Time Cordial (A Toast To Friendship)" and "A Night Watch Prayer" were first presented at The Montana Cowboy Poetry Gathering, in Big Timber, Montana, during August, 1989. "An Old Time Cordial (A Toast To Friendship)" also has appeared in an original painting with the same title and hangs in a private collection. "Cactus, Yuccas And Rocks" was written for the Montana Legends of Rodeo Association, and first appeared in their Seventh Annual Legends of Rodeo Enduring Heritage Commemorative Calendar for 1990.

The poem "The Badlands" was written by John D. Munn and is reprinted in *EPIC TRAILS* with the authors permission. We especially wish to thank Mike Korn, formerly Folklorist for the State of Montana and now with the Montana Department of Fish, Wildlife and Parks, for his assistance in tracing and varifying information.

The names, "Latigo," "The Great Montana Centennial Cattle Drive of 1989" and "The Big Drive of '89" were originated by Latigo Corporation, along with the official "$\frac{M}{89}$" Cattle Drive Brand. These entities appear in *EPIC TRAILS* with the express permission of Latigo Corporation.

Silver Sage Impressions and the authors of *EPIC TRAILS – Endless Tracks Across Centuries* also wish to thank those who gave permission for the publication of the personal letters in the "Letters" section of *EPIC TRAILS*.

Any omissions or errors with regard to appropriate credit for any other material used or referenced in the publication of this book are the responsibilities of the authors and are unintentional.

DEDICATION

Dedicated to the memory of my mother, Bertha Sargent Cox, (April 24, 1909 - November 19, 1985); and dedicated to my wife, Margie, and sons, Casey and Clinton, and daughter, Charlene, and their families; and to my good friends, and I consider them family, too, Vic and Verlie Hanson. These people especially, are the ones who have made my life what it is today.

Dedicated also to the memories of those old time cowboys and homesteaders who came to Montana 100 years ago to start the foundations upon which we have been able to build. Without those foundations there would be much less of the likelihood of a Montana Legacy to share with the generations whose responsibility it will be to provide the continuing stewardship of that Legacy. For Tia, Cash, Cassidy, Cayla, and Calli's, generation and those to follow I wish happy trails and bright horizons, because the responsibilities being passed on are not easy.

And dedicated, as well, to my rodeo cowboy friends, who I rodeoed with from 1953 to 1973.

C. L. C.

Dedicated to Daphne, whose courage, fighting spirit, and positive outlook serves as inspiration to us all during some very trying times, to Daphne's big brother, Jim, who has been just that, a big brother and friend, and especially to their mother, Lillamay, my bride of nearly three decades, who married me for "better or worse" in 1962. She has endured and forgiven a lot of the "worse" and still has the light in her eyes and lilt in her voice that first made her so beautiful to me. They are all waiting, if not with complete patience, at least with kind understanding, for me to find a bit of the "better" to share. Without my family, this book could not have been written. Thank you, and God Bless you.

Dedicated, also, to those other generations of pioneering women whom I have been so privileged to be loved and taught by, and from whose presence and memories I continue to draw strength, as I have since I can first remember my mother's hand on my shoulder, foot by my chair, and voice saying, "Come, now, it's not so difficult, and you can do it!" To my mother Lyndall (March 14, 1901 - November 14, 1983) and Lillian, my mother-in-law, who is still very active and vivacious, and to grandmothers, now gone, Jessica and Flora, and Elizabeth and May, my heartfelt thanks for what you do and did to lighten the loads of others and brighten the lives and home fires of all who have known you.

Dedicated as well, to the same generations of men, whose fortunes were best marked by sharing those home fires. Respectively, my dad, Kenneth E. Scott, who at 86, so wanted to participate in the "Big Drive of '89" and would have, had circumstances been different, my bride's dad, Lawrence E. Mascall (December 9, 1907 - November 23, 1971), and our grandfathers, now also gone, Walter H. Deming, John M. Scott, James Cant and Billy Mascall. Their hard work, integrity, and steadfastness provided the foundation for the best inheritance future generations could have; the ability and ethic to use one's head and hands.

And dedicated finally to Lou's pet cow, "April" and her decade and a half of contribution to the fullness of our family's life while re-creating through the generations of her own descendents of Longhorns and Longhorn crosses, a bovine family representative of the 100 years of the cattle industry on these plains and ranges, which "The Great Montana Centennial Cattle Drive of 1989" commemorated. While you and I didn't always agree about some of my meager, but well meant, professional ministrations to you and yours, "Dear Old Girl," I know you know, I meant for the best, and we thank you for what you taught us about love and family and patience and kindness. Thank you for helping us to empathize better the true and rewarding relationship possible among all creatures, great and small!

J.A.S.

INTRODUCTION

It is not often we have the opportunity to read and enjoy a book that is as authentic as this one. I can think of no one person who has a closer relationship with this land than cowboy/author, Connie Cox.

Connie Cox of Whitewater, Montana, knows these trails. He is a man, a cowboy, stockman and rancher, who was born of this land, and has ridden over it on good horses. He is a husband, father and grandfather, who married and with his good wife, Margie, has raised his family on this land. With this book, he has helped to preserve, and to pass on to future generations, the values and knowledge that only God and open ranges teach.

Connie Cox is the living spirit of the West and it was qualities such as his that settled the West and which will continue to sustain this Great Nation. There is a little touch of the cowboy in every American.

Connie Cox is a true son of the West and I call him friend. Enjoy!

Conrad Burns
United States Senator, Montana

FOREWORD

EPIC TRAILS – Endless Tracks Across Centuries, is a brief look into the story of the authentic West, as seen through the eyes of Connie Cox, Montana cattleman who's ranched, rodeoed and raised a family in the always beautiful, but often difficult Big Sky country. This Montana land, rich with history, vast under its awe-inspiring sky, ready for those who live here to celebrate its first century birthday as the 41st state, is a land of rugged breaks and mountains. Hence its name, a Latin derivation, meaning "Mountainous Regions." It is also a land of high plains, rolling prairies, stark buttes and the headwaters of many streams and rivers so vital to Montana and those who live here, and contributing life-giving waters to wide other regions far beyond Montana's immense borders.

This brief look allows one to follow the tracks of teams and wagons and of Connie Cox's Longhorn cattle as they retrace trails of earlier times and as they trail some 240 miles from Connie's ranch on Frenchman Creek at the Canadian Border to the town of Roundup, Montana, settled on the banks of the Musselshell River. Roundup is at a location on the Musselshell where Buffalo once watered and crossed, and near points where the Western Trail, which succeeded the Chisolm Trail of the 1870s, spilled thousands of head of Texas cattle onto the Montana ranges and many on into Canada.

Roundup is thus a fitting place to serve as trailhead for assembly of a drive of cattle, wagons and riders which will be reminiscent of those arduous treks North of more than a century ago. Here Connie Cox's Longhorn cows will join up with other cattle and a wagon train to trail into Billings on the rims of the Yellowstone River with the "Great Montana Centennial Cattle Drive of 1989."

The "Big Drive of '89" will not only commemorate Montana's 100th Birthday as one of these United States of America; it will also commemorate a historic tradition, a life-style built on hard work ethics and often maintained with nothing more than sheer determination and a deep love for the land. The event does not begin to describe the people who live here; generations of hard-working ranching folk who battle the winds of fortune and the whims of nature to survive. Who are these people?

– Endless Tracks Across Centuries

Connie Cox is one of them, and *EPIC TRAILS* is his story in part, a window giving a brief glimpse into a unique lifetime; but it is also the story of his friends and neighbors. It reflects a way of life cherished by many and yearned for by many more. It's a western saga of Montana ranching and an effort by a ranch family to forge a living from the land despite obstacles.

Connie's story is that of the many who have prevailed, as those before them did, with skills handed down from generation to generation, from father to son, often with the only other help being that of a reliable saddle horse and a good and faithful cowdog, and on occasion, a willing neighbor. Often all a man had was his saddle and tack, a sharp knife and lariat rope. The only tools at hand were those he could carry or make from what he could find along the trail.

Trailing the 34 days from Frenchman Creek to the Yellowstone River, Connie kept a journal where he recorded events of the trail and thoughts and reflections on this way of life, long cherished, but in many ways in danger of extinction. The notations are often brief and like Connie's conversation, one may need to read what is left unsaid as importantly as that which is noted. This Drive, little adorned, and in most ways not much changed from those of a hundred years ago, bridges the years between old tribulations and new challenges, but the struggle to preserve the timeless values remains.

Share the experiences of the old and the new; the vision, feelings and observations of a western cattleman who loves his heritage. Independent and self-reliant, he doesn't seek hand-outs, rather only to tell his story. And through the doing, to share with others the importance of life: Family, friends, self-respect and love of country; and of the simple things: Grass, water, livestock, wildlife and the open sky. He asks only the freedom to continue the God-granted stewardship of the soil that sustains all living things.

J.A.S

– Endless Tracks Across Centuries

LETTERS

Roundup, Montana
September 9, 1989

Dear Connie and Crew,

I guess one is never too old to write her first fan letter so at age 59 I'm going to give it a try. I want to tell you how much I enjoyed the Cattle Drive this week as one of the thousands of spectators, and I really appreciated all the efforts that you and people like you made in order to make the Drive a reality. It was so great that I was absolutely speechless and emotionally stunned as I watched the spectacle. Nothing in my life ever matched that tremendous scene and, unless there is another Drive, I doubt if anything ever will.

When I heard about the Drive and the people who were getting publicity for it, I honestly believed it would be a disaster. Until the *Roundup Record-Tribune* published the names of those signed up and I saw names like yours, I was skeptical. Once I read the *Gazette* article and your bringing your herd from the Highline, I became a believer, and from then on I've just enjoyed everything.

You said people thought you were crazy of others thought you were a hero. It takes a lot of both to become a Legend and you fellows are part of an Epic event.

If you decide to make it an annual event to keep this part of Montana life alive, I'd like to volunteer to help even if it is with the most menial tasks. I'd consider it an honor.

I've ordered the Latigo video, the Roundup cable video of the Roundup parade, copies of Channel 2 News coverage of the Drive, and videos taken every day by some young fellows. If you'd like to borrow them to make some copies just let me know. Since I don't have T.V. or video V.C.R., I haven't seen them all yet, but I'm working on it.

I know I speak for thousands when I say thanks to you and yours for the part you played in the Cattle Drive. I appreciate it greatly. Good luck to you all.

Sincerely,

Mary Sweeney Brower

Mary Sweeney Brower

Dr. James A. Scott
Bar Two Research & Development
193 Gerber Road - P.O. Box 6370
Great Falls, Montana 59406

September 23, 1989

Latigo Corporation, Directors of
The Great Montana Centennial Cattle Drive of 1989
P.O. Box 1989
Billings, Montana 59101

Friends at Latigo:

The Great Montana Centennial Cattle Drive of 1989 is History! As Chairman of the Montana Veterinary Medical Association ad-hoc Cattle Drive Committee and Member of Latigo's Advisory Board, I want to thank each and every person who cooperated in true grass roots Montana spirit to bring about one of the greatest, most colorful, memorable, and proud events in Montana's 100 years of Statehood.

I especially wish to thank my M.V.M.A. Cattle Drive Committee Members who worked on detail after detail to coordinate what proved to be a very smooth and effective Animal Health and Emergency Care Plan. This work preceded the Trail Drive during the entire period of nearly 20 months and continued right through staging, processing, the Drive and Wagon Train, themselves, and until after the sales in Billings on Monday and Tuesday, September 11 and 12.

M.V.M.A. Cattle Drive Committee Members are: Dr. Ray W. Randall, Bridger, Montana; Dr. Brent D. Thompson, Roundup, Montana; Dr. Diana Scollard, Absarokee, Montana; Dr. John A. Beug, Red Lodge, Montana; Dr. John P. Murphy, Deer Lodge, Montana.

The above wonderful people all pitched in and carried on for the M.V.M.A. and Latigo when my summer of 1989 became very disrupted by a major medical emergency in my family.

In addition to my Committee, we had an exceptional group of veterinarians who volunteered a tremendous effort at the County level, during the staging and processing into the Trailhead at Roundup, participated in the Drive and Wagon Train, as riders and with teams and wagons, or provided back-up Veterinary medical support and services with mobile veterinary ambulatory clinics, and opened the doors of their veterinary hospitals for haul-in patient care.

This group includes: DR. E.S. (GENE) ABY, Glendive; DR. ORLEY ARTHUR, Roundup; DR. ROGER BAXTER, Chinook; DR. DAVID BERST, Billings; DR. VICTORIA R. BOKUM, Shepherd; DR. JERRY BILLQUIST, Great Falls; DR. WILBUR CLARK, Dept. of Lvstk,, Helena; DR. DUANE C. COLMEY, Livingston; DR, JIM CURTIS, Malta; DR. DON FERLICKA, Dept. of Lvstk,, Helena; DR. JOHN W. GEE, Stanford; DR. E. ERIC GOULD, Laurel,; DR. MICHAEL J. HAALAND, Billings; DR. FRANK HOULE, Dept. of Lvstk., Helena;

Continued on next page

DR. OWEN JAMES, Dept. of Lvstk., Helena; DR. LAUREL KELLY, Corvallis; DR. RICHARD KINYON, Conrad; DR. RAYMOND LIEN, Columbus; DR. JUDY A. LYNCOLN, Roundup; DR. CHARLIE R. NOLAND, Circle; DR. N.D. (PAT) PATTERSON, Miles City; DR. BILL P. PATTON, Cascade; DR. WILLIAM R. RATHS, Lewistown; DR. FRED R. SCHMIDT, Billings; DR. ROBERT C. SCHMITT, Chinook; DR. J. GREG TOOKE, Ekalaka; DR. ROBERT WELBORN, Broadus; DR. D. E. WOERNER, Laurel.

In addition, this group had the help of DR. ROB MYERS, M.V.M.A. Secretary/Treasurer, Bozeman, Montana; DR. VERN TRAIL and DR. GAIL TRAIL, Moose Jaw, Saskatchewan; DR. BAXTER BLACK, Brighton, Colorado.

Latigo and Cattle Drive participants owe a particular "Thank You" to the Montana Legends of Rodeo Association of Great Falls, Montana, and Legends of Rodeo President, Bill Davis, of Great Falls, for donating the courtesy use of a brand new 4 place Jackson Horse Trailer and 4 Wheel Drive pickup to serve as an Emergency Animal Care Transport Ambulance and Mobile Command Post for Veterinary Services, during the "Big Drive of '89." A thank you is due also to G.T.A. Feed Company of Great Falls, for allowing Bill Davis the time to serve as driver of this Ambulance and to assist me in transporting sick, injured, or otherwise distressed horses and cattle to Veterinary Hospitals at either end of the Trail Drive, when these animals needed additional care to that which our doctors provided right on the trail or in camp at night.

We transported a total of 27 horses to either Roundup Veterinary Clinic or to Billings Heights Veterinary Hospital, who kept their doors open 24 hours around the clock during the entire Drive to accommodate and care for these animals. A number of cattle were also transported by support vehicle to either Roundup or Billings. Most of these horses and cattle were able to return to the Drive to complete the trek into Billings.

I wish to especially thank the following Veterinary Products Companies for donations of a good many thousand dollars worth of Animal Health Products to Latigo through our M.V.M.A. Cattle Drive Committee. These products helped the volunteer doctors to care for sick or injured animals on the trail, helped prevent problems from occurring; as with pre-immunization of cattle and horses with vaccines at the County level, prior to the Drive; or added value to Consigned Trail Drive Cattle when they sold at Billings Livestock Commission Co., or at Public Auction Yard Sales Co. in Billings: Norden Laboratories, Lincoln, Nebraska; *"Cattle Master 4 Vaccine;"* The Upjohn Co., Kalamazoo, Michigan; *"Naxel" Antimicrobial;* Northwest Veterinary Supply, Portland, Oregon, and Great Falls, Montana; *I.V. Fluids, Bandages, Topicals;* Merck & Co., MSD/Ag-Vet, Billings, Montana, Distr.; *"Ivomec" Cattle Dewormer;* Walco, International, Billings, and Great Falls, Montana Distrs.; *Topical wound dressings and Bandages;* Parker Livestock/Intermountain, Billings, Montana; *I.V. Fluids, Wound Dressings, Sutures, and Sports Medicine Products;* Fort Dodge Laboratories, Fort Dodge, Iowa; *Anesthetics, Sedatives, Analgesics;* 3-M Companies, Minneapolis, Minnesota; *Support Wraps and Bandages;* and numerous others; including the attending volunteer Veterinary Doctors, and Clinics for materials and supplies donated out of their own Mobile Clinic Stocks.

Continued on next page

A special "Thanks" to Motorola Communications and all their good people for untold help and use of equipment.

And also, a special "Thank You" to Drovers, Wranglers, and all Support Staff who by being alert and communicative, noticed lamenesses, or other problems, averted many injuries or other mishaps, and kept serious animal injury and health problems to an absolute minimum.

The following provided Veterinary Services Support Wagons, Mobile Veterinary Clinics or other support vehicles and Staff: Neil McKinnon, High River, Alberta; Radio Command Post Back-up, and Veterinary Supply Dispensary, with the Chuckwagon Camp, Main Herd; O.E. (Gene) Johnson, Sand Coulee, Montana; Veterinary Supply Wagon, Drovers' Camp, Main Herd.

Wagons and Teams with the Wagon Train were provided and staffed by the following: YELLOW WAGON CIRCLE–Dr. Ray Lein; BROWN WAGON CIRCLE–Dr. Roger Baxter; GREEN WAGON CIRCLE–Dr. Gene Aby; PURPLE WAGON CIRCLE–Dr. Charlie Noland; ORANGE WAGON CIRCLE–Dr. Jim Curtis; BLACK WAGON CIRCLE–Jack Hash, and Dr. John Beug; PINK WAGON CIRCLE–Ken Connor.

Mobile Veterinary Clinics providing back-up included: Dr. Ray Randall, Dr. Duane Colmey, Dr. Vicki Bokum, and Dr. Judy Lyncoln.

Additional Support Vehicles were provided and manned by: Chet and Moe Duffy, Lewistown; Jess Satterfield, Lewistown; John Denning, Lewistown; and Ray Smith, Great Falls.

Thanks. It was a great Cattle Drive and a great week for Montana, September 4-9, 1989.

Sincerely yours,

Dr. Jim Scott, Chairman
M.V.M.A. Cattle Drive Committee

cc. MVMA Annual Meeting
    Report and Files

Chicago, Illinois
November 17, 1989

Dear Mr. Cox and Family,

Here and now in Chicago it is early evening. My husband, Al and I watch the day moving going West just as we did this past August and September.

About 20 years ago our friends, Cliff and Nancy Banks, gave up Chicago for Sand Point, Idaho. We made constant elusive promises to visit them. We finally kept our promise this year, driving through parts of Wisconsin, Minnesota, North Dakota, and the wonderful, beautiful surprise of our lives, Montana.

And there was and remains the bonus memory of the Great Montana Centennial Cattle Drive. Lucky we purchased many extra copies of local Montana newspapers, bringing these accounts of this event back home to families and grandchildren and friends. Every time I read and view the pictures of this Great Cattle Drive, I realize the awesome responsibility, the awesome job, and the happiness of all the families and all the men who provide, by their labors and sacrifices, to grow the food for the entire world.

Also I see in these pictures the pride of the men for their job, "WELL DONE."

There is a train that rides its rails in our area; sometimes when dawn stretches awake this train whistle sounds an awakening voice that seems to say, — MONNNNTAAAANNA — MONNNNTAAAANNA — you know the way a train can do such a thing. When we hear that train whistle or when we see a sunset that has the colors of the West in it we hope some day again to see Montana.

We did not see the Great Cattle Drive arriving in Billings, Montana, as we had other commitments, but you may be sure that you, your family and friends were thought of with kindness. In the meantime we are thankful that we have seen Montana once upon a very special time.

AGAIN I MUST SAY ... Mr. Cox, when I see your picture on the front page of the *Billings Gazette,* dated August 31, 1989, on this Thanksgiving Day I will see all that you and your family provide so many with, not only food, but PRIDE in a job well done, AND THE FEELING OF HAPPINESS IN THE DOING OF IT ALL.

Thank you for the food that sustains body, mind and heart.

Cordially,

Dorothy Majer Sky

Marjorie Cox
Cox ZN Ranch
Box 124
Whitewater, Montana 59544

(Letter Undated - 1990)

Dear Jim -

Hope you are doing okay. I know you are really busy, but I'm sure it will be worth it.

Sent a few pictures of kids and Connie roping. I'm sure you won't be able to use very many, but thought it might give you a few ideas of Connie and kids competing. The kids have given us some great moments in our lives. They started young and won in the NRA, College, and Casey qualifying for the National Pro-Rodeo Cowboys' Association Finals in 1988, at Las Vegas, Nevada!

This isn't anything that a lot of other people haven't done, but they had to do it on their own. They bought their own horses and when Casey was 15, he went roping all summer and roped against and with the top men competitors and had to pay his own way.

I guess the main thing is they all had the ambition and try instilled in them at an early age by Connie and (it) seems to have helped them become good solid citizens. Connie was a great Dad when the kids were growing up – he took all three with him all the time and is now getting to enjoy the grandkids.

I'm sure you're finding out writing this book how many people Connie has met, or they have heard of him. We had a hunter that was here for the first time last Fall and he took a trip to Wyoming a couple of weeks ago. He is from North Carolina, and phoned when he got home. He said he ran into people from Wyoming and Montana and everyone he asked if they knew Connie, and many did. He is coming back this Fall and said he, "didn't know he was staying with someone so well known when he was here the first time!"

Also, when the Flatwillow Christian Community Hutterite girls came all the way from Winnett just to sing for Connie at his roping school – they said, "We wouldn't have traveled that far for anyone else!"

In 1960, Connie went to Chicago to ride at a rodeo – he stayed at a motel, and across the street was an Italian restaurant that they ate at. Connie got to visiting with the owner and the next year I went with him when he went back – they treated us like royalty. They took us all over Chicago – wouldn't let us pay for hardly any of our meals – they had lived all their lives in the same home and didn't hardly know their next door neighbor, but yet they took to Connie.

(continued on next page)

We have met so many wonderful people rodeoing and have really been blessed with our family and doing the things we like.

We were at a roping this weekend and quite a few of the ropers had heard what a good roping we had this year. I was telling them we would probably quit after 2 more years, as that will be 20 years. They all said Connie should keep it going as Connie has kept it going when almost all the other ropings have quit after a few years because they take a lot of work and planning. They said even if they couldn't make it every year, they always hear about the good time everyone has. I think this says a lot. Connie has always been more concerned that people have a good time and go home with some good memories even if he comes out short putting the roping on.

I wrote on back of some of pictures. We have a tape taken of Connie feeding cows from his airplane. He's feeding blocks – dropping them from the air – you might want to see it some time.

If you need any help just let us know. Hope you can read my scribbling. –

Take Care –

Marjorie

Marjorie

ALLEN C. KOLSTAD
LIEUTENANT GOVERNOR

State of Montana
Office of The Lieutenant Governor
Helena 59620
(406)444·3111

October 1, 1990

Dear Readers,

Montana's exciting Centennial Year, 1989, was celebrated by Montana citizens and visitors alike. Individuals and cooperative groups planned and developed thousands of events throughout Montana; and visitors returned to, or arrived in Montana for their first look at, our beautiful 100 year-old Big Sky State. Centennial activities ranged from family reunions to publishing community histories never before put down on paper, from bell ringing ceremonies to Centennial balls, and from wagon trains to operas; but, possibly the largest, most complex, historic, Centennial undertaking, was the Great Montana Centennial Cattle Drive.

As Chairman of the Montana Statehood Centennial Commission and as Lieutenant Governor of Montana, I was privileged to participate in numerous Centennial activities including the Great Montana Centennial Cattle Drive. I've been told that the "real" Centennial Cattle Drive was nothing like any seen in the movies or on TV, and I can tell you that this was true. There were a variety of serious and humorous experiences from the trip that I'm certain will be shared with friends and neighbors and enjoyed and remembered for years to come. Montanans can say with pride that this once-in-a-lifetime adventure was a reflection of the true Western spirit and enthusiasm which made our State and our Country the great place it is today.

The eyes of the world were focused on Montana for a short time as viewers in nearly every corner of the globe witnessed scenes of the epic Centennial Cattle Drive and caught glimpses of the beautiful Montana scenery. I am proud to have been privileged to participate in Montana's Centennial Celebration, and particularly the Great Montana Centennial Cattle Drive.

Sincerely,

Allen C. Kolstad

ALLEN C. KOLSTAD
Lieutenant Governor

ACK:cl

Sheraton Great Falls
The hospitality people of **ITT**

Dear Jim

    I've sent a lot of Pictures but you may be able to use one or two also sent NRA Rodeo News shows of past Winner's you may be able to use some of it or you may not, sent along some Pictures of Kids, also one of Margie in her Prime

    Hope to see you Before July 16

      Best Regards

      Connie

THE TALLY BOOK

Acknowledgments and Preface

This book would not be written had it not been for many and varied influences and people. To give acknowledgment is to express gratitude for help and encouragement; it is to avow or own up to receipt of such help and to render recognition of the efforts of those providing such help and encouragement. In short, to give acknowledgment is to give credit where due. An acknowledgment may also be an admission, though conceded possibly with some reluctance, to having made a mistake.

Undertaking the writing of *EPIC TRAILS – Endless Tracks Across Centuries* was not a mistake. The idea and the subject matter were there and the need to express recognition of the uniqueness of an industry, of a way of life and of even a small part of the fabric which bridged the 100 years leading to Montana's celebration of her Centennial of Statehood was there. This fabric has many frayed edges left over from all sorts of attempts to grasp and tell of the structure or fiber of this uniqueness that is Montana, is her part of the history of that suspenseful era that encompassed the great cattle drives, is her ranching and cattle industry of today, and is her people. Most of those frayed edges are still there for the hands and minds willing to take them and continue to trim them and to weave them into more stories which need to be told. The mistake made in the writing of *EPIC TRAILS* has been that some thought it would be a story easy to do in the telling and writing. What an education!

The strands which have been taken here, starting with Connie Cox's observations and notations, adding the experiences of others, including facts and documentation provided by Latigo Corporation, tied together with the artfully illustrative images from Cal Sorenson's camera and others, have all been woven together into the merest suggestion of the entire story. What we have in *EPIC TRAILS* is a gossamer whisp resulting, and it floats on a slight current which we hope will bring the reader a faint inkling of all the stories and images that are still out there and untold, and that still need to be told. *EPIC TRAILS* is in no way an attempt to be the documentary which should yet be chronicled and recorded about the Cattle Drive as an important facet of Montana's evolvement and history.

The fact that in the preparation and planning for "The Great Montana Centennial Cattle Drive of 1989," involving all the many people without whose efforts this epic event would not have happened, Connie Cox was the one Montanan to go to the extra effort he did to do his part, is not unique in itself. Many people talked of driving cattle to the Trailhead at Roundup. A number made serious plans to do so, only to have unavoidable circumstances make it too difficult or, apparently, impossible. Connie Cox did it, and part of the acknowledgment of this fact, and to Connie and his crew for doing it, has to be prefaced with the additional fact that the uniqueness is really in the man, or is the man, himself, and to some, this uniqueness expresses, in encapsulated form, the true Spirit of the Drive itself, of the entire Centennial Celebration effort, and of Montana grass roots capabilities.

Knowing the man, I understand, and hope to have conveyed in this book, that he does not consider himself unique, nor to have done anything out of the ordinary. He did what he did because he wanted to, because he thought it should be done, and because, in the doing of it, he felt there was a personal experience or adventure which in some way others, who might not get to do it, would enjoy and appreciate. To not share it in his estimation would be selfish. Connie Cox may be many things to many different people; some may understand him and some may not and I know people who agree with him and others who disagree with him. But to a person, I have not encountered a single individual who considers Connie selfish or small. What I have encountered, and I've had to go to a lot of trouble and different sources to do so because it is not easy to get much out of Connie in a direct interview, is that he is a sharing and caring person. Thus, I would like to specifically acknowledge and thank Connie for calling me during the summer of 1989 to say he was going to definitely make the trail drive from Frenchman Creek to Roundup, and asking for help in writing an account of it. *EPIC TRAILS-Endless Tracks Across Centuries,* is the result of Connie's wishing to share – nothing more, and hopefully, nothing less.

In the sharing, it is our hope that Montanans and the rest of the world might know and enjoy a bit more about this beautiful land as it was prior to "The Big Drive of '89" and want to learn even more as Montana's second Century of Statehood is embarked upon.

It was possible to piece together parts of this book and to develop segments about Connie's life from numerous telephone conversations with Connie over the past year and a half. While not interviews in any sense of the word, these conversations did serve to give a point of orientation from which "reading between the lines" could progress. One of the most complete written communications I received from Connie is reproduced in the "Letters" section of this book. The best way to describe trying to get Connie to stay put long enough for an in-depth discussion about Connie would be to compare the effort to that of "keeping a bug on a hot skillet!" For this reason it has been particularly gratifying to have his permission to print his letter in the book.

I would also like to thank Mary Browers, Dorothy Majer Sky, Margie Cox and Lieutenant Governor Allen Kolstad for the permission to print additional letters appearing herein. To me the views presented express a cross section of thinking that is America.

A special thank you is in order to Connie's sister, Norma Dell Brown, and her husband, Wayne, for the help given in filling in some of the details needed, which even when reading between the lines, were not forthcoming from Connie. A similar note of appreciation is due Connie and Margie's daughter, Charlene Coleman, for the perceptions she shared about growing up with her cowboy dad as a loving, but sometimes, exacting mentor. Now, in more recent years, she is seeing her own children experience a mellowness in Granddad, as he tutors them, which is both gratifying and amusing. The insight and awareness apparent in her conversations about her dad reflect a maturity that came about in large part from the loving family relationship and early requirements for accepting responsibility which she grew up with. It was and is a real world, even way out in the sticks. There is no more sobering or humbling experience in the life of the most loving and conscientious dad or mom than that moment when they first know that their child knows they are not really perfect, that they are just normal, real people, and can make mistakes just like normal, real people! It is at such a time that a given family is most fortunate to have childhood fantasies replaced with friendship and caring and forgiveness – naturally becoming adult actions, responses and emotions – where the parent-child relationship preceded. Connie and Margie truly have good friends in their daughter and sons.

It is fitting that acknowledgments the authors and publisher feel should be a part of this work should include recognition of those sponsors and others which helped Latigo Corporation and Montana see "The Great Montana Centennial Cattle Drive of 1989" become a reality. It is emphasized here, one additional time, that EPIC TRAILS is in no way intended to be an official documentary of all the more than two years of detail and effort which was undertaken to plan, stage and execute the Cattle Drive.

Latigo Corporation is under no obligation to Silver Sage, nor conversely, does Silver Sage have any commitment to Latigo. However, the official documentary which Latigo had planned, and which would have provided them the forum by which to recognize these deserving entities, did not, for whatever reason, become a reality. A number of people in Latigo, and many other Montanans, for that matter, have been chagrined that help and assistance which was so generously brought forward to assure getting the job done, had not been formally acknowledged. So, as with a couple of cowboys concluding a horse trade with their handshake being the only thing necessary to bind the deal, the authors of *EPIC TRAILS*, and Silver Sage, on behalf of themselves, on behalf of Latigo Corporation, and on behalf of the people of Montana, and all those who were able to enjoy the "Big Drive of '89" in any way, extend thanks to the following for helping to make it all happen.

(NOTE: The following listings may be incomplete due to additional sponsor or volunteer donations which may have been generated directly to the Montana Rural Development Fund too recently to be included in this publication.)

NATIONAL SPONSORS:

Anheuser - Busch
Billings Chamber of Commerce
Billings Gazette
Billings Plaza Holiday Inn
Breakfast Exchange Club
Cellular One of Billings

Coca-Cola Bottling Co., West, Inc.
ConAgra Companies:
    Agri Basics, Monfort, Northwest Fabrics,
    Scentry, Transbas, Western Ag Chemicals, Inc.,
    Yellowstone Valley Chemicals
Conoco

Entre Computer Center
Lyle Johnson, Sculptor
Motorola Communications
Toshiba
U S WEST Communications

STATE SPONSORS:

Agri-News & Western
    Livestock Reporter
Charles Bailly & Co.
Billings Livestock Commission Co.
Corporate Air
Dover Shorthorns
Executone
First Bank System

First Interstate BancSystem of Montana
Hands Across the Table IV
Jay Contway, Sculptor
KGHL – 790AM
KOA (Kampgrounds of America
Leachman Cattle Company
Mrs. C.W. Lippard (*in Memoriam*)

Midland Printing & Supply
Paine Webber
PAYS (Public Auction Yards)
Transmountain Land &
    Livestock Company
United Tote
Yellowstone County Postal
    Cancellation Project

CAMPSITE SPONSORS:

Connolly Saddlery
McCoy Cattle Company

Padlock Ranch
Scheels Sports Shop

There are a number of other ways in which it had been and is possible to be a special part of the Legacy Mission of the Cattle Drive and to ensure the perpetuation of its success. This includes Memberhips as follows:

THE STAN LYNDE CLUB:

Membership $100. Benefits include a signed and numbered print of the official Cattle Drive painting by Stan Lynde, entitled "Train Crossing," and an official Cattle Drive Calendar:

Mike Murphy
Bull Mountain Outfitters
    Musselshell, Montana
Allen's Electric Tool Repair
    Billings, Montana
Sundance Gallery
    Billings, Montana
Ray and Patty Dietz and Family
    Billings, Montana

Breakfast Optimist Club
    Billings, Montana
John James Barker
    Rafter JB Ranch
    Lorida, Florida
Guy and Shirley Doubleday
    Pompano Beach, Florida
Frank and Connie Pelican
    Billings, Montana

Col. David D. Bissell
    Ellsworth Air Force Base,
    South Dakota
Fergus Electric Cooperative, inc.
    Lewistown, Montana
Frank Sandford
    Missoula, Montana
Leo Sas
    Billings, Montana

STAN LYNDE CLUB: (Continued)

Paul Mayo
  Harlowtown, Montana
Lloyd G. Schermer
  Pleasant Valley, Iowa
Continental National Bank
  Harlowtown, Montana
Jim Walker
  Billings, Montana
Kathryn and James Powers
  Englewood, Colorado
Fairmont Hot Springs Resort
  Ed Henrich, General Manager
  Anaconda, Montana
Fred J. Endsley
  Barrington, Illinois

James R. Chambers
  Dillon, Montana
Jim and Mary Ann Canan
  Billings, Montana
Garber Land and Livestock Co.
  Ismay, Montana
Edgar and Matilda S. Lister
  Missoula, Montana
Billings Optimist Club No. 13-010
  Billings, Montana
Jerry Travis
  Withee, Wisconsin
Caroline Stanart
  Elverta, California
Emma Jean Stevenson
  Billings, Montana

John and Grace Leuthold
  Molt, Montana
W. J. Jameson
  Billings, Montana
Donald and Bernice J. See
  Billings, Montana
Ray Krone
  Soap Creek Cattle Company
  Augusta, Montana
Ben R. Arnold
  Arnold Ranch
  Broadview, Montana
Jack (Slug) Millis
  Boyes, Montana

THE J.K. RALSTON CLUB:

Membership $500. Benefits include a numbered J. K. Ralston print from Ralston's original work entitled "The Steer Outfit;" a copy of Ralston's biography, "The Voice of the Curlew;" an official $\frac{M}{89}$ branding iron and an official Cattle Drive Calendar:

Ron Simon
  Billings, Montana
Bruce Simon
  Billings, Montana

Kelly Hagerty
  Orange, California
Stanley J. Yoder
  Boalsburg, Pennsylvania

Donald A. and Phyllis A. Odell
  New York, New York

THE CHARLIE RUSSELL CLUB:

Membership $1,000. Benefits include a numbered C. M. Russell print from Russell's original work entitled "Charlie Russell and His Friends;" a commemorative Cattle Drive Documentary; an official $\frac{M}{89}$ branding iron and an official Cattle Drive Calendar:

Mrs. Charlean Keller
  Billings, Montana
Charles E. Kerns
  Mount Martinez, California
Calgary Exhibition Stampede
  c/o Wayne McKinnon,
  Calgary, Alberta, Canada
Stanton L. Brannin
  American Fork Ranch,
  Two Dot, Montana
Byron Logan
  Hickory, North Carolina
Jerry Hanson
  Billings, Montana
Montana Silversmiths
  Columbus, Montana
Transcisco Industries, Inc.
  Mark C. Hungerford,
  San Francisco, California

Heritage Solid Wood Homes, Inc.
  William F. Pierce, General Manager
  Kaj D. Nereaux
  Santa Rosa, California
Dan Lee
  Latigo Corporation
  Billings, Montana
Charles Bailly & Co.
  Billings, Montana
James R. Scott
  c/o First Interstate BancSystem
  of Montana,
  Billings, Montana
Robert L. Nance
  Billings, Montana
Pete Hoiness
  Billings, Montana
Dave Auer
  Billings, Montana

Benchmark Printing
  Billings, Montana
Rollins Burdick Hunter of Montana
  Billings, Montana
Mr. and Mrs. Bernard J. Brown
  Morrill, Nebraska
Thomas W. Vogel
  Billings, Montana
Norwest Bank Billings
  Billings, Montana
Jane Glennie
  Two Dot, Montana
R. E. Turner
  c/o One CNN Center
  Atlanta, Georgia
Craig Pierson
  Billings, Montana
First Citizens Bank
  Billings, Montana

M89 SPONSORS:

Dave Auer
Benchmark Printing
Big Sky Beeper Co.
Billings Exchange Club
Crowley, Hanson, Haughey, Toole,
  & Dietrich, P.C.
Deaconess Medical Center
Fergus Electric Cooperative

Beverly Bates Hall
Jerry Hanson
Pete Hoiness
KCTR - FM/AM
KTVQ - 2
Nance Petroleum
North American Resources Co.

Northern Ag Network
Norwest Bank
Nutrilix
Safeway Supply
James R. Scott
Robert H. Waller
Wirth Design Associates

– Endless Tracks Across Centuries

IN-KIND AND CASH DONATIONS:

Montana Farmer Stockman Magazine
Big Sky Business Journal
A. L. Clancy Creative/Technical Services
Chuck Christiansen
Janine Stenehjem
Star Office Machines

Advanced Office Services
Moorman Feeds
Loomix
Sage Advertising
NILE (Northern International
Livestock Exhibition)

MVMA (Montana Veterinary
Medical Association)
Neil McKinnon LK Ranches
Jay Thompson
Pat Goggins
Mrs. Ralph Shane

OTHER ADDITIONAL CASH DONATIONS:

Ralph Lauren
Yellowstone Basin Properties
Jim Birginal

Melvin H. Schlesinger
Arthur O. Erickson
Wolery Farms, Inc.

Howard and Ruth McGuigg
Kurt H. Lueck

In addition, a special thank you and acknowledgment recognizes the efforts and contributions of over 1400 volunteers with 2700 riders who consigned cattle to the Drive, and:

Fifty-Six Montana Counties
City of Billings
City of Roundup
Yellowstone County
Musselshell County
Montana Highway Department
Montana Highway Patrol
District Inspectors, Montana Brands Enforcement
Montana Department of Livestock
Montana Army National Guard
Montana Air National Guard
Yellowstone County Sheriff's Department

Musselshell County Sheriff's Department
Billings Police Department
Roundup Police Department
Roundup '89ers
Governor Stan Stephens
Lieutenant Governor Allen Kolstad
United States Senator Max Baucus
United States Senator Conrad Burns
United States Congressman Ron Marlenee
United Stated Congressman Pat Williams
Montana Statehood Centennial Commission

And on behalf of Latigo, a special thank you also to all the other thousands of people, both from Montana and from around the world, who helped make this a memory to treasure.

The authors of *EPIC TRAILS* and Silver Sage Impressions wish to particularly thank the following Latigo Corporation officials for the extra effort they have made in communicating information to the publisher in order that these acknowledgments could be made possible:

LATIGO CORPORATION EXECUTIVE COMMITTEE:

James R. Scott, Chairman
David Auer
N.C. (Pete) Hinson, Jr.

J. Kim Kuzara
Cal Winslow

All the people who were able to enjoy the Family Night and Nashville entertainment on Thursday night of the Cattle Drive owe an extra thank you to National Sponsor, Coca-Cola Bottling Co., West, Inc., for especially sponsoring this event, making that night's Wagon Circle camp temporarily the seventh largest settlement in the state of Montana.

Then, as part of the Saturday, September 9th, Grand Finale, another National Sponsor, Anheuser - Busch, is gratefully acknowledged for especially sponsoring the Trail's End Concert in the Billings Metra. This festive Western Saturday night featured Lee Greenwood. Also appearing courtesy of Budweiser were Hoyt Axton, Sheb Wooley, Ed Hunnicutt, Brenda Williams, The Gairrett Bros., and Suzi Maki and The Cattle Drive Band.

Pertinent amongst the acknowledgments rendered herein, a point of clarification is in order. There have been at times, certain degrees of confusion relative to who the "real Jim Scott" might be, as matters of the Cattle Drive are concerned. Four different individuals by this name occur within the cover of this book. At least one additional party by the same name appeared on

– Endless Tracks Across Centuries

the roster of riders traveling with the Cattle Drive Wagon Train. Besides this writer, whose volunteer duties had primarily to do with planning and coordinating veterinary health matters and animal care concerns prior to, and during the Drive, the following bit of information about each of the other Jim Scotts should elucidate this question for the reader.

James R. Scott, Chairman of the Latigo Corporation Executive Committee, and Latigo Board Member, helped with many, many facets of the Drive, not the least of which had to do with helping get the generous support of the numerous fine sponsors recognized here. His concerns will also be ongoing as he serves on the Board of Directors, along with David Auer, of the Montana Community Foundation. This body, as indicated elsewhere in this book, will have the continuing responsibility of seeing that the Legacy of the Cattle Drive is perpetuated into the reality of the Montana Rural Development Fund. The Mission Statement of The Montana Community Foundation appears in Chapter 21 of *EPIC TRAILS* on pages 111 and 112. This Jim Scott and his family call Billings home.

Readers who would like additional information about the Rural Montana Development Fund are urged to contact The Montana Community Foundation directly by writing to:

Montana Community Foundation
Power Block Building, Suite 4-P – 7 West Sixth Avenue
Telephone 406-443-8313 Helena, Montana 59601 Fascimile 406-449-3668

Also at home in Billings, and a member of the Volunteer Medical Doctors who provided Emergency Medical Services on the Cattle Drive, is another Jim Scott, James R. Scott, M.D. He was horseback with the Drive, traveling with the Wagon Train.

Jim Bode Scott, one of the Official Drovers with the Trail Herd, calls Shepherd, Montana, home. This Jim Scott is a top all-around cowboy, having competed successfully, and for a number of years in the top standings, in the rodeo events of Saddle Bronc Riding, Steer Wrestling and Calf Roping on the Montana Professional Rodeo Circuit of the Professional Rodeo Cowboys' Association. Jim is a working ranch cowboy, as well, and is active in the sharing of inspiration to other fine young athletes through the energies of the cowboys' Christian movement, Cowboys for Christ.

While he was not able to participate in the "Big Drive of '89" in body, at least one other Jim Scott was with me in spirit. James W. Scott, my own son, is another Montana cowboy of whom this father is very proud. I recognize Jim here for more than this reason, however. As mentioned regarding Connie's family, our son, Jim, and daughter, Daphne, are the best friends their mother and I have. Jim has been a Registered Radiology Technologist with special tracking interest in the Heart Catheterization Laboratory at Providence Hospital in Anchorage, Alaska, for the past few years, He is a good case in point exemplifying Montana's exportation of her young people. After completing his education and training, which he paid for himself, Jim found it necessary to "cowboy up" and seek opportunity beyond Montana's borders. He misses Montana and we miss having him here, but we understand. And in the understanding, we can acutely relate to what the Cattle Drive Legacy could ultimately mean to rural Montana, and her future generations.

Suffice it to say, having made this point of clarification about "the real Jim Scotts" for the readers of *EPIC TRAILS*, this writer is not sufficiently oriented in the study of genealogy to have an idea how far back on the Scott family tree one might have to go to find, if possible, a common branch or branches. I do know something of the reasons why I find fascination in the history of the trails that led to Montana 100 years and longer ago. The acknowledgments herein would be incomplete without brief reference to those responsible for these reasons.

My great grandfather, Rice Campbell Scott, was a "bullwhacker" wagon freighter who brought wagon trains over the Western Trails during the 1860s and 1870s. Great-grandfather was born around 1844-45. He joined the Union Army in 1863 at the approximate age of 18 years and was a member of the Seventh Cavalry. Fortunately for me, he apparently decided upon other endeavors, I believe due to injury or illness, considerably prior to the Seventh Cavalry's ill-fated trek to the Little Big Horn, June 25, 1876, under the Command of General George Armstrong Custer. Rice Campbell Scott's maternal grandfolks were supposed to have been part of the Feuding Campbell clan of Kentucky or Illinois. He married Katherine Cormany in 1864-65 and my grandpa, John Michael Scott, was born November 20, 1869, one of four children.

Great-grandfather was wagonmaster of freight wagon trains west from St. Joseph, Missouri, hauling over the Smoky Hill Trail to Denver. An account relates his wagons were, on one occasion, 27 days attempting to go 9 miles through deep winter snow with heavy mine equipment destined for the mountains west of Denver. The cook with the wagon train was said to have been able to go back to the embers of the previous campfire to get coals with which to stoke his cookfire at the next camp. Other treks included travels over the Oregon Trail and the Bozeman Trail. Great-granddad Scott was in the employ of the Freight Division of the Company, Majors, Russell and Waddell, which also embarked the Pony Express westward from St. Joe. On one wagon train west, great-grandfather received word that Katherine was gravely ill, so he left the freight wagons in charge of his assistant wagonmaster, returning to St. Joseph by steamboat from Miles City. This was around 1874, and that wagon train fell to a bad fate at the hands of hostiles shortly thereafter. Katherine Cormany Scott died in 1874. Rice Campbell Scott lived until 1908 and is buried at the Natonal Military Cemetery at Fort Leavenworth, Kansas.

John Michael Scott farmed in Missouri, Kansas, and Arkansas, spent some time building railroad in the Ozark Mountains, and homesteaded in Oklahoma and Colorado. He married Flora Harris, and my father, Kenneth E. Scott, was born September 15, 1903, the middle of three sons born to John M. and Flora. Dad still lives on the home ranch at Kiowa, Colorado. Grandmother Flora Scott died in 1934, and my grandfather Scott was nearly 90 years old when he passed away. My mother, Lyndall Deming Scott, was born, March 14, 1901, the fifth of seven children to Walter H. and Jessica Pease Deming. Mother's family migrated westward from Ohio to California, homesteading and farming in Iowa, Nebraska and Colorado on the way. She and my dad were married in Colorado in 1927 and lived and ranched on Comanche Creek in Elbert County most of the years from that time until mother died November 14, 1983.

Dad owned and operated a commercial trucking business along with farming and ranching from 1926, until selling the trucking business to my older brother, Kenneth E. Scott, Jr., in 1976. Ken continued the trucking business until his health failed. He is survived by his wife, Virginia Herrick Scott, and one son, Gregory. Mother attended college two years in Nebraska and taught country school in Colorado. I was born the middle of three sons in 1934 and my brothers, Kenneth, Larry and I attended The Lost School District "one roomer" until it consolidated. We and our sister who came along too late to go to a one room country school all graduated from Kiowa High School and had the opportunity to attend Colorado State University. There were five students in my High School graduating class. My younger brother, Larry, is a soils chemist with his degree in animal nutrition. My sister, Mary, has a dual degree in mathematics and physics. Larry operated an independent soils and plant tissues testing laboratory with partners from 1957 until 1989. He and his wife, Evie Novak Scott, continue to live in Colorado. They have a daughter, Tracy, and two sons, Brett and Todd. Mary and her husband, Richard Filson, have a son, Scott, and daughter, Stephanie, and they also make their home in Colorado.

Withstanding my brother Larry's admonitions that "if people would listen to his recommendations concerning proper nutrition, there would be little need for my ministrations as a veterinarian," I prevailed and somehow doggedly managed to hang in there to get my D.V.M. degree from Colorado State University the same year Larry became an animal nutritionist. Having always liked what I saw in Charlie Russell's painting, I wanted to see for myself what had so inspired Charlie to preserve as he did his images of Montana. This is what brought me to Montana to begin veterinary practice. Fortunately for me and my children, I had an opportunity to return to the Veterinary Clinical Teaching Staff at Colorado State University to do special tracking in the field of beef cattle obstetrics and breeding soundness for a period of time. It was during this time that I had the privilege to meet students, graduate students and a number of the ranching families it has been my good fortune to know, work with and share learning experiences with since returning to private practice.

Most importantly, it was at the same time that a friend asked me to go with him to help a damsel in distress and it was my happy destiny to meet my bride of now nearly thirty years. "Lou" was a United Airlines Stewardess flying out of Denver, and her car had had a breakdown. Thank you forever, Richard Maxfield, for asking me to help respond to that call for help that wonderful day! This lovely girl who has been the light of my life for now more than half of it was born the second child to Lawrence and Lillian Cant Mascall of Grant County, Oregon. They named her Lillamay Christine, but her brother, W. C. (Bill) Mascall, promptly nicknamed his little sister Lou. Coming to know and love Lou's family doubled my fascination with the trails of the West and the frontier spirits which forged over them to chance new ranges.

Lawrence E. Mascall was born December 9, 1907, the last of nine children, to Billy and May Mascall. Billy Mascall was an early day sheep rancher in the John Day River country of Eastern Oregon. His family settled in Grant County near Dayville around the mid 1860s. They'd discovered the value of the good but sparse bunchgrasses and sweet fresh water springs in that rugged land east of the Ochocos, close to the same time gold was discovered in 1862 at Canyon City. Sheep ranching, like everything else in the Fall of 1929, and on into the middle 1930s, kind of "went to Hell in a handbasket," and Lawrence and Lillian struggled for many years putting back together the Mascall Ranch which Lillian and Lou's brother, Bill, continue to operate, still with a few sheep, but mostly with cattle. Bill has a daughter, Susan, and a son, John. Both make their homes in Oregon.

Lou's dad passed away November 23, 1971. Lillian Cant Mascall was the fourth child born to James and Elizabeth Cant who had homesteaded and ranched on down the John Day River through Picture Gorge (so named because of Native American hieroglyphic inscriptions and pictorial characters found on the canyon walls) in Grant and Wheeler Counties. James and Elizabeth were both Scottish immigrants to this raw Oregon landscape, James by way of first having made a couple of passages to Argentina, and Elizabeth, a few years after James had started to establish roots in Oregon, by way of ship to Montreal, train across Canada, and wagon to Grant County. She was a tiny little lady, and she responded to my mother's inquiry at the time Lou and I were married, "Lizzy, how did such a wee slip of a girl like you brave the trip from your home in Scotland, all by yourself to travel to this wild, unknown land?" by answering simply, "My mon was here!" in her sweet Scottish brogue.

James and Elizabeth Cant are gone now, too, but memories of them, along with all the others, remain and will be cherished. Our children were blessed to be able to spend wonderful moments with these great-grandparents, as well as with loving grandparents. The home James and Lizzy built with lumber they hauled in by wagon before there was a road stands as a memorial to the hands that built it and the home fires it sheltered. It is now the museum and information center of the John Day Fossil Beds National Monument.

The expression of gratitude to those responsible for much of the inspiration leading to *EPIC TRAILS-Endless Tracks Across Centuries* can in no way be entirely complete because to acknowledge everyone I should would be a sum total equivalent of additional books. The circle which my trail followed back to Montana was a bigger one than once intended and the friendly doorways along the grubline have been many and diverse. The shelters along the way afforded by snug roofs and warm hearths have been an experience as heartening as if they were the exhilarating aromatic spirits of a cordial deeply quaffed. One of the most rewarding experiences of my life has been the association it has been my privilege to have with these loved ones and others, as well as with a number of ranchers, colleagues, former students and graduate students with whom it has been my good fortune to work.

It has been possible to work professionally and as friends with many of these people for two and three, and even in some instances, for four generations of the same family, while they have constantly strived for improvement of their livestock and overall ranching operations. They have done so to meet the challenges imposed by environmental concerns, food safety concerns, health concerns, generally increasing animal agriculture antagonistic forces of, all too often, an ill-informed society, and, plain and simply, to meet the challenges of survival. Just a few of these families or individuals, some of whom are also regrettably no longer with us, and to whom I owe a great debt of gratitude include:

The Doherty families of the Mesa de Maya and Capulin Mountain areas of Colorado and New Mexico; most especially the John J., John F. (Tanky), and Billy Doherty families, and Loreen (Tiny), and the John A. Doherty family; Bob and Thelma Bowers, known over a trail that took us from Colorado and Nebraska to Manitoba and finally to Ontario, Quebec, France, Germany, England, Brazil, and back to California (one day people will recognize your *Econergy, Concept of Plenty*, Bob); J. E. Rouse and Roma, of the One Bar Eleven on the North Platte in Wyoming (John, September 18, 1892 - November 27, 1990, wrote the trilogy, *World Cattle* and the book, *The Criollo, Spanish Cattle of the Americas*); Drs. Floyd Cross, Rue Jensen, Bob Davis, Harold Hill, Lloyd Faulkner, Bob Adams and H. H. Stonaker of CSU, and particularly of the times and experiences at the Four Corners Experiment Station near the San Juans; the McKinnon, Ward, Copithorne, Ewing, Gilchrist and Cross families of Alberta (CSU Beef Cattle A.I. Short Courses, Western Stock Growers Short Courses at Banff, and mile after mile after mile of hot, dusty, or cold, snowy bull testing roads/the writings of Lachlin McKinnon, Charlie McKinnon, George Ward, and Sherm Ewing and others, offering great insight into more endless tracks/the first volume of Sherm Ewing's trilogy has just been published, entitled, *The Range*; the other two volumes, *The Ranch* and *The Roast*, follow).

I am deeply grateful, also to: J. J. (Bud) Prosser; Richard Goff; The E. W. (Bill) Serrell family; the Bill Sinclair family; the Jolly families, Culbreath families; and many other wonderful friends in Colorado; and especially to the G. D. (Gib) McGarvey families and Lee Stark for years of friendship, encouragement and support, as well as, endless interesting trips of gustatorial sensation and superb service through the steak menus in "The North Forty" or at "The Rear Of The Steer" in the CharcoBroiler of Fort Collins and the Black Steer of Loveland, respectively; also to:

Daphne Davis; the Jim Roeser family; the Drs. Charlie Vail; G.M. Beeman, A. W. (Wright) Dickinson; and Alan Rice families, all of Colorado; and the Carl and Marian Trick family of North Park, Colorado. The Dr. Larry Rice and Dr. Charles Nichols families of Oklahoma; Burt and Ginny Guenin and family; and Dr. Joe and Diane Jeffrey; and the Merlyn and Janice Carlson family of Nebraska. Also, the Dr. George Platt, Ron Davenport and Nolan Henson families of Texas and Sid and Thelma Warner and family of Kansas.

A special thanks also to the Dan Lindblom family of South Dakota, the Art Brandvik family of Montana and to G. A. (Furgy) and Boots Furgason of Florida for all their many kindnesses and friendship the years with Norris Cattle Co.

Remembered, too, will be the Mosher familes; the Schmitt families; the Leadbetter families, the Mitchell families, and the Bailey familes of Montana, along with good friends and neighbors, including, the Thrasher, Johnson, Udall, Vining, and Cobb families. Thanks, also the David and Karen Carlson family, the Max and Florence Schumacher family, and the John and Vicki Ropp family. Dan and Deb Leadbetter of the Valley Garden Ranch at Ennis, Montana, will make endless tracks across the hearts of flower lovers everywhere with their beautiful "Montana Roses."

A lot of rough trails and not a few cold and sometimes dry camps have been weathered with friends like Dr. Jim and Shirley Baker, Dr. Paul Draper, Dr. Jim Bailey, Steve Mansker and Cadet and Eva Oxandaburu. Dr. J. J. (Jake) Batty and Dr. Michael P. Doran were in a lot of those camps, too, and we'll miss the stories those two could tell and the fun they were around the campfire!

A special thank you, too, to John and Avgi Stewart-Smith and their family; to the Neil and Robin Harvie family; to the Dan and Donna McKinnon family; to the Dr. Andrew and Geri Bronson family; to the Alvin and Ann Kumlin family; to the Marshall and Teresa Copithorne family; to the Charlie and Sherry Ewing family; to the Chuck and Nina Ewing Travis family; to the Wayne and Leslie Ewing Kriz family; to the Hugh and Betty Lynch-Staunton family; to the Tom and Lois Gilchrist family; and to Jim Burns for all their sharing hospitality and kind friendship these many years. And a very special thank you to Neil and Lucille McKinnon and family; Sherm and Claire Ewing and family. George amd Mabel Ward and family and Jack and Eleanor Ward and family for keeping the latchstring out for the best part of thirty years as I made endless tracks through their part of the world.

I wish to thank John Stewart-Smith of Beefbooster™ Cattle, Ltd. for the permission to explain a bit of the Beefbooster™ Beef Cattle Genetics Improvement Program for the benefit of everyone involved in agriculture. If you eat – you are involved in agriculture!

Finally a very special thank you to Ted and Carol Beam, to Keith Watkins and to the Margaret (Mrs. Glen) and Ann (Mrs. Tom) Scott families and the Bill Colfelt family for all the love and help these many years.

There are many others to whom all I can say is, "Thank you and God Bless you!"

I learned a book is not just merely "written" –one has to think a book, then nurture it, edit it, re-write it, scrap some of it, type set it, size it, paste it, strip it, get it printed, published and distributed. Hopefully, then it will be sold and read. It is a real manufacturing process and experience.

In order to complete all this I would like to thank, additionally, Byron and Colette Bennett of Bozeman, Jerry Brekke, of Brekke Photography Studio in Livingston for his help to Cal Sorenson; Jeri Walton of Outlaw Publishing, Bozeman for help in many ways; Stan and Lois Burgard and all their fine staff at Color World Printers, of Bozeman; and Anne Smith Sperry of Bozeman without whose warm kitchen, and round oak table for a final editing desk, the job could not have been completed. Thank you all once again, very much!

J.A.S.

TABLE OF CONTENTS

TABLE OF CONTENTS (Continued)

–––––––––

EPIC TRAILS —

JOURNAL
OF
THE TRAIL DRIVE OF 1989

DAILY HISTORY OF CATTLE DRIVE FROM CONNIE COX RANCH OF WHITEWATER, MONTANA, 240 MILES – 21 DAYS TO ROUNDUP, MONTANA, TRAIL HEAD FOR THE GREAT MONTANA CENTENNIAL CATTLE DRIVE OF 1989 – ROUNDUP TO BILLINGS.

START TRAILING AUGUST 11, 1989 FROM HOME RANCH ON FRENCHMAN CREEK AT THE SASKATCHEWAN BORDER TO THE TOWN OF ROUNDUP ON THE BANKS OF THE MUSSELSHELL.

SOME SAY THAT 'THE BIG DRIVE OF '89' TO CELEBRATE MONTANA'S 100TH BIRTHDAY OF STATEHOOD WILL NEVER TAKE PLACE, BUT WE'LL NOT KNOW UNLESS WE TRY. SO WE'RE PUTTIN' THIS SET OF LONGHORN COWS SOUTH DOWN THE TRAIL WITH THE FAITH THAT TWO YEARS OF PLANNING BY A LOT OF GOOD MONTANA PEOPLE WILL RESULT IN A CATTLE TREK TO BILLINGS THAT WILL NOT BE FORGOT.

THERE LIKELY MAY NEVER BE ANOTHER ONE LIKE IT.

Connie Cox

— ENDLESS TRACKS ACROSS CENTURIES

Trails Past Relic.

Dodson ~ Zortman Stage.

© 1989
R. Contway

Photo circa, courtesy of Rose Contway

The coach was a 'Mudwagon' type with fast '4-up' hitch hooked up and ready to run.

EPIC TRAILS —

THURSDAY, AUGUST 10, 1989. THE DAY BEFORE —

"GETTING EVERYTHING READY TO GO. COWS ARE BEGINNING TO SETTLE DOWN AFTER WEANING THEIR CALVES. COWS HAVE BEEN BY CREEK NEAR CORRALS AND THEY'VE BEEN WEIGHED AND WILL BE READY TO MOVE OUT EARLY TOMORROW MORNING. SHAVED FOR THE LAST TIME FOR A MONTH AT 3:08 PM AND WEIGHED MYSELF — WEIGHED 188 POUNDS. HAD SUPPER - MAYBE LAST HOME COOKED MEAL FOR A WHILE - AT 7:40 P.M. BARBEQUED STEAK, BAKED POTATO AND CORN ON COB - GOOD! ALEX McDOUGAL, KEN SCHOKER, SANDY OLSEN, WINSTON BASCOM, DENISE COX, DANNETTE MONTGOMERY (DENISE'S TWIN SISTER) AND HER 4 KIDS, DARWIN, CHRISTOPHER, BECKY AND COLIN AND MYSELF."

"TURNED IN EARLY. TOMORROW THERE'LL BE NO LOOKIN' BACK."

—ENDLESS TRACKS ACROSS CENTURIES

PROLOGUE

ENDLESS TRACKS AND THIS FRENCHMAN CREEK COUNTRY

The pre-dawn blackness gave no clue as to the whereabouts of the horizon ahead as I sat straining to see toward Starkey Ridge. The gate with the ZN monogram brand over top had been passed so I knew the dirt trail I was following was the right one leading to the ranch home of Connie and Margie Cox. The direction headed was right because the morning star was that way, giving the only indication where the horizon might emerge with the break of gray dawn. Polaris, which had beckoned me northward from the High-Line, had swung the handle of the Little Dipper in a wide arc, and was steadfast off to the left.

People have always wondered at the pull of the North Star, at the treks of many an explorer and wanderer as they were guided by it; and at the myths and legends of ursine nature passed from generation to generation of the indigenous natives throughout the northern hemisphere. From the Native American hunters in quest of the Buffalo to the bucolic drovers of the great trail herds of yesteryear to the astronaut traveling on wings and rockets, mankind has followed this pull. The horizons are crisscrossed by his tracks and by the tracks of the animals he followed as he kept his eye on the star. From the Buffalo and Antelope of the native prairie and the Longhorn descendent of the Criollo, to the modern day herd of beef cows so vital to today's world food needs, these tracks and the courses they have wended have meant survival to the various peoples who have followed the trails.

These thoughts and many others gave way to concentration on the moment as darkness was gradually replaced by the dawn. The ridge ahead down which the trail lay was now visible and it was as if looking toward the toe of a great horseshoe shaped basin. The near horizon stretched off to the right into breaks that would be Connie Cox's winter country. To the left the rough breaks extended on to a plain that would be to the north of the U.S. and Canadian border along the 49th parallel. Those breaks hide the wanderings of Frenchman Creek as it comes from the Saskatchewan side and twists ahead to where the ranch headquarters lay.

Dawn breaks clear and beautiful. You should be able , it seems, to see all the way to the end of the world from this high ridge were it not for a haze. The gray light of early morning becomes laced with hues of mauve and gold as the sun rays reach up from behind the far horizon and spread through the haze. All senses seem keen at this hour. The haze was borne aloft by the winds of yesterday and of the day before and the day before that. This dry country is seldom without the wind and the dust that rides on it. For a moment, however, there is no wind; not even a breeze stirring. Listening intently, one can almost hear the stillness. If there is a definition of the "Big Open," it is here to be felt, even, if not explained. One knows what is meant by the "Big Sky" feeling or "Big Country" feeling because it envelops the body and spirit completely. As the edge of the sun burns a hole in the distant horizon it scatters the last blue-gray of dawn into a million shadows and the breaks awaken to the new day.

The rose and violet colors of a moment ago evaporate into the morning sky and a breeze now stirs the silence. With it there's the buzzing of a fly and the "cluck" of a partridge as she stretches from her roost under a sage brush and warily leads her nearly grown brood out for the day. The smell of the sage is heavy as the sun warms the early morning air and a magpie rudely brings the rest of the morning awake as he scolds the little partridge family darting beneath his perch on a yucca spire. Doves, prairie chickens, song birds and a rooster pheasant all add a voice to the morning. With exception of the pheasant and the magpie, all the rest are content with a modest announcement of their presence and most fade into the lightening day in their re-

Petrified remnant of prehistoric rain forest on the dry prairie along Frenchman Creek.

From ancient times to now, trails led to watering places and shelter.

The buffalo and antelope and Native American made tracks which were replenished each season. These tracks were altered little by the elements, the hunt or even the Pishkun.

Then the settlers came and they changed many of these trails forever – but some have prevailed – etched by time into the landscape.

Endless Tracks Across Centuries.

5

spective field dress. Not so the rooster. He's regal in his bright attire as it reflects the morning sun and he wants everyone to know it. The raucous magpie acts as if he'd stayed out all night, in his formal evening tuxedo appearing smartness, and fusses at every sign of the new day.

With the day thus started it is time to move on down the dusty road as it winds off the top, descending a narrow hog-back and switch backs through shadowy recesses to the willows along Frenchman Creek. The ranch home and headquarters buildings are on a small knoll-like rise which is actually like an island with Frenchman Creek curling nearly a full circle around the homestead site. Frenchman Creek is not big in the sense of many creeks and rivers in Montana but it has spring fed live water along much of its course and is a wonderful oasis along its bottom through these dry breaks. Many creeks in this country are for the most part just dry washes the majority of the time, or if they do have live water in them, may be only a few feet wide and inches deep. In time of heavy thunderstorms or rapid spring melt after unusually accumulated snows, however, these usually dry washes can become treacherous flooding torrents. When asked about this, Connie replied, "A dry wash can have a wall of water come down that can run from 6 to 600 feet wide an' deeper than a man standin' in his saddle, but this rise is high enough that Frenchman Creek's never flooded these buildings since we've been here. Far as I know, never in the history of the ranch. It's cut across during flood time where the crick circles back nearly to itself but the round corral here must be close to a hundred years old and its still standin'!"

Besides the family home, the headquarters site consists of a few old original log buildings, a feed storage shed and shop, large barn with working corrals and arena, an older house that serves as bunkhouse and hunter's camp and the old original round corral. The arena has served over the years as the family's playground where Connie taught his sons, Casey and Clinton, and daughter, Charlene, to ride and rope and school horses into well trained ranch working horses and rodeo mounts. While used as a playground when time

permitted the arena more often functions along with the rest of the corrals as the place where much workaday handling of cattle and horses must be done if they are to be managed efficiently to provide the livelihood necessary to the ranch survival.

Around and beyond the homestead site, the bottoms along Frenchman Creek have been developed into hay meadows and the willows provide winter shelter for stock and habitat for deer and other wild animals and birds. High on a bluff overlooking the homesite and bend in the creek, the American flag waves a heart tugging greeting to the traveler who visits there. On matters such as desecration of our flag Connie states very matter-of-factly, "If someone is hell-bent on burnin' her they'd better have themselves wrapped up in her first!" And with his jaw set and his usual quick good humor darkened for a moment he continues, "Or else they respect our flag and our country, they better be on a boat for somewhere else – there should be one leaving about every five minutes that'll accommodate 'em!"

What is "right" to Connie and what is "right" about this Frenchman Creek country are very important if one is to understand this man and his love for the way of life that is his. There is an honesty to both that is exacting and without compromise. Early settlers found the area that is this part of Montana and similar country in neighboring Saskatchewan to be good cattle country by and large but not without its hardships. The "Big die-offs" of 1886-87 and 1906-07 from unusually hard winters, and later a nearly as hard winter of 1938, following the drought years termed "The dirty thirties," provided ample evidence of how harsh life can be in this land. Application of common sense business and management expertise provides a buffer which allows modern day inhabitants to survive and even occasionally have a year or so of prosperity. But the whole person who experiences and savors such years knows a constant vigil must be kept if one is to get through the 8 or 10 years that often prevail in between. While Connie's life and times are essentially of this modern day, the spirit with which he relates to this land could well have been from those earlier times when all there was was native prairie and no fences.

Connie's formal education (or lack of it) is an important factor in the relating of his story because while he thinks and writes in a phonetic context, his mind reflects what he sees and hears as it is. This may not necessarily be as you or I would perceive it if someone else were trying to say the same thing. Having this book render what is "right" to Connie may not be what is grammatically or literarily and literately correct, but "Eye to eye, mouth to mouth and toe to toe, head screwed on right and feet on the ground common sense is what I'd like to be able to explain," says Connie.

The senses stirred by the early morning break of day back up on the high ridge included a hunger that put me to looking for breakfast smoke and the smell of boiled coffee and frying bacon. No place in the world excels our American West in the offering of kind hospitality to the traveler, be he a stranger or frequent visitor. Margie Cox and her kitchen are no exception, as many a cowboy, rancher neighbor, hunter or other wayfarer can attest to. All are received and treated as guests and nobody leaves Connie and Margie's home hungry. And nobody leaves without a bit of enlightenment if he has any ability or sense to listen at all. Connie mixes a lot of physical activity and nervous energy with some deep psychic feelings, simple philosophy and sly sense of humor.

Much of the time, while always sincere and actually seeming extremely serious, he can get a good joke over on you. A "greener" or dude has a hard time telling whether his leg is being pulled or whether there really are "Snipes" out there to "hunt???" Connie tells people, "I only got to the third grade in school by the time I was sixteen years old and then the school board kicked me out 'cause the teacher started bringing me apples!"

People that know Connie from his earlier years know he progressed past the third grade in school but he doesn't elaborate upon how much beyond and makes no bones about appreciating the education he got behind a saddle horn more than from conforming to formal academic pursuits. Nonetheless, he and Margie saw that their children all completed high school and all had the opportunity to go to college. Connie feels life is much less

confusing when seen from the back of a horse or looking over the tail ends of a bunch of trailing mama cows and their babies. He's quick to allow, "The trail isn't always straight and there's always going to be some bumps in it!"

If you have the opportunity to watch Connie on horseback working cattle, it is an education in itself. His neighbors say of him, "If it's an expert at handling stock you need or want, Connie is as close as you'll find. He often works alone and he always works 'em easy! He's always ready to help a neighbor but will jokingly assert, 'If you want a helping hand, you'll find it at the end of your elbow!'"

Knowing that Connie had been born and raised in the Havre area and that Margie was originally from the Lone Tree Bench community south of Chinook, I inquired as to what brought them to this ranch in the remote basin on Frenchman Creek. Connie replied, "It was from flying cross country on week-ends to get to rodeos." He reminisced as he looked off into the northern distance; "If I hadn't learned to fly a plane I likely wouldn't have been able to get to very many rodeos and I'd probably never known this Frenchman Creek country even existed. I got on my first rodeo bucking horse in May of '53 when I was 20 years old. That was at Maple Creek, Saskatchewan and over the years I went to a lot of rodeos in Canada, as well as throughout Montana and elsewhere. In order to get to as many as possible and still work through the week, the airplane was the only way it could be done. I'd fly across these breaks and look down at what still looked like wide open country and imagine how little it appeared to have changed since it must have been the bottom of some ancient ocean. You could almost see where the high water marks must have been along the ridges and sometime there must have been a rain forest because I could see the remains of what looked like big petrified logs. As I flew along I could imagine some of the trails followed now by cattle and game may have been started by animals which became extinct way before the Buffalo had their day and then nearly lost out, too."

Off the bedground at break of day in this Big Sky Land of 'Epic Trails.'

"I'd go home and tell Margie about this place I could see where the creek wound around a little island rise and the homestead on it looked to be old and sturdy as the breaks nearly. It looked to me as if those breaks provided good shelter and feed for open wintering most years and I'd heard old timers tell that this was country where cattle had been able to make it better than other places they could remember back at least to the time Charlie Russell painted his famous picture sketch he called "Waiting for a Chinook," or some call it, "Last of the 5000." I'd dream about this Frenchman Creek country and we'd talk about it, but the kids were little and we were just getting a start. The idea that we might someday be able to buy the place was about as remote as the ranch itself, but then we learned it was for sale and somehow in January of 1968 we managed to mortgage about everything but the kids and our souls and we bought it!"

Acquiring the ranch on Frenchman Creek was one thing. Making it work was quite another. Work it has been. Connie traveled back and forth from the place where the family was living north of Havre. In January of 1968, the three Cox children were midway through the school year. The cows were getting heavy and would be starting to calve in a couple more months. The road from the ranch where they were living to the newly acquired place east of Whitewater could be especially long if the weather was bad. The days were short and seemed lots of them, about all that could be accomplished from before daylight until after dark, was to get those old cows fed and make sure the ice was broke long enough for them to all get a good drink of water. And there was lots of fence to fix and other things that needed tending to before the Frenchman Creek place was really ready and workable.

There would be wisdom in getting to know the country and the lay of the land before committing to just exactly what type of operation might best fit on Frenchman Creek. Connie's eye for conditions and seasonal affects of the weather and year to year cycles were put to the test of deciding whether this would be a cow-calf outfit or if yearlings would work plus pairs or if it would be better as a steer grazing deal without pairs. It looked liked it would be well suited to a cow-calf set up because of the winter protection Connie felt the breaks and bottoms afforded. If enough grass could be saved for winter grazing of the cows after their calves would be weaned each fall, and the cows would learn the terrain after a few seasons; it looked to Connie as if it were country where the right kind of cow could really earn her living. "This has always been 'next year' sort of country, all along this north 'High-Line' area and farther east, the drier she usually gets," states Connie.

"You usually don't have to worry none about dry cycles and wet cycles in this country – It's mostly just dry and drier!" he continued. "Lots of growing seasons you're lucky if the grass ever gets more 'n a bite and a half high all summer long so it takes lots of acres to run an ol' cow and her baby for half the year and still have enough grass to get the cow through the other half of the year in good enough shape to bring another 'coupon.' If a man was really inclined as an inventor and could come up with a crossbreed cow that had a 5 foot sickle bar for a mouth and a cruisin' speed of 35 miles per hour for grazin', he could prob'ly make his fortune sellin' replacements to his neighbors in this dry country!"

"Not too many of the average people on the street realize what all is involved in production of the steak or hamburger they think is too high priced as they take it for granted at their super-market shelf," Connie adds. "Few really understand that their beef comes from grass primarily or grass in the form of roughage that is harvested as hay or fodder or silage; nor do lots of people realize when they get up on their 'soap-boxes' about cows competing with humans for grain they think should go directly into the cereal box, that an old cow makes their steak out of some pretty rough stuff!" He allows, "Matter-of-fact, if it weren't for the efficiency of that old natural leather bound self propelled hay baler we call a cow walking around in too tough country to stick a plow into, there'd be a heckuva' lot more starvation in the world than there already is. Let some of those 'do-gooders' take on a big feed of ol' dry grass when they run out of hamburger to go with their 'helper' and see how long it takes them to form a cud and then learn to chew it."

– Endless Tracks Across Centuries

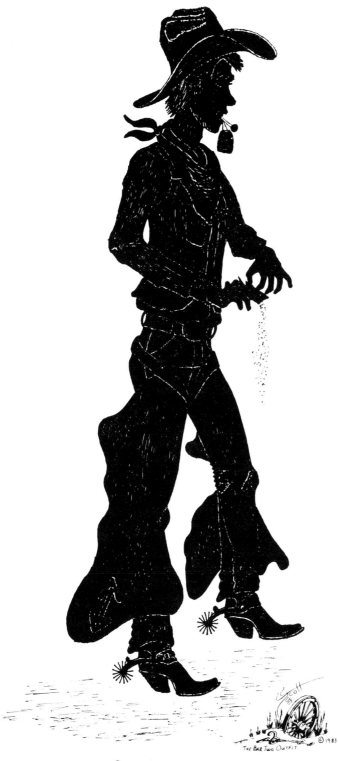

Somethin' to Ponder.

In truth, besides the cow and her production of meat and milk and leather and a wide variety of other life sustaining materials; such as, insulin, only the sheep and goat and domestication of wild ruminants or otherwise harvesting of them, allows man to have food, fiber and sustenance from land which would efficiently produce little else. It is very "nice" to think that we should only grow soybeans or beansprouts or other "vegies" on lands where God only intended enough rainfall and tilth for the cloven hooved ruminant; such as, the ox or his cousin to track and get by. It is also very naive and very ridiculous! Connie sums it up pretty well when he says, "People should never go pointing an accusing finger without they realize for every one finger they point there are three others pointing right back at the accuser!" Try it. Interesting little exercise in the all too often neglected quality known as humbleness, isn't it? It is something to ponder.

Time really flies, especially when one is having fun! And actually it was a fun time even with all the hard work. The spring of 1968 came with the new calf crop. Calving time is renewal time. The rancher with a concern for his bovine charges really lives with his cows during the weeks and sometimes months in that period in cow country that seems to start too soon before winter is past and leaves not enough time to get everything else done the rancher calls "spring work" before the heat of summer is upon him. He particularly lives with the "first calf" heifers if he expects to have a good percentage of the newborn calves survive or doesn't want to lose some of these new little mothers to obstetrical difficulties. Living with them means very constant surveillance 24 hours around the clock. Extra help is sometimes afforded to take turns at the night shift, but more often than not, the man just getting a foothold in the ranching business finds that extra help from his wife and helpmate and from the children quite often at a very early age.

Speaking of the quality of humbleness or humility, there is nothing any more equalizing than to be standing looking at one's handiwork with pride and compassion after having successfully assisted a heifer through a difficult delivery; only to have the new mama "tree" you atop a too low fence rail or behind a spindly shed support

– Endless Tracks Across Centuries

Tracks along the 49th Parallel
friendliest fence line in the world.

Basics of cowboy gear –
his saddle and lariat rope.

A cowboy and his best 'Hired' Hand.

Two of a cowboy's best Workin'
outfit – A good horse and faithful dog.

because she's angry from the hurt and trauma of the birth and is, at the same time, asserting her new found "mother instinct" as she "protects" her baby from the only "enemy" in sight. And here all the time you thought you were her "friend." It is equally disconcerting and goes a long way toward "unmaking your day" to save mother and calf through such a difficult birth only to have the calf totally ignorant of the next step in its progress toward survival, that if instinctively nursing the vitality giving first milk – the colostrum. In the first few hours after the calf is born, this first milk is unusually high in protein and immune bodies so necessary to the calf's immediate well-being and future survival against neonatal illness. Or it will totally unmake the rest of your day, besides using up precious time needed for all the other chores that have to be done every day without fail at this time of year, if the new lil' mama decides after waiting the 285 days that have just culminated in this "blessed event," she'd just as soon not be a mama anyway – "no way!" She decides she won't claim her calf or even takes her baleful eye and charge off of you and now chooses to consider her own flesh and blood "the enemy!" You now have to become protector, contortionist, educator, survivalist; alternating between quick offensive and quicker defense, depending who's momentarily the "winner," as you try to get the calf to suckle or try to keep the now very upset little cow from injuring or killing it or you! Oh, it is lots of fun! Fortunately, the majority of the time, nature's instincts work out to avoid a lot of this fuss, but there are always enough of these incidents to make life exciting.

As one of Connie's helpers summed it up after being flattened and run the full length of by a big old snorty heifer with "nothing but ugly on her mind – and this being the umteenth time, I've enjoyed just about all this 'fun' I can stand!" Of course Connie had already asked him what he was doing on the fence when only a moment before he'd been in the pen trying to push the unwilling calf up to an equally unwilling mama's flank. "What are you doing? – don't run from her – yuh'll make her think yer 'fraid of her – why don't you get back down in there and get 'em mothered up?"

With the upset heifer working over his backside on

the too low fence rail, the hired help replied, "I can't b'lieve she'd be mad at me after I was so nice to her but I can't get back in the pen 'cause I'm too busy bein' on this fence!" And all the time he's thinking, "Why am I doin' this when I could be working some place nice and warm like the Savin's 'n' Loan or good and safe like drivin' in a demolition derby?"

Anyway time does fly and the summer of 1968 flew with it, as did the fall and weaning, shipping calves; and all of a sudden winter has passed into the 1969 calving season and it has come another spring. In June of 1969 Connie and Margie with their three small children all making pretty good "hands" to help by now – after all Casey "was 11," Clinton "was 10," and "our little girl, Charlene, was 'bout 8-9," – made up a trailing crew of 5 to trail their cow herd with young calves at side from the ranch north of Havre to their new range on Frenchman Creek. "We were ten days trailin' that time," Connie recalled. "The kids started school in Whitewater the fall of 1969."

In the twenty years from the time of trailing their cows to the new location of Frenchman Creek to Montana's statehood Centennial year, Connie's family saw a lot of change. The children have all grown up and made lives of their own. Connie and Margie have improved and expanded the cow herd. In 1969 it was not uncommon to experience a 75% calf crop and weaning weights of 375 pounds. In 1989 the percentage calf crop had improved to 93% and the calves averaged better than 500 pounds at weaning time. Cow numbers have increased as carrying capacity has been improved through good management of the grass and water. "The only thing we have to sell off this ranch is grass and the best way, if not mostly the only way, to sell grass is as pounds of beef represented by live calves. Every cow must produce a calf every year and that calf has to survive and thrive if we are to survive, pay the bills and mortgage, and hope to maybe have a little left over for the tax collector or do any improving," says Connie.

It is not possible in the cow business, or for that matter, in ranching and agriculture generally, to make a decision about your operation today and realize any benefit if it's a good decision (or detriment if it turns out a bad decision) in less than a thousand days. In round figures a thousand days is just about three years. To make much change in a cow herd takes 8 or 10 years. That's only 3000 days. By the time you've spent 20 years or nearly 7500 days you've hopefully made enough more good decisions than bad and have had not too many years of dust instead of rain and not too many grasshoppers or blizzards or poor prices so that you could actually benefit from the right decisions. This is then called progress. Not one to stand in the way of progress, Connie says, "The trouble with progress is it's kinda hard to recognize at times and it may then just plumb run over you and iron you out if you are standing in the wrong place."

As has been said, time flies, and while change is continuous and ever constant, the analogy of days to years puts a perspective on this land and the lives affected by it that makes one know the story there is to tell is like the tracks that cross and recross the land. It is a story that in truth will never end. We are admonished to live one day at a time and one is encouraged by the wisdom of this advice as wind whisp clouds cross the sky and the colors of the willows along Frenchman Creek show change beginning from summer to autumn dress. There is a feeling about this land and the shaping it has had on the man that is not possible to explain. But the tracks up in the breaks that lead me back out of Frenchman Creek from Connie and Margie's home are not unlike the weather and humor lines in Connie's face. There is a depth of character in both that is unchanging and you know there is a unique steadfastness behind a decision such as the one to pay tribute to Montana's 100th birthday by taking the time and effort to trail a herd of Longhorn cows retracing tracks of over a century ago. It makes for something special in the celebrating of the Centennial.

It just seemed the right thing to do at the right time and there was the gut feeling that if it weren't done there'd be gnawing emptiness for not having made the effort. This then is not intended as a documentary of the entire Great Montana Centennial Cattle Drive of 1989. It is merely a sketch of a small fragment of the transition from one century to the next as viewed by an individual who would have liked to have been living at the beginning of Montana's start as a state. Not having been able to do that, the reliving of a few moments of that era seemed to become a very important effort.

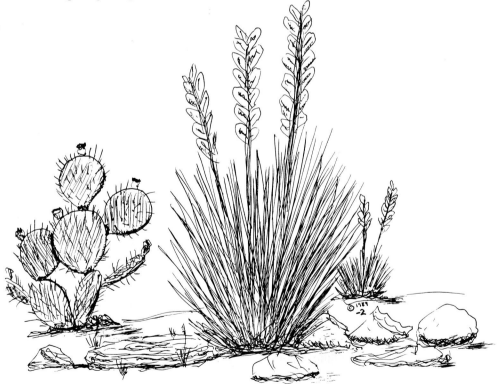

Rough Stuff – Cactus, Yuccas and Rocks.

– Endless Tracks Across Centuries

The Man.

The Country.

EPIC TRAILS —

FRIDAY, AUGUST, 11, 1989. THE FIRST DAY —

"It's 3:02 A.M. Couldn't sleep. I'm only one up. Larry Simpson, Ric Olsen and Andy Mueller pulled in yard at 2:30 A.M. and are waiting for me. They'd had a break down before leaving Saco last night. They brought Larry's team and wagon. We ate breakfast at 4:30. Beautiful morning. Left ranch at 6:45 A.M. with cows headed south on Frenchman Creek. Trailed 7 1/2 miles by 10 A.M. and stop to rest at Lyle Broadbrook's. Got to our first night's camp on Louie Depuydt's place a little after 7:00 P.M. It's a beautiful place to stay overnight. Saw two rattlesnakes the last mile into camp. Dwayne Reitan's boy, Sam, riding with us a little ways.

Ric Olsen and Alex McDougal left to go to their homes. Mel Smith came to camp at 7:30 P.M. to help trail tomorrow. Weather hot — in the high 90's today. There are 225 miles left to Roundup."

— Endless Tracks Across Centuries

Chapter 1
WILD HORSE LAKE YEARS

"Better for a man to wear out than to rust out" was more of a thought outloud rather than a reply as the question was raised to Connie Cox. "Why in the world are you putting yourself out to do this trail drive to Roundup, when all indications from the news reports say the big Centennial cattle drive is probably not going to happen anyway?" Well, what if it doesn't come off? If someone hadn't shown some faith, the West would have never been won either. Sure, it is taking extra work and planning but a lot of people have been involved for two years in preparation for this "Great Montana Centennial Cattle Drive of 1989" and a tried and favorite "Connieism" was the actual completed reply, "How're you gonna know or less you try?"

He'd acquired the Longhorn cows to replace in numbers some cows which he had been running on shares for another man. There'd been a hundred head of black cows in the deal and it had been one of the ways Connie had been able to help build up his numbers along with improving the Herefords, Angus and black-whiteface crosses he'd been working with since the move of the herd from the ranch at Wild Horse Lake to Frenchman Creek twenty years ago. These Longhorns were good hardy cows and he'd been using Charolais bulls with them. The calves they produced were darn good ones and the Longhorn-Charolais cross even made Connie dream that there might be a way you could have an 800 pound cow bring in a 700 pound calf at weaning time in the fall. The owner of the share cows had left him short of numbers when he'd decided to run those cows again himself, but Connie wasn't disappointed in the results of his experiment with the Longhorns. They'd proven very competitive in making their own living in the rough breaks and he figured he owed them a little recognition.

What better way than to try to recount a little of their own history by retracing some of the tracks of their Texas ancestors? What the heck if no one else showed up for the Big Drive of '89 in Roundup, anyway? The plans had been made, the calves weaned early and arrangements completed to put them into a feedlot with Ward Fenton down on the Yellowstone. If nobody else had cattle at Roundup when they got there, they'd just go ahead and trail them on into Billings and then decide how to get ready for whatever would be

next! The old adage that "there's nothing quite so good for the inside of a man as the outside of a horse" was something Connie had always pretty much believed in as a beneficial catharsis. He could do with the emotional rejuvenation and chance for some reflection that concentrated time in the saddle on this trek would provide. It was time to open the gate and count them onto the trail.

As early as Connie could remember all he'd ever wanted to be was a good hand as a cowboy and ultimately as a cattleman. It hadn't been easy but no one had ever promised it would be and he'd never looked for guarantees, only opportunity. Connie's sister, Norma Dell Brown, recalls Connie's early bent to be just a good cowboy and reflected, "If Connie could have lived a hundred years ago his ability and love of that era would have made him feel he was in seventh heaven. Connie has a natural sensitivity to his surroundings and a keenness of perception that more than makes up for what he may lack in formal education." She continued, "His general knowledge, free spirit and a certain charm of personality is unlike anyone else I'm acquainted with and these qualities have made me feel that Connie really has yearned to have lived at an earlier time." Fortunately the pensive bittersweetness resulting from these traits is tempered with an active sense of humor.

Connie was a restless youngster and he and his father, Arthur Cox, were never close. I sense that he had a great love for his mother and tried to be a help to her at home but because of conflict with his father, sought to be away from home much of the time when his father was there. Connie left the home place at Wild Horse Lake when he was 15 and stayed with friends south of Havre. He worked at putting up ice during the tough winter of '49-'50 when he was 16 years old, both in Havre and at Columbia Falls. His father would be gone a lot so Connie would go back home to help his mother. "I'd go home when dad was gone, then he'd come back and I'd leave again. Besides Ann Manuel and her folks who I stayed with off and on from 1948 'til 1957, I also stayed with my uncle and aunt, Herschel and Alice Fox, in Havre for a while and went to school, and I stayed a lot with Vic and Verlie Hanson, who were very good to me and like parents to me. All these people helped me a lot and the Hansons are still like my folks – they are much more than friends."

When Connie was 19 his uncle co-signed with him to get him started with some cows. The home place was at the east end of Wild Horse Lake and a lease was made on his granddad's place for the start up cow operation. This was in 1952. He'd worked with horses in about every respect; mostly riding at cow work, but with teams, too, haying and winter feeding, even breaking and starting to school some according to their aptitude (and attitude!). Connie got his first pickup truck when he was 20, the same year he decided to try his hand at rodeoing. "I never got on a bucking bronc in a rodeo arena 'til the one I mentioned about in May of '53, at Maple Creek, Saskatchewan. Oh, I knew I could ride a bad one some, but I'd been bucked off hard at home enough just in the routine course of ranch work to be pretty leery of taking rodeo up fulltime in the rough stock events. But I liked it and I liked a lot of the folks in rodeo, both the hands and the stock contractors and people behind the chutes who worked so hard at making it work for the people who came to watch and enjoy."

"Casey Tibbs, from over at Fort Pierre, South Dakota, was doing okay on the (Professional Rodeo Cowboys' Association) Pro-rodeo circuit and I liked his style of riding broncs. I also liked the way he was adding color to rodeo. 'Stead of hanging around back of the chutes after a rodeo was over or limpin' on down the road to the next one with a few 'haywire' buddies in a balin' wire ol' outfit, like most were having to do, you'd see Casey downtown with the crowd, signing autographs and visitin' with people. He was great P.R. for the sport. And there were others at the time who were top hands and who influenced my decision to try my hand at contesting. Bill Linderman, the Reynolds brothers, John and Benny, Ray Jacobsen and Merle Boyce; all good Montana cowboys. Some, like Casey Tibbs, were hitting the professional circuit full time, others were ranching cowboys and stayed mostly in the Montana Circuit. One of several such fellows that I traveled down the road with quite a bit was Dr. John Gee, veterinarian from over at Stanford. John worked as hard as anyone I can think of at everything he did and was good at it all. He still lives and practices at Stanford, runs a feedlot and you can still find him at some of the Old Timers' Rodeos in the Steer Wrestling."

"One thing that lots of people today may not know about rodeo or just take for granted is how much of the sport evolved out of regular day to day ranch work. It has changed a lot over the years but when I was young and enthused about starting into the rodeo game people sort of automatically figured the better Saddle Bronc and Bareback Bronc riders came from the north country; Montana, Canada, Wyoming, the Dakotas. Your better Calf Ropers and Team Ropers would be expected to come out of the south country; Texas, Oklahoma, California, Arizona and such. There were many early exceptions, particularly in events such as Bull Riding and Steer Wrestling. Many of the early-day contestants did not specialize nearly so much as they appear to nowadays, so there has always been a lot of crossover between rough stock events and timed events. But there was a sort of practical background to the generalization that 'good riders came out of the North and good ropers came out of the South'."

"Cowboyin' like the cattle and even the horse business originated out of the South with the trail herds. To be true I think the earliest trail herd into Montana came from over in Washington Territory in the early 1840s but those cattle of the Northwest had either originated out of California or with the migrants who'd moved west along the various emigrant trails. The men who worked the trail herds of the '60s and '70s were naturally, many of them, handy with a rope, and the climate in the South allowed for year around practice of their craft. They truly honed it into an art. The early native horse stock which came with these trail herds into Montana and on into Canada mixed with some native stock and some brought by the military and settlers from the east. The native range horse that developed was not big, was light to medium of bone, but had to develop a tough ability to survive the winters and so became surefooted and resourceful. Much of the more outstanding horseflesh that developed from the central plains from Wyoming through Montana and into the Canadian prairies were three way crossbreds. A native mare would be mated to a draft type sire, such as a Percheron, Belgian or Clydesdale. These breeds were short coupled and stout. The resulting cross, if a filly, would be bred in her time to a Thoroughbred. The 3 way result was a horse with bone, size and conformation combined with hardiness and stamina. These horses were

Mixing cow business
and rodeo was two
full-time jobs
rolled into one.

Connie Cox in good form
in rodeo's classic event,
The Saddle Bronc Riding.

The best part of a long day ahead.

usually very spirited but fortunately had good dispositions, and it was this type animal northern Montana ranchers strived for and broke into the good useful working ranch mounts they needed."

Unfortunately, not all of these horses had the usual good disposition, or could be spoiled by mishandling, and early day bucking horses often came from the resulting situations. Many an early day rodeo rider developed his talents from having to ride a lot of good but green horses of the type that did make good ranch working stock as well as some of the latter type "bad ones." Growing up and working in northern Montana, in the Wild Horse Lake and Bears Paw Mountain areas, proved Connie to be no exception. He had the hands and touch that have made him a good trainer of working horses and ones he had very capably been able to rope off of doing ranch work or contesting in the arena. At the same time he had the balance and athletic ability to fit a good ride on the ones that found it was a better life to work 8 seconds at a time trying to buck the rider off than to spend hours trailing or gathering or doctoring on the range or dragging calves to the branding fire. Horses may be considered "dumb brutes" but ask any qualified Saddle Bronc or Bareback Bronc's Union Rep and he'll be quick to ask the question back, "Which do you think makes more sense, a few seconds output a day in front of a cheering bunch of fans, or day after day of sweat and labor, often way out there by yourself with nobody to care or notice but your rider?" Sure a good thing there's still a good work ethic among horses as there is among men in this ranching business or all there'd be would be rodeos!

The following tale related about "Old Timers" by a cowboy who knew both the horse and the man illustrates a little of what makes up the mettle and fiber of people the likes of Connie Cox, and of the horses such men come to "know," respect and love.

The cowboy had pulled into a ranch yard to help with some cattle work for a neighbor but had been made late by a breakdown so the rest of the riders for the day's gather had been long saddled up and gone. All except one fellow busied with trying to get on an unwilling appearing mount of which he had one front leg dallied up to the saddlehorn to gain a bit of advantage. The rider was warily trying to get a foot in the stirrup while having his left elbow tucked well inside the near rein and a good mane hold. The arriving neighbor noticed right off that neither the man nor the horse were "colts," In fact they were darn "long in the tooth," both of them, and to see this type sparring contest between two "Old Timers" was strange and made him inquisitive. Needing to ask directions as to the day's ride anyway, he walked over to the pair, neither of whom had seemed to have noticed his arrival nor seemed to care about him being there. Only when he spoke as he approached did he hear the old cowboy conversing with the horse, and he received no reply to his greeting, "Howdy, Pardner, you reckon you can point me in the direction the other boys took off to?" Stepping a little closer to the two he was about ready to repeat the question when he heard the old cowboy say to the horse.

"Ol' hoss, ah wish you was still jist 7 er 8 years old an' Ah was still man enough t' ride the har off'n yuh?! And with that matter-of-fact declaration he was finally able to get his stiff old knee bent sufficiently to get his foot finally in the stirrup and deftly swing on. Even on three legs the old horse still tried to whirl from under him and would have bucked if he could. Only when the tied up leg was slowly released to the ground and the two nearly crow-hopped over the top of the observer did they seem to realize his presence and acknowledge him. "Oh, h'llo there, didn't see you come up. What kin Ah do fer you?" With explanation made both cowboys headed out the gate for the range they were to help gather and with further questioning the younger man learned an interesting course of events which had led up to the scene he'd just witnessed.

"Ah wuz workin' fer a guy named of Piper in Wyoming 33-34 yars ago and he had me break out a string of purty rough hosses. This'n wuz one of 'em. Ah got 'em kinder green-broke and went on to another outfit. Jist a couple yars back Ah went over into that Chugwater country to pay ol' Piper a visit and as't him 'bout that string of outlaws he tried to kill me off with, the ones Ah'd tried to green-break fer 'im?"

"Tried, is kerect!" the old man snapped back, "Them hosses all turned out bad and ah sold ever' one of 'em but one Ah couldn't ketch to a buckin' horse string!"

"That a fact? What happened to the one – blizzards or buzzards get 'im?"

"Hell no, he's still rangin' out there in those dobie breaks, smarter 'n' ornrier than the devil – plumb wuthless!"

"That so? Well, if Ah kin ketch'm, kin Ah have 'im?" Ah as'ts, an' ol' Piper says t' me, plenty surprised but not so snappy now. "Yuh bet! Don't think yuh kin ever ketch th'

Two Old Timers.

The Classic ("Wreck!").

Champion Bronc Rider – Plains, Montana 1959.

Photo Courtesy Margie Cox.

23

7   7
Brand
right hip & right rib
is Connie Cox Ranch
stamp of ownership
on cattle.

If the iron is right
an instant touch
results in a good mark.

Old time ways with head & heel
ropers providing restraint.
New ways may add use of
mechanical squeeze chute.

A good cowpony and a
willing working dog
are a cowboy's right 'Hands'
on roundup gather.

Cherry red hot iron
in a wood fire takes
only a touch.

ol' cuss but yuh kin shore have 'im and plumb welcome!" With that Piper made out a bill of sale with the added note "Range delivery" and the deal was done.

"Ah did manage to trap this ol' hoss and it waren't easy but Ah got him back home and got him so Ah could ride him some. Seemed like he could remember some of my ways from b'fore and Ah could shore remember some of his'n, 'specially a couple things _ he don't like you to git on an' never miss more'n one loop if yuh try to rope off'n 'im or he gits mad an' will buck yuh off shore!"

The cowboy relating this story calculated that the two "Old Timers," the man and his horse, had to be in their late '70s and mid to late '30s respectively, and both would put in a hard day's ride "jist helpin' the neighbors."

While not entirely depicting how "the West was won," this story does suggest the patient bonding between the man and his horse that people like Connie have come to know and to rely upon for getting many of the day-to-day things done that did add up to the "winning of the West" and keep things moving along with ranch and livestock work even with today's technology.

Another young Chinook area cowboy that Connie traveled to rodeos with some in the '50s and '60s was Bob Sivertsen. Bob was one of several Sivertsen brothers Connie was acquainted with and they had a pretty auburn haired little sister by the name of Marjorie. Between trying to get a start in the cow business and taking his rodeoing very seriously the next few years after his start in '53, Connie talked Margie into marrying him in 1957 and they lived in the Simpson Community at the west end of Wild Horse Lake. With starting a young family they were both busy, and when asked about why he never decided to rodeo full-time for a while on the Professional Rodeo Cowboys' Association circuit, Connie replied, "If I was going to do so I should have gone pro my second year at the age of 22. I was really riding bucking horses pretty good by then and was roping and bulldoggin' – they call it steer wrestling now, not too bad either. But I got to thinkin' when you are old you are old for a long time or at least hope you will have a chance to be and I figured if I was going' to mix ranching with rodeo I'd better work darn hard at both but not let one interfere with the other if I felt like I was losing the edge either way."

"I like a really good time but riding broncs is like flying an airplane. You have to have all your marbles about you when you get on one end and besides working at it I know I had a lot of good luck. It was enough to become involved in the sport of rodeo on a regional basis in the Montana Rodeo Association and the Northern Rodeo Association. I was fortunate to be starting into rodeo at about the same time the Montana Amateur Rodeo Association was organized under the leadership of Harry Dawson. Later on, close to the time we made the move from Wild Horse Lake to the Frenchman Creek ranch, I'd had the opportunity to serve as President of the Northern Rodeo Association in 1967-68. The Montana Amateur Association evolved into the Montana Rodeo Association in 1969, and in 1982 the MRA and the NRA joined forces to become the largest regional rodeo association in the world under the banner of the Northern Rodeo Association. Besides the association affairs, I was lucky enough to be able to contest weekends during each season, for 10 years in the Saddle Bronc competition, and for 17 years in the Bareback Bronc riding. I quit getting on bucking horses intentionally when I was 37 because I could feel the edge wasn't there like it had been. I continued to steer wrestle for a time and still do team rope in the "Old Timers' Association rodeos."

Because he was serious about trying to enjoy being old when the proper time came Connie said he was never very much "interested in riding bulls." He continued: "And that's just my way of thinkin' what I b'lieve is only common sense for me – maybe not for the next cowboy — but darn sure for me. I hope when I die, my home will be in Heaven, but I'm sure not homesick yet!"

Calm in the Hurricane Eye – but I'm not homesick yet!

EPIC TRAILS-

Saturday, August 12, 1989. Day Two —

Up and gone at 5:45 a.m. Cows trailing good. Stop for breakfast at 10:00 a.m. Cows are trailing about 2 to 3 miles per hour. Watered cows at Hilmer and Edna Bakke's and let them rest 'til about 1:30 p.m. Got to Milk River bridge at 3:00 p.m. and had a lot of trouble trying to get them to cross bridge. After more than 1 1/2 hour of refusing to take bridge, Carl Stahl brought some hay and scattered it on the approach and on bridge. Cows followed across in just a few minutes and were all across by nearly 4:30. Let them water again at Milk River and correled cows for overnight at Saco Roping Arena.

'Swede Olsen brought a big dun colored steer to trail with our cows. Looks like this steer might weigh a ton. He's sure big and tall at the shoulders!

At 5:30 p.m. we all went to the 'plunge (Sleeping Buffalo Hot Springs) to swim and eat supper. Really 'roughing' it! Stayed overnight camp at the Arena with the cattle. ~~Mesgos~~ Megedos bad! — nearly to eat us up! Weather was hot again — high 90's with hot wind blowing. Larry Simpson's granddaughter, Amber, 7 years old, rode all day with us. Made 15 miles today, even with hold up at Milk River bridge. 210 miles yet to go to get to Roundup.

Endless Tracks Across Centuries

A cow is nature's leather bound hay baler —
she'll build you a steak out of pretty rough stuff!

Chapter 2

THESE DARNED OLD COWS

There's probably not an animal that can be any more contrary or stubborn than an old cow when she takes a notion she wants to do what she wants to do or doesn't want to do what you might want her to do. It is a good thing they are gregarious and have a herding instinct so that right or wrong a given bunch generally sticks together in whatever they decide to do at a given moment. There are the exceptions and those usually end up causing the rancher or cowboy more work than the rest of the herd put together. These are the ones that'll brush up when they see a rider come into view, or will always find a bog to cross at the most inopportune time. Or she may be what is termed "breachy," or the proverbial "fence crawler," in that she's always through the fence into the crop or at the neighbors field and obviously not where she's supposed to be. If she is a "loner" this may not cause too much consternation most of the time. If she happens to be pretty well up in the pecking order and a "ringleader" as well, she can deal quite a lot of misery into a cowboy's everyday life.

This kind of cow will not only lead others astray but she'll also lead them into refusing to do what you need or want them to do on a herd basis at times. This old girl can see the smallest opening in a cut-bank to duck into, or crawl the tightest fence and never seem to get a nick or loosen a staple, so it's hard for you to find out where she gets out, but open the gate to put her back where she belongs and she can't see the open gate for love nor money. Or she'll jump through the fence right next to the open gate and tear enough fence down to have you mending it for the rest of the day. She will lead the others up to the opened gate and break and run back or by with a bawl and a snort that puts all the rest of the bunch into a spooky mood so you end up "spilling" them and have to go about gathering them all together again. Another action which will disturb the composure of even the most patient of hands is to have a gathered bunch of cattle willingly moving toward or through a gate only to have an old boss cow or boisterous bull stop in the middle and challenge "anybody to set foot across this line," disrupting the whole flow of traffic.

While circumstances will vary, it seems that critters, much the same as people, have quite a sense of imagination. So, it seems, was the case with this set of Longhorn cows of Connie's as they perceived some sort of spook or "troll" of bovine Teutonic folklore to be lurking under or about the Milk River bridge and refused to cross. But, necessity being the creator of invention, and where there is a will there is a way, it is often possible to lead the beasts where they cannot be driven. So it was in this crossing that the cows readily followed the bite of hay, when more prodding or pushing could have resulted in a scatter that would have ended the rest of the day's progress. Although the afternoon was hot and the wind searing, the smell of the hay and a rote sense of having followed similarly on many a cold winter day behind a feed of some sort got things moving again, with whatever bugaboo the bridge may have held temporarily forgotten. The wind also helped to minimize another aggravation. The swarms of mosquitoes (Connie terms them "megeetos") prevalent along the streams and low or marshy areas can put the cattle in a frenzied rush for willows or other brush to seek relief.

All in all the drive seems off to a good start and earlier in the day with the cows trailing well it was obvious which ones wanted to be the leaders and which were content to follow. Those that would prove to be dawdlers and lollygaggers the whole trip were making their impression on the drovers, too. It would be their lot to serve as practice targets for the "trap" of many a thrown heeling loop as the riders would try to encourage them to get back on the trail and to keep up with the herd. A big horsefly attempting to get a bite through the hide of one of the "drag" critters could expect an attempt on his wellbeing from the honda end of a well aimed rope, too. It was a time for thinking and reflection as the senses perceived somewhat outside a conscious awareness, the moment at hand. The smell of the sage, the acrid feeling of the dust in the air as it combined with the sage and the wild primrose to penetrate the sinuses and assail the eyes; the creak of the saddle leather rhythmically uninterrupted as the ear caught the note of a distant meadowlark and a not so distant warning buzz of the tail of "Mr. Whizbang" warning your horse to "don't tread on me" and the distant dance of a little whirlwind "dust-devil" twisting toward the shimmering mirage-like horizon with its blue hills and far off buttes; all served to transport the mind away on its own nostalgic journey.

There were mixed feelings about trailing these Longhorn cows away from home. As mentioned earlier, they had been acquired to keep the count up when some share cows had been returned to their owner. These were hardy animals, and their crossbred calves sired by Charolais bulls were good ones, but the varied color patterns of their hides created an enigma when it came market time. No matter what kind of cattle it seemed a man had to sell at that particular moment, the order buyers and others who tended to "make" the market invariably wanted something a little different! If you had whitefaced cattle with red hides, advertised in years past as being from the "breed supreme," the buyers wanted blacks because they were being advertised "blacks are better." If you had straight blacks you were informed they didn't suit the feeder who preferred "baldies" or black whitefaced or brockle faced calves to background or feed out. If you started with a straight Hereford or Angus set of cows and spent the 1000 or 2000 or 3000 days necessary to get what you thought you'd understood the market wanted in the way of the "baldie" or good black whiteface cross calf you were then told, "Gotta have some exotic blood in these calves so as they'll grow faster. Boy, thats what the feeder wants; some big good-doin' Simmental or Limousin or Gelbvieh or Chianina or Salers or one of 'them other European' crosses – but these calves are too big so we'll have to buy 'em on a weight break and discount the real heavy ones 'cause they ain't 'green' enough to suit the order we have." Or, "Man-Oh-Man did your calves ever do good for that ol' boy that fed 'em out but the packer wasn't happy with 'em 'cause the carcass was too big to fit in the box'?????" Whatever that means?

Funny thing, a lot of the different breeds or crosses and resulting types become rather difficult to identify in the current system of marketing once the hide comes off, so that what's underneath suddenly looks more alike; more like muscle or red meat, fat and bone. And the color of the money it does bring no matter how it is sold, nor how it's purchased at the meat counter, is reasonably uniformly green. Nevertheless, it had to be faced that the Longhorn cross calves were a challenge to merchandise for anywhere close to the same price per pound at weaning time as the baldies or other calves of more uniform color.

And then there was always the problem of just what to keep and grow out as replacement breeding heifers to maintain numbers as older cows or ones that quit producing efficiently were of economic necessity removed from the herd. Most commercial cattlemen have been so busy trying to keep up with the whims and wants and likes and dislikes of the market place that they have not had the time to plan and develop a systematic plan of genetic improvement, if they are attempting to crossbreed to produce what they hope is the desired market calf. If they have tried to stay with a straight breed or a herd stemming from one specific purebred source they have often found they were losing ground out in the "sticks" of their real world ranching environment because the seedstock they were depending upon for their herd bull purchases and to produce their future range cows from were not functional cattle. They were more, shall it be said, "ornamental" cattle that were selected as much or more on show ring "glitter" than on performance capability or economic merit. Connie was reminded of the grinding process it had been to make improvement from the weaning weights and percentage live calves to sell compared to the number of cows maintained from the Wild Horse Lake years to now. He was reminded that with all his efforts to invest in improved genetics, based upon what he thought he'd come to understand about what the marketplace wanted, he was still forced to sell any improvement he'd made on "an average." That tended to give the buyer all the advantage of his progress rather than see an appreciable return to his own pocket for the extra effort.

He knew he liked the cattle business and had never thought of being in anything else but didn't much like the too frequent reminder that these darned old cows were more a way of life than a way of making a good living from a strictly business sense point of view. He

Cuttin' some of the trail dust off the outside.

31

hoped that continued attention to managing his grass and improving the genetics of his cow herd would keep the necessary edge to make a little headway. In these changing times there was talk of things like "retained ownership" or maybe partnering with the guy who would feed the calves out so that if there was improved profit potential in the calves from his efforts to produce better ones he might share in that return. Getting the banker to look with him at something of that long range nature was another matter to be contemplated, and not lightly, it might be added, matter of factly. Niche marketing or integrating from the ranch production level forward into the sale of a "branded" beef product that could be recognized back to its source or origin was another thing he'd been reading quite a lot about recently. Boy, it was kind of good to get away and just look out over old Blue's ears and just think about the whole big picture.

Connie had worked hard at being a good cowboy and hoped the equally hard work he was continuing to do might leave him remembered or known as a good cowman, too. Not that he figured the world would note many legendary figures in the cow business; at least among rangemen. Such notoriety most probably was reserved for the purebred man or the scientist or stockman turned politician. He would be happy just to maybe someday get far enough ahead to pay the ranch off and to live past this time of health-nut-anti-red meat negative propaganda that just seemed to add confusion unnecessarily. He was seriously reflecting on all the people he knew who had lived to an active and healthy old age with nutrient dense beef as a major staple in their diet when Blue quickly sidestepped to avoid a rattler. Connie looked into the dense sage thicket where the warning "buzz" of the snake was coming from but Blue did not wish to venture closer, so taking his cue from his horse, Connie rode on, his thoughts still on how to get equal time in the media for his industry to tell their side of the nutrition and health story. He was reminded of the story a friend had told of an old cowboy lamenting on a frosty September morning; "Folks jist don't re'lize all the good a ol' cow really does."

This was at a Fall roundup camp and a couple of the older cowboys were swapping yarns in the chill of the morning while the chuckwagon cook was tending to a

breakfast of fried steak, spuds and onions, all being done up in a cast iron dutch oven and about ready to be washed down with coffee boiled in an old granite pot. Moving away from the smoke of the cook fire, the old cowboys were watching the wranglers jingling the loose horses into the rope corral, and one sat down on a big old dried cowchip to protect his gaunt old haunches from the cold ground. He continued, "Yup, take this hyer dried up meader muffin fer instance; the cook kin use it fer kindlin if'n he's a need to or given a little rain 'r snow to dissolve it and when the sun warms enough the dung beetle kin go to work, It'll git spread aroun' natural-like to make more grass next spring." He knocked the ashes out of his ancient pipe and proceeded to refill and light it up again when his cowchip seat started to move! Realizing what was causing it to move the other old gent and the cook held their breath a moment as a big rattlesnake started to squirm out from beneath our old cowboy's perch. Before either could utter a warning, the seated cowboy sprang up as if propelled by coiled steel. Realizing the rattler was cold and sluggish and that he hadn't been in much danger because of this, the old cowboy added the philosophical note; "Yuh see there, boys – you've know'd of fresh cow flop bein' used as a poultice to draw pizen out'n a wound – wull bet yuh didn't know when it dried up it could be used like armor to pertect yer backside from snakebite in the fust place!" With a final authoritative flair, he added as the cook rang the triangle, "An' jist see how it natur'lly kept that ol' 'whizbang' from freezin' to death las' night." The rattler crawled down a gopher hole while the rest of the hands stood dumbfounded. "Yup, the ol' cow is sure mankind an' nature's natural born protector, bless her durn'd ol' hide anyhow!"

Waitin' for things to warm up on a frosty mornin'.

– Endless Tracks Across Centuries

EPIC TRAILS—

SUNDAY, AUGUST 13, 1989. THIRD DAY ON THE TRAIL —

    EVERYBODY UP AT 5:30 A.M. AND COWS ON TRAIL BY 6:15. HAD TO GO THROUGH TOWN OF SACO AND HAD TO WAIT 'TIL AFTER 7:30 TO CROSS RAILROAD TRACKS AS 2 TRAINS WENT THROUGH. COWS CROSSED TRACKS REAL GOOD AND TRAILED THROUGH TOWN CAUSING NO TROUBLE. DAN GARRISON WENT IN FRONT OF LEAD COWS WITH HIS PICKUP TRUCK AND SOME CAKE. COWS FOLLOWED RIGHT ALONG.

    LET COWS REST SOUTH OF TOWN AND WENT BACK INTO SACO TO HAVE BREAKFAST. AFTER RESTING COWS A COUPLE HOURS WE TRAILED ANOTHER 5 MILES AND PUT THEM INTO GRAZING ASSOCIATION CORRALS. WE ARE INTO ROUGHER COUNTRY AND MADE 11 MILES TODAY. SANDY OLSEN WENT BACK TO MALTA TO GET READY TO LEAVE TOMORROW FOR ALASKA WHERE SHE TEACHES SCHOOL. SANDY HAS BEEN TEACHING AT PILOT STATION WAY WEST OF ANCHORAGE.

    NOT QUITE SO HOT TODAY. WEATHER IN THE 80'S WITH A LITTLE BREEZE. 199 MILES TO ROUNDUP.

—ENDLESS TRACKS ACROSS CENTURIES

Chapter 3

RODEO WEEKENDS

Getting the Longhorns through Saco and heading into rougher country on a pleasant Sunday morning gave Connie and his riders a sense of a milestone passed as they went back into town for breakfast. The trail would now be moving again into more native prairie and there would be miles ahead between here and the Missouri River, where about the only sign of modern times would be the fences. They would be trailing in a southwesterly direction now until crossing the Missouri, and the view ahead was as beautiful as this day itself was turning out to be. The wait at the railroad crossing in Saco and the way things were moving this Sunday morning reminded Connie of the many rodeo weekends in the '50s, '60s and into the '70s. Thinking back and adding up the weekends and number of bucking horses he'd got on nearly every weekend for 5 months or so each year for nearly a dozen years with saddle broncs and a dozen and a half years for bareback broncs, he could believe why the joints creaked and ached a bit these cooler mornings. Oh, he had contested some in the bull riding until about the middle '60s but as mentioned earlier, self preservation seemed to be a pretty strong instinct, so the combination of the two bronc riding events and the timed events of steer wrestling and roping made the best sense to Connie. Statistics of past NRA event champions and All-Around Champion Cowboys during those years bear out the fact that this combination was a good choice for this cowboy.

Researching Northern Rodeo Association records for the decade of the '60s lists Connie Cox in the year-end All-Around Champion Cowboy standings at least seven times with five first place wins, a second and a third. He consistently placed high during those years in the bronc riding events and steer wrestling with some placings in the calf roping, team roping and even the bull riding to compile the necessary points to place up in the All-Around competition. These placings were in competition with a lot of very good cowboys who were also tough competitors. In a long list of NRA winners which would make up a large regional USA rodeo who's-who,

such competitors and standings included names like Merle Boyce, Bud Connelly, John Gee, Ray Jacobsen, Wes Stoos, Joey Malsam, Bill Nauman, Jim Jacobsen and many, many others. Many names published in the winners listings by the NRA and in the regional media during these years included, as with the Jacobsen family name, multiple family members or two generations of competitors at the same period of time. Family names included Fraser, Gustafson, Nelson, Brown, Songer and again many, many others of public record. Names which appeared on some of the winners lists during these years are familiar today in other walks of Montana life, but especially in ranching, or some facet of the livestock industry. The list includes names such as: Taylor, Gollaher, Pursley, Anderson, Dear, Hough, Perry and Murnion. Some came from ranching to rodeo, depending upon the generation; others went from rodeo to ranching, or such industry related endeavors as livestock auction marketing and livestock supply services. Others, like Dr. John Gee, successfully combined rodeo with his veterinary profession. Jay Contway, noted Native American sculptor of western art, sharpened his keen observation of detail in and around the rodeo arena and won some calf roping competitions at the same time.

Most interesting in the review of winners listings during the years in which Connie Cox's name appeared frequently was the appearance of the second generation names on the standings roster. In the youth or kids events of roping and barrel racing names like Casey Cox and Clinton Cox and Charlene Cox were beginning to show up. Tip Coleman's name appears frequently in the early '70s. Tip is today the son-in-law of Connie and Margie Cox and it would appear he and Charlene have a third generation of potential ranch and rodeo hands developing with their children, Tia and Cash. Connie says some of the rodeo highlights over the years for him have included the span of time from his own winning of the Amateur Saddle Bronc Championship at Cheyenne Frontier Days in 1955 to teaming up with son, Casey, then 15 years old, to win the 1973 "10 Head" Roping at Lewistown, "when a lot of tough ropers were there," to seeing Casey go on to being a champion National Collegiate Team Roper and seeing him qualify for the National Professional Rodeo Finals at Las Vegas in 1988.

In the Cox home at the ranch on Frenchman Creek one has to look in a quiet corner in a back room to see a modest display of just some of Connie's rodeo championship trophy buckles and other awards. Some of the trophy saddles have seen a lot of use and are polished and seasoned from the work they've done, not as a show piece. Typical of most people in the rodeo business, Connie's brusque affability covers up an innate shyness that is very matter-of-fact and which would just as soon leave accolades unspoken or left to the imagination. When asked one time why his trophy buckles were not more visibly displayed after the questioner had examined the engravings and counted more than 100 of the championship awards, Connie replied, "I s'pose there may be that many there but in a hard winter you can't eat a one of 'em; I even tried once and broke a tooth in the bargain!" He had no further comment. Changing the subject he said, "The thing that's meant the most to me from rodeoing are the friendship and the memories of the good and fun times. To be sure, there was fierce competition at times, and it wasn't all fun, as there'd be lots of rodeos with no pay day and pretty bleak prospects of how to get to the next one where you hoped your luck would return. The code is much the same as with your neighbor in the ranching business. You haze for a fellow steer wrestler, knowin' he may very well put you out of a winning time. Or you help your buddy get on a rank horse making sure his rein and stirrups are adjusted just right to give him every chance of beating you. You feed your neighbor's cows when they're trapped in a storm and he can't get to 'em or pull his cow out of a bog or fix his fence. Mostly he'd do the same for you. When it's all said and done you hope you've got enough really good friends so's you won't have to hire somebody to pack the box they put you in to carry you to your final reward!" He concluded, "I know I've got a few such friends, like Joe Big Knife, for instance, an' I hope they feel they could depend on me the same as I know I can depend on them."

Another highlight that has developed into an ongoing thing for Connie from those earlier rodeo weekends has been the Cox Ranch Annual Team Roping held at Frenchman Creek each spring or more recently at the Whitewater Arena. Team ropers come from all over to participate in a few days of competition and fun and to renew old acquaintances. Besides drawing cowboys and their families together for what has become somewhat of a reunion of many NRA hands, this annual event sees them coming from several Canadian provinces and from states as far away as Georgia. Connie says, "We'll have our Twentieth Annual Ranch Roping in 1992 and by then I think Clinton will carry it on."

Where there's smoke. . . . 8 seconds paid off for the old "Refugee From A Cultivator" this time. He's only worked three-and-a-half minutes in the past two years but he's good at his job and likes it, too. Bucked off 19 cowboys and only been qualified on a half-dozen times!

– Endless Tracks Across Centuries

Connie Cox calf roping at Wood Mountain Saskatchewan, July, 1970.

Connie Cox on a bareback bronc at Augusta, Montana, 1957.

If I hadn't been flying to rodeos on weekends, I may never have found Frenchman Creek.

Silver Sage And Silver Clouds.

37

Connie Cox at Havre in 1969 shaping up a steer for a fast wrestling time . . .

*. . . But the good time all belongs to the steer this trip.
The old "Rubber Neck" refuses to cooperate!*

EPIC TRAILS —

MONDAY, AUGUST 14, 1989. FOURTH DAY OUT —

LEFT ASSOCIATION CORRALS AT 6:00 A.M. COWS TRAILING GOOD. COOL BREEZE BLOWING FROM THE EAST. GOT TO JIM SALISBURY'S CORRALS AT 10:15. STOP FOR BREAKFAST AND TO LET STOCK REST. BACK ON TRAIL AT 1:10 P.M AND WENT ONLY ANOTHER 2 MILES TO A PASTURE WHERE FEED IS REALLY GOOD. CAMPED THERE TO LET COWS GRAZE AND REST 'TIL 5 P.M., THEN TRAILED ON TO FRANK MARTIN'S PLACE. DID NOT GET TO THIS CAMP 'TIL 10:30 P.M. COWS TIRED AND SO ARE WE AND OUR HORSES.

MEL SMITH AND KEN SCHOKER LEFT TO GO BACK HOME AND MARGIE COX AND BRUCE BLACKMER ARRIVED IN TONIGHT'S CAMP. MY WIFE, MARGIE, DROVE FROM HOME AND BRUCE CAME FROM MALTA. THE WEATHER WAS BEAUTIFUL TODAY WITH THE COOL BREEZE. WE COVERED 20 MILES SO HAVE 179 MILES TO ROUND UP.

—ENDLESS TRACKS ACROSS CENTURIES

Connie Cox and his team roping rodeo family.

With Casey, heeling '73.

Clinton, heeling.

Charlene, heeling.

photos pgs. 40 - 41 courtesy Margie Cox.

40

Casey, heeling '83.

*Clinton,
heeling '83.*

*Charlene, roping
the heels, '83.*

Chapter 4
THERE'S ALWAYS MONDAY MORNING
Didn't He Know. . . . . ?

Out of this Montana country of cold and snow,
    Came a free spirited cowboy I used to know;
A consistent top hand of rodeo renown,
    Known through the land and every western town.

        Wagons, teams, saddle horses, bedrolls and tack,
            Trailing a herd of Longhorn cows and steers,
        Just like Teddy 'Blue' did in the early years.
        Trailing them to the '89 rendezvous–
        Experiencing the 'Fiery' and 'Snuffy' from horseback;
            and legendary things just known to a few.

                Driving them to the Great Centennial Cattle Drive,
                    Hoping to make it with every one well 'n' alive.
                One fine night when the cattle was all bedded down,
                    A friend stopped in camp–hauled them all into town.

In a little bar to cut the dust they settled down,
    Having a drink or two, their thirst to drown.
The barkeep listened to their yarns for a while,
    Then he said, "Fellers", with a smile–
"I know you all must be heckuv' good hands,
    But tell me something I can't understand?"

        "You have fought the dust, mud, 'skeeters and alkali,
            'Til every son-of-a-gun of you's got the red eye.
        By lookin' at you I'm surmisin', but it's my best guess;
            If you was to cry, you'd surely all bleed to death!"

                "You have crossed bogs and dangerous prairie dog holes,
                    Fought wind, rain, hail, rattlers and God only knows;
                Your cattle are tired, horses jaded–you're all saddle sore,
                    Now you say you have several days more?"

"I'm just a bartender–not any way a cowhand,
    But I know somethin' of the misery of this land.
Now then fellers don't get all in a huff;
    And please don't sneeze–I'm allergic to dust,
But why do you suffer and press your luck,
    When you could do it so easy with a truck?"

        Connie looked at him over top of his glass;
            Not sure to believe what by his ears did pass?
        How could you answer a livin' body so dumb?
            Didn't he know...? They was havin' fun?

                Next mornin' at camp, when the sky grew gray,
                    The coyote yippin', "It's the break of day."
                Connie slowly crawled and loosed the kinks from his bed,
                    With a burnin' thirst and an achin' head–
                "Ouch!" He muttered as he drank the water bucket down;
                    A cowboy enjoys a lot with friends when he's in town!

– Endless Tracks Across Centuries

EPIC TRAILS—

TUESDAY, AUGUST 15, 1989. FIVE DAYS ON THE TRAIL—

SLEPT IN. DID NOT START COWS ON TRAIL 'TIL 7:30 A.M. GOT TO BIM AND SONNY OXARART'S PASTURE AT 10:00 A.M. FIXED SOME BREAKFAST. FRANK AND HENRY MARTIN STOPPED BY CAMP TO VISIT AND TO LOOK AT LONGHORNS. WE ARE CUTTING 2 COWS OUT WHICH ARE SHOWING FOOT-SORE AND A BIT LAME. OUR START THIS MORNING HAD ALSO BEEN DELAYED BECAUSE WINSTON HAD PUT A COLT IN THE CORRAL TO USE FOR WRANGLING THE HORSES BUT HE DIDN'T CHECK THE FENCE SO THE HORSE GOT OUT AND WE HAD NO WRANGLE HORSE. I THINK WINSTON MOSTLY USES HIS HEAD FOR A PLACE TO PUT HIS HAT AND TO GROW HAIR. IF HE IS LIKE THIS IN A FEW YEARS, HE SHOULD BE ABLE TO GET A GOOD JOB SOMEDAY IN WASHINGTON, D.C. WORKING FOR THE GOVERNMENT!

AS WE GOT READY TO MOVE COWS OUT ON TRAIL AGAIN AT MID-DAY, BRUCE BLACKMER WENT TO LEAD SADDLE MARE TO WATER AND HAD A MISHAP. HE PLACED A HALF-HITCH OVER HER NOSE AND SHE REARED UP AND STRUCK HIM ON THE ARM. MARGIE TOOK BRUCE TO DOCTOR IN MALTA. THE REST OF US TRAILED ON TO TWEET AND BETTY OXARART'S RANCH. GETTING THERE ABOUT 4:30 P.M., WE PUT THEM IN A 200 ACRE PASTURE WITH GOOD FENCE AND A NICE PLACE TO BED THE COWS OVERNIGHT.

WILLIAM ANDERSON, NANCY BARNETT AND BILLIE JO ANDERSON CAME FROM LARB HILLS TO VISIT AND LOOK AT LONGHORN COWS. WILLIAM AND I TOOK PICKUP AND TRAILER WITH MY HORSE 11 MILES EAST AND CHASED 44 SHEEP AND 1 LAMB ABOUT 2 MILES

—ENDLESS TRACKS ACROSS CENTURIES

AND PUT THEM IN A CORRAL FOR LEO BARTHELMESS. THEN BACK TO OXARARTS WHERE WE RAN TWO MILK COWS IN THEIR CORRAL FOR THEM. I'M GETTING TO BE QUITE A 'COWBOY', HERDING SHEEP AND CHASING MILK COWS!

LARRY SIMPSON HAD SUPPER READY WHEN WE GOT BACK TO CAMP. FRIED STEAK, BEANS AND BREAD — GOOD. THIS HERDING SHEEP AND NURSEMAIDIN' MILK COWS CAN SURE MAKE A HUNGRY HAND OUT OF A PLAIN OL' COWBOY.

IT WAS HOTTER WEATHER AGAIN TODAY BUT A COOLING BREEZE IS PUTTING A CHILL INTO THE NIGHT AIR. WE MADE 12 MILES TODAY SO HAVE 167 LEFT TO GET TO ROUNDUP.

Chapter 5

40 HOUR WEEKS . . . ?

"You can lead a horse to water but you can't make him drink" is an old saying most everyone has heard at one time or another. What would have been a routine day of just moving the wagon and cows down the trail sure turned out to have a lot of little extra happenings and mishaps. Winston's wrangle horse being gone when needed at the beginning of the day started things off. Poor Winston had to take a lot of good natured ribbing and practical jokes, but he was possessed of good humor and a pretty crafty practical joker himself so took it all good naturedly. Bruce Blackmer's difference of opinion with the saddle mare hopefully hadn't caused serious injury but the crew would have to wait for the report to come back from Malta to know. Most of the cows were getting trail wise and seasoned into the trek, and unlike the trail drives of old, the cows that became lame now could be loaded in a trailer and given a lift. Getting into camp at 10:30 p.m. the previous night had made a long and tiresome day out of Monday and Bruce, who was taking time off from his regular job with the BLM and calling the trail drive his vacation had reflected that the hours doing cow work weren't very regular. The diversion of moving the sheep and milk cows for Leo Barthelmess and Oxararts had actually taken a little longer than Connie made it sound when he joked about "chasing" them. Herding was a more accurate term in both instances as hurrying sheep in hot weather could lead to serious problems and if you wanted an old milk cow to do her job – that of providing a little cream for your coffee – you'd better treat her with respect, kid gloves and tender loving care! As many an old timer would attest; "Anybody who'd look after sheep or tend milch cows would be better at runnin' a hospital pen than at cowboyin'."

Writing a job description for a cowboy's work could be quite a varied effort. Depending upon the season or the given ranch he might work on, his job was usually several part to full-time endeavors wrapped into the general term of cowboying. Of course, preference would have every task performed from the back of his saddle horse, and cows and calves and bulls and yearlings or older stock or grazing cattle and other horses should be the sole objects of a cowboy's attention. Mending fence, greasing windmills or wagons, doing the haying, cleaning the barn, feeding in winter, anything but a "hospital bunch," irrigating or tending any other species than a cow were all evils that had to be done on occasion, but you didn't admit to liking to do these things, and by a cowboy's definition these tasks didn't belong as part of true life cowboy work. To be sure, the cowboy usually handled these evils with quick dispatch just to get them done and out of the way so that he could get back on his horse and ride out over the hills to do important things, like take tally "repping" for his boss while roping and dragging calves to the branding fire at Spring roundup. He'd even take a reluctant turn at milking a cow if the cook threatened him sufficiently, but as few and far between as he could keep those times the better. A 40 hour work week, it seemed, could be spent several times over in a given 7 day period with lots left over to still be done! A cowboy didn't worry much about the hours he put in if he liked what he was doing.

You kept at the job 'til it was done regardless of the hours it took!

EPIC TRAILS—

WEDNESDAY, AUGUST 16, 1989. THE SIXTH DAY—

IT RAINED DURING THE NIGHT. UP AT 5:08 A.M. AND THERE'S A DAMP COOL BREEZE. NEED TO WEAR A JACKET AND THERE'S SOME HUMPS AS BLANKETS AND SADDLES GO ON THE HORSES. COWS ARE STARTED DOWN THE ROAD AT 6:18. WE GET TO LEO BARTHELMESS PLACE AT CONTENT BY QUARTER TO 8:00. WE PUT A FOOT-WEARY LAME COW INTO LEO'S CORREL (SIC) TO REST. SHE'LL PROBABLY GET TO RIDE IN A TRAILER TO HELP HER OUT SOME. THIS IS ONE MODERN DAY ADVANTAGE 'TEDDY BLUE' COULDN'T SHOW A CRIPPLED CRITTER ON HIS TRAILS NORTH.

GEORGE AND EDNA HAYNES FROM MALTA AND BILL AND BETTY LUCAS FROM CALIFORNIA DROVE OUT FROM MALTA TO TAKE PICTURES. WE TRAILED WEST TO GEORGE ROBINSON'S OLD PLACE, VACANT NOW. WAGON BROKE DOWN. A BOLSTER PIN BROKE. LAUREN GREEN PICKED WAGON UP WITH TRACTOR AND WE GOT IT FIXED AND ON THE WAY AGAIN. WE STOP FOR BREAKFAST AT 10:05 A.M. AND I'M THE COOK THIS MORNING. FIRST TIME I COOK ON THIS TRAIL, BUT FIGURE AS LONG AS I CHASE SHEEP AND BRING IN MILK COWS I MIGHT JUST AS WELL COOK TOO!

THEN TIMBERCREEK BILL, NANCY AND B.J. ANDERSON HELPED US TRAIL UNTIL MID-DAY. AMBER AND B.J. HAD A GREAT TIME. THEY HAD QUITE A FEW HORSE RACES. WE MADE CAMP ON A BIG RESIVOR (SIC) WEST OF GEORGE ROBINSON'S ABOUT 1:30 P.M. TO LET STOCK DRINK. KEN AND LAURIE ANN WATSON AND BEVERLY KEONCEFORD RODE OVER FROM THEIR PLACE AND VISITED OUR NOON

—ENDLESS TRACKS ACROSS CENTURIES

EPIC TRAILS —

CAMP. WE PUT THE CATTLE ON THE TRAIL AGAIN ABOUT 3:00 P.M. AND JIM POND AND HIS FOLKS, WILLIE AND LYDIA, CAME FROM BILLINGS A LITTLE AFTER 4:00 O'CLOCK. JIM WILL RIDE WITH US 'TIL SUNDAY. AFTERNOON IS GETTING HOT AGAIN.

WE CAMPED TONIGHT ABOUT 8:00 P.M. ON BILL FRENCH'S RANGE. JANA AND CLINT SIMPSON VISITED OUR CAMP FROM SACO AND JANA COOKED SUPPER FOR US. IT ISN'T COOLING OFF MUCH THIS EVENING. WE TRAILED ABOUT 14 MILES TODAY. HAVE 153 MILES TO ROUNDUP.

-ENDLESS TRACKS ACROSS CENTURIES

Chapter 6

. . . . AND 18 HOUR DAYS??

Trailing more in a westerly direction today, the drive is crossing land that proved too unyielding in homestead days. Seeing and passing by places that are now vacant can be a stern reminder of just how difficult it can be to wrest sometimes even a marginal living from these eastern Montana prairies. The ruins of what were once the barest of homes have been slowly settling and rotting and drying up as they return to a level making them, year by year, less discernible from the landscape. The grass and cactus and wild rose grow, albeit patchily, where the settler's wife one time tried to nurture a garden. She put in long hours carrying water from a well which sometimes was more unyielding than the land so that the water had to be rationed between that used for the house and needed for the few chickens, the milk cow, saddle horses and team. The horses had to be kept up to do the work. The garden got what little there might be spared. Just when there was the encouragement of a bit of green and the hope of some vegetables or maybe even a flower to brighten the drab kitchen, the wind came with the blowing dust and sand turning the little garden, and the hope it fostered, to despair. Retreating inside her house, the woman would still try to prevail against the filtering dust. Her children remember, years afterwards, her attempts to keep some of it out by soaking torn strips of a tattered blanket in a dab of water in the granite wash basin. They vividly recall their mother's futile efforts, going from window to window, forcing the dampened bits of cloth between the loose sash and the window sill.

They remember, too, that this effort, while very vivid to them because they were small and this was the focal point of their world, was only an extension of the battle their father waged as he saw the same thing happening to a failed crop and watched what little grass there was eaten up by grasshoppers. The stock had to be moved off the home place, and this time a long way away, in hopes of finding enough grass to keep them going until they could be sold. There had been times past when this had worked out to at least keep the basic herd intact so the cows could be brought back home to produce another calf crop. Other times they'd all have to be sold because the dry persisted too long, or the market was so bad that the year's increase wouldn't pay the mortgage. They could think back to those times when it would have been fun to have gone to a community picnic at the little settlement where their folks went to purchase staples and the few supplies they might afford. But they remembered that the wagon was broken down and their father had even had to send the extra riding horses away to pasture. Hopefully there might be enough feed by late summer so they'd be able to bring the horses back to have them for riding to school.

Many of these families prevailed and others found the elements and the seasons too harsh. Those that persisted developed, in many instances, a work ethic that has passed from generation to generation through determination. It is a work ethic that underlies and provides the foundation for the lifestyle seen today when it comes to getting things done with the demands of day to day ranch work. These people truly know there are days and weeks that in order to get the things done in the time there is to do them, they literally have to "trade their bed for a lantern!"

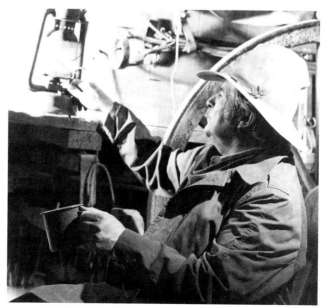

.... times when you have to trade your bed for a lantern.

– Endless Tracks Across Centuries

EPIC TRAILS—

Thursday, August 17, 1989. A Week on the Trail—

This is our seventh day headed for Roundup. Up at 5:30 a.m. and I wrangled the horses. Ours were close but Larry's gray team and his saddle horses drifted about 5 miles away in the night. We were an hour finding Larry's horses so didn't get cows on trail 'til about quarter to 7:00. We trailed on Bill French's land to a county road and then headed south again. Had our stop for breakfast at 10:00 a.m. and camped 'til 2:30 in the afternoon to let cows graze and rest.

Bruce returned to camp. He had a dislocated elbow from his little difference with the horse so Doctor in Malta had sent him to Havre to have elbow put back into place. Glad he's okay and that his injury was not more serious and good to have him along on the drive again.

We trailed 2 miles south, watered on Greg Oxararts, then traveled 5 miles west and another mile south. We made camp 4 miles south of Noel Emonds. Clint, Jana and Phyliss Simpson came out again from Saco and cook supper for us. Later on Noel and Sharon Emond came by camp to visit. Garth Bascom and his mother drove out to camp to pick up Winston and take him home. We will miss his jokes, wit, and dry sense of humor. We'll miss his laugh. He was fun help. Larry Simpson, Andy Mueller and myself are the ones left that started last week from the ranch. Weather is real cool with northeast wind this morning. Went 12 miles today, 141 miles left to Roundup.

—Endless Tracks Across Centuries

Chapter 7
THE THREE "R's" – EDUCATION AND TUITION

Will James told a story of a boy and his bout with formal schooling. It has been many years since I last read the book. I believe the title of James' story was "Big Enough," and it related the boy's adventures with a colt that grew into a smallish to medium size adult horse while the boy also was growing up. My recollection is that the boy considered being in school similar to imprisonment, so took his small horse and ran away from home and school. They were gone a good long while, much to the consternation of those who loved them and feared for their well-being, but were "Big Enough" to deal with the many adventures or mis-adventures that being on their own dealt them. I think of this story often when I think of Connie's own stint at schooling. To him, it was a chore, an unpleasant task at best; and more of a run in, where he felt he was being bushwhacked, rather than benefited by "readin', 'ritin', 'n' 'rithmetic."

Although I spent considerable more time in pursuit of a formal education than my friend did, I can relate to some of the frustration and confinement or restriction he felt at times. Don't take what I say here in the wrong context. Education is important and it provides untold opportunity in the unlocking of doors. What one finds when the doors are passed through, however, often depends much more on how education is used, rather than from whence it may have been obtained. Some people seem capable of becoming educated way beyond their knowledge. Unfortunately, when this happens, the grasp of what is termed "common sense" or good judgement tends to become altogether uncommon. The elements of an academic education mixed with the experience gained behind a saddle horn or tempered in some other manner by the school of hard knocks appear to make the recipient a bit more observant and maybe more capable of truly judging rather then merely being judgemental.

"I got my start in school in 1939 at a little school called Spring Coulee, and I believe the teacher was Mrs. Olson," Connie relates. "It was a summer school. I went to the Delvin School at Havre for a few grades to a Miss Cunningham, and grades 5 through 8 to Lakeview School. I believe the teachers were Miss Haymaker and Mrs. Whitson. That was about it. I know about tuition, because the education from the school of hard knocks can be very, very dear."

Admitting to the meager academic pursuit to which he'd availed himself, Connie encouraged his children not to be satisfied with so skimpy an education. In fact he insisted the kids finish high school, and all three had the opportunity to go on to college. Casey attended Blue Mountain College at Pendleton, Oregon for three years. Charlene studied for three years at Eastern in Billings and Clinton attended Dawson College at Glendive, briefly, before going to work full time at ranching with a neighbor in the home community of Whitewater. All three also got an early start in learning that there was responsibility that had to go along with having good horses to ride and rope off of. Connie and Margie saw that they were mounted on good, well trained horses from the start, but they had to care for their own and they signed notes along with their parents so they learned that they'd have to earn their keep and pay for those horses as time went along, too. About education and men, horses, kids and dogs, Connie philosophizes a bit.

"I've had men who were supposed to know somethin' come here to work an' just havin' one of 'em around was like havin' two good men gone! You've got to start a youngster out with a broke horse – you can't take a green kid an' a green horse and teach either one of them anything at the same time. I'd as soon have one good dog to help work cows as ten know-nothin' men. If it isn't goin' well, you can at least tell the dog to 'go lay down or git in the pickup!'"

The classroom of Connie's preference.

– Endless Tracks Across Centuries

EPIC TRAILS—

FRIDAY, AUGUST 18, 1989. BEGIN THE SECOND WEEK —

Up at 6:00 in the morning. Easy wrangling today. Horses only a little way off. Had coffee and donut and got cows started trailing by 6:45 a.m. Only a couple minutes later Amber Simpson came loping her horse up road, horse turned sharp and she fell hard to ground. Knocked the air out of her but she got right back on her horse and rode on. She's sure a nice little girl — tough too! Rode every day but the first one.

At 7:45 a.m. Clarence and Shirley Blunt and Bob and Theresa Frye stopped and showed us which way to head. They then went on before us to close some gates. We sure have met some nice people so far on this trail. Shirley Blunt came back and rode a few miles with us.

A little later, Jess Robinson and his son, Clyde flew over and landed to give us more directions which way to go. Jess took pickup and trailer about 14 miles on ahead to where we will camp on the Robinson Ranch tonight.

At 12:30 p.m. Jim Pond's horse bucked him off hard and stepped on him. Bruce took him to hospital in Malta. We made camp about 6:15. Everybody really hungry as we have not eaten since coffee and donut early morning. Larry fried ham and potatoes. With this and some cold beans and bread we got filled up. We had cool breeze all day — had to wear coat. We made 20 miles today. We're 121 miles from Roundup — half way there. Hope Jim Pond is okay.

-ENDLESS TRACKS ACROSS CENTURIES

*Much about an education comes with how it's used –
maybe as much as where it is found.*

The school of hard knocks is not without tuition.

Chapter 8

THANK GOSH IT'S FRIDAY

Half way to Roundup. It's been good trailing, for the most part, this far, and the people along the way have been wonderful. Everyone living where our trail has crossed has been most helpful, showing the directions, opening gates, letting us water the stock and just plain being friendly good neighbors. The people who've been just traveling through have been just as friendly, wanting to see the Longhorns and the wagon and just visiting camp. It's a good all around feeling even though there have been a few bumps along the way. Bruce had no more than got back from having his dislocated elbow fixed when there were the shake-ups with Amber and her horse this morning and Jim Pond getting bucked off his horse at midday. Amber has had a busy time. She's ridden all day, every day but one. She would have raced horses all day Wednesday with B. J. if she could have, and bounced right up after her tumble this morning. Oh, to be that young and full of vim and vinegar again!

Connie, Larry Simpson and Andy Mueller agreed that since it was the half-way mark and a Friday night they ought to do something to sort of celebrate. After all, they had made it over a week now, and they joked about how the old time drovers must have drawn lots and vied and swapped night guard when they'd have their trail herds on the outskirts of Dodge City or Ogalalla or Miles City. Trouble was, Connie's herd wasn't on the outskirts of anywhere this Friday evening, and they weren't where they could see the lights of any kind of settlement to beckon them in. They agreed that whether they could see any lights or not, they'd wait until tomorrow night when they'd be able to bed the Longhorns and loose horses in a fenced field and they'd go into Mobridge for supper. Hopefully they would hear how Jim Pond was by then, or better yet, he and Bruce would be back to go with them.

Larry Simpson took a turn at fixing supper at camp and since it had been such a long day and everybody was really hungry his talents as camp chef for the evening were much appreciated. They all felt like they could have enjoyed an old shoe fried up if that would have been all he could have served. No cow town lights to beckon them but as they settled down under the stars and a big moon they could really feel they were somewhere "close to the middle of Montana" and not that far from heaven!

Our little cowgirl, Amber,
gets a helping hand from Grandpa.

EPIC TRAILS —

Saturday, August 19, 1989. The Ninth Day —

Sun rose over the ridge at 6:24 this morning. Last night was beautiful. Big moon, cool, lots of stars. Slept good. Started cows on trail at 6:45. Two cows pretty foot sore but most are picking footing okay and are grazing good along way and at rest camps when stop to fix our own chuck.

Bruce and Jim Pond came back from Malta. Jim did not get hurt seriously yesterday when he got bucked off. Thankful for that and Jim cooked breakfast of bacon and eggs, bread and coffee. Sure beats a donut. At 11:00 a.m. Clyde Robinson came back with his plane and flew Larry over the trail while we were camped to eat. We saw another big rattlesnake. Don't mind them too much if see them first, but sure don't like to be surprised by one or have horse ride right over top of him. Just as soon they don't camp with us too!

Little Rocky Mountains look really close this morning. Sure are a pretty sight. Taking closer look around, realized our 2 dogs that have come along to trail with us are lost. 'Killer' and 'Blaze', don't know what we would do without them so went back to where I last saw them. Found them right there. Guess it's the last place they saw me too so they figured I was the one lost and they'd just stay there 'til they found me!

We got cows on trail again at about 3:20 p.m. and went for about 2½ hours before making camp at Robinson's

— Endless Tracks Across Centuries

Somewhere in the middle of Montana.

EPIC TRAILS-

FIELD. WE CLEANED UP AND WENT OVER TO MOBRIDGE. NOBODY THERE SO WE DROVE TO ZORTMAN AND HAD A STEAK FOR SUPPER. WENT BACK TO CAMP. OUR LITTLE COWGIRL, AMBER WENT HOME THIS EVENING WITH HER DAD AND HER UNCLE, LARRY ROSS.

WEATHER WAS FINE TODAY. COOL THIS MORNING AND GOT PRETTY HOT MID-AFTERNOON. HIGH 80's BUT HAD A LITTLE BREEZE SO GNATS AND MEGEDOS NOT TOO BOTHERSOME TO US OR HORSES AND CATTLE. WE MADE CLOSE TO 13 MILES BEFORE MAKING CAMP THIS EVENING SO HAVE 108 MILES LEFT TO ROUNDUP.

Chapter 9
REFLECTIONS ON BUILDING A RANCH

Arising to a cool morning after a really good night's sleep under the moon and stars, Connie and crew had the cows back on the trail within a few minutes after the sun topped the horizon. Bruce and Jim Pond returned from Malta and Jim's experience with a bucking horse had fortunately resulted in only a pretty good shaking up, and he'd have a few sore places a day or two. The Little Rocky Mountains were beautiful and looked like you could reach out and touch them. Cows were grazing as they moseyed along and were happy to be left to do so as Connie and Andy stopped to have their own breakfast. Bruce and Jim were not only back to camp; Jim had also cooked breakfast and by mid morning it really hit the spot. Realizing his dogs were missing made Connie abandon the view of the Little Rockies for the moment while he went back to see if he could find them. It put him to thinking about all that had happened the past 20 years as they'd worked to build the Frenchman Creek place into a good working ranch.

He reflected that there seemed to be a lot about ranching and the beef raising business that was imagined by folks who just didn't know. It seemed to him that a lot of the people off the street who were being quoted by the media or appearing as authorities in TV interviews, and even at hearings back in Congress, about things like food safety, the beef and health controversy, or that orchestrated scare deal about the apple business, were way off beat. Many of these do-gooders were not just uninformed; they were misinformed, had their narrow viewed little minds made up and were not about to be confused by any real facts. These same people, many of them very often in the public eye, had the attitude a ranch just happened, and the cows didn't cost anything to keep because, after all, they just ate grass, and they seemed to figure the grass was "free." Connie could assure them the only thing "free" about the grass was the freedom of choice of a body to ride out where it grew and the freedom to try making it into something people could use. This is what he thought education should be all about. These know-it-alls, who in truth were often know-nothin's, didn't seem to know or care that most working ranches had been built with blood, sweat and tears. They didn't seem to know or care that to build a ranch and still hopefully be able to have a little fun with your family on

it and in doing it – that it took a lot of love – love of the land and love of the challenge of trying to get Mother Nature to cooperate with you, at least once in a while. It took money – lots of it, and often borrowed over a long term with needed decent prices each Fall for the calves, just to break even – yet mixing money talk and talk of profitability seemed to raise the ire of lots of people. And finally, to build a ranch into a useful, working business operation took a lot of stouteartedness, kindness and repetitive effort. Lots and lots of tracks, yes, endless tracks; some would hopefully remain to serve as a pathway for posterity, but more would be repeatedly wiped out by the whims of Mother Nature or the foibles of manmade storms such as the politically and fiscally arguable Food Stabilization Program. How many of these people who would tell him how and where he could or couldn't graze his cows, Connie wondered, knew the extent of such a tax supported government effort toward assuring they had the cheapest food in the world. He wondered also when they didn't have money to buy this most bountiful and high quality life's sustenance, if they knew they were getting their food stamps courtesy the very same Food Stabilization Program?

Turning his thoughts back to the quest of the moment, Connie's spirits lifted as he spied his missing dogs, "Killer" and "Blaze." They were awfully faithful and good help, and they didn't ever question, but did appreciate a pat and a kind word once in a while. They were genuinely glad to see him. Yes, kindness was part of building a ranch, and the people who hadn't experienced the bonding which occurred between children and pets or between animal friends of different species, like Blue and Blaze, for instance, had plain and simply missed something of life. A ranch was a unique kind of home – not only to people, but to many, many different creatures. A balance was important and Connie felt as if the years of effort at Frenchman Creek were hopefully beginning to arrive at that balance.

While they had been striving to improve the grass and water on the place, and to develop more productive cows, there had also been the effort to care for the wild things by making sure there was food and cover for the deer and antelope, upland birds and migrating birds. It seemed to be working because some of these denizens

– Endless Tracks Across Centuries

A lot about a ranch is imagined by folks who just don't know – A ranch is built with blood, sweat, and tears – and love, fun, kindness and endless tracks. It's a unique kind of home – not only to people, but to many, many creatures.

THE MISFIT

While working in the unemployment office,
        I tell you this happened–just the other day.
A very nervous fellow came in;
        I noticed his hair was silver gray.

"I know you think that I am old," He spoke,
        "But I'm really only twenty-four."
"My hair turned white when I worked for Connie Cox;
        Some think I was in the Second World War!"

"I asked Connie Cox for a job;
        For to be a cowboy was my goal."
He said he would give me a chance,
        That was the best way to really know."

I thought I was a man of nerves,
        They called me 'Killer' on the football team;
But it takes more than nerves to work for him!
        I'll tell you just what I mean."

"I had to feed all kinds of cattle,
        In the wind, the cold and blowing snow.
I was sure that I would freeze to death,
        As sometimes it was forty below."

"I had to help in calving time.
        Connie would yell at me with a frown.
'Don't be runnin' from those cows, Boy,
        You've gotta stand yer ground!'"

"I had to ride his saddle horses and
        He would often say to me with a grin,
'Git yer carcass up off the ground;
        Don't let him think yer scared of him!'"

"He tried to teach me how to rope,
        But I guess I was just too plain dumb.
He said, 'Yuh'll prob'ly git a lot better;
        Jist as soon as you lose yer thumb!'"

"I had to cross some flooding streams,
        That were a boiling mass of mud and limbs.
'Don't worry none', Connie would yell at me;
        When I didn't know how to swim."

"I had to drive over icy roads and ridge back trails,
        With hundred foot cuts on either side;
I dared not put on the brakes_
        Just prayed to God, don't let it slide!"

"I had to ride in thunder storms,
        With sizzling lightning popping down.
I knew I'd soon be electrocuted;
        For there was no shelter for miles around."

"I had to ride in strange country;
        Then Connie would ride up to me and fuss,
'How yuh 'spect to find any cattle, Boy,
        When all you do is look at yer compass?'"

"Well, he put up with me for a year,
        And I'm sure he is a good cowboy teacher.
When I left he said, 'Good luck, Boy,
        I think you should really be a preacher.'"

"So I up and sold my tack and saddle;
        I gave my spurs to my friend, Hank.
You wouldn't have a job that's safe and warm,
        Something like working in a bank?"

– Endless Tracks Across Centuries

appeared bent upon eating him out of house and home at times. Connie mused at his recollection of a neighbor's comments on a meeting he'd attended where an official of the FWP Service, new to the area, had made the declaration at the public gathering, "I do not know where some of these complaints originate? It is a known biological fact that deer will not eat the rancher's alfalfa." The neighbor had walked out of the meeting figuring he sure wasn't going to learn anything from this erudite fellow. Connie just chalked it up to another case of a poor misguided servant of the public being educated way beyond his knowledge or of, "being sort of low rent in the gray matter district of his anatomy." For the most part Connie had a good working relationship with most such officials where his ranch was concerned and he worked hard at keeping it good. Perhaps this new chap had observed Whitetail on the haystacks turning their noses up at the alfalfa after they'd fouled it. The man was precisely correct if that was the case – the deer wouldn't touch a mouthful of it – no self-respecting other animal would either! This didn't change the fact that the deer had ruined the whole stack, however, by urinating on it, leaving their droppings and trampling it. Tracks like this one could do without, and the foolproof fence to protect against such traffic had yet to be invented. Some of these animals were regular Houdinis when it came to being capable of being where they didn't belong! Some things you just learned to live with.

Getting back to the herd with the dogs, and moving the cows back on the trail after their midday rest, Connie's thoughts turned again to his efforts at genetic improvement of his cow herd over the years. It was kind of intriguing, where the Longhorns were concerned, that ancestors of these cows had been the earliest cattle in the Americas, having come with the Conquistadores. The breed had nearly died out, only to be now on the increase again, as cattle breeders searched for such traits as calving ease, disease and parasite resistance and hardy, frugal rustling ability with strong inherent maternal character. Connie was sampling several avenues of genetic adventure, hoping to find the right nick to fit the conditions of his range and the requirements of his, and his banker's, economics. In the first two to three years of their life on Frenchman Creek, Connie supplemented available winter grazing for newly weaned replacements and coming first and second calvers on the meadows close to headquarters

with some hay and protein. By the time a young cow reached the age of four years she was expected to be capable of earning her own keep out in the winter breaks, and with the exception of terribly severe blizzard or prolonged drought conditions, she might not see another bite of prepared hay in her productive lifetime. She did get access to a protein and energy supplement in block form to gnaw a bit from along with the grass and browse she rustled. Connie used to load two or three hundred pounds of these blocks in his airplane and drop them off one block at a time in the protected areas along the brushy coulees, but found they were better utilized and weathered better if hauled out once every other week or so, and placed in strategically located wooden troughs. These would be moved from time to time through the breaks, to encourage more uniform grazing utilization. Range bulls, after being removed from summer breeding pastures, were also kept close to home where they could be monitored through the winter and given supplemental hay or blocks as conditions indicated.

Connie studied various cattle crossbreeding reports and visited a number of seedstock herds and performance test stations over a period of years. He found the calves off his black and black baldie cows and sired by Charolais bulls to be fairly popular with the buyers. However, he questioned the use of heifer calves of this cross as replacement prospects. They got a little big for good self maintenance on his range, compared to the efficiency with which they, in turn, would produce a calf of their own. He admired and respected the efforts of such noted cowmen as Tom Lasater, of Matheson, Colorado, credited with developing the Beefmaster breed (a 3-way cross utilizing Hereford, Shorthorn and Brahma cattle in a prescribed set genetic mix), and Neil Harvie, of Cochrane, Alberta, one of the founders of a beef cattle genetics improvement group of commercial cowmen, known as Beefbooster, Alberta. In studying the results obtained with Beefmaster cattle and by the Beefbooster group (two entirely different entities not be confused by the name similarity), Connie became acquainted with Sherm Ewing, a seedstock breeder with Beefbooster, and at that time from Claresholm, Alberta. Sherm developed a strain of cattle known as the Beefbooster M_4, and Connie began using some of these bulls along with some Brangus bulls from his friend, Bill Gilchrist, of the Cypress Hills area in Saskatchewan. Building a ranch and cowherd is a long, slow process.

– Endless Tracks Across Centuries

SUNDAY, AUGUST 20, 1989. TEN DAYS SOUTH —

Up at 5:08 a.m. Made coffee. Everything pretty quiet so had to stir a little action up. Served Andy a cup of coffee while he was still rolled in his bed. He thought we had better room service than 'Hollowday Inn'.

Sunday morning. Lot of people will go to church today. Of those maybe 5 percent would be on the square and you could depend on them if needed to go to the end of the road with you. In our crew we have five people and we all would go to the end of the road together, 100% for each other. Beautiful morning. Little Rockies off to the northwest — breaks to the south — and Judith Mountains way south across the Missouri. No wind and about 60° above.

Man never made a church as beautiful as God made this. As Bruce and I sit on our horses and with hat in our hands, give Thanks, we are truly blessed. Time is 6:32 a.m.

Got cows started on trail and headed them southwest. Went back to camp and Jim Pond and I took pickup and trailer back to Barthelmess corrals to pick up cow we left there Wednesday to rest up her lame foot. Jim is still hurting quite a lot from the shaking up he got getting bucked off his horse. We got back to camp at 11:30 a.m and Jim went on to the river bridge to meet his folks to go back home. I went southeast of Don Robinson's to wait for cattle and

THE CREW. TIME IS 12:33 P.M. WHEN THEY SHOWED WE WENT ON AND DIDN'T MAKE CAMP 'TIL 5:00 P.M.

BRUCE COOKED UP A HASH OF POTATOES, BEANS, CORN AND HAMBURGER AND BOILED UP SOME COFFEE. WE ATE SUNDAY BREAKFAST AND SUPPER AT SAME TIME. DAYS LIKE THIS ARE PROBABLY WHAT GIVES THE BUREAUCRATS SOME OF THEIR BRIGHT IDEAS 'BOUT THINGS LIKE 'SAVIN' DAYLIGHT'!

IT WAS HOT DURING THE AFTERNOON AGAIN TODAY UNTIL ABOUT HALF HOUR BEFORE WE MADE CAMP. THEN WE GOT A GOOD RAIN AND IT COOLED WAY DOWN. CLEARED OFF AND NICE EVENING. TONIGHT WE CAN SEE THE LIGHTS OF ZORTMAN AND WAY TO THE SOUTH THE LIGHTS OF ROY SHOW UP. WE MADE 10 MILES TODAY LEAVING 98 MILES TO ROUNDUP.

Chapter 10

WHERE CHURCHES GROW

Among other wonderful poems and lyrics written by Badger Clark is one of the West's favorites: A Cowboy's Prayer. This poem, and the other beautiful works of this talented man, won him the title of Poet Laureate of the State of South Dakota. Connie had to have had a similar feeling as he and Bruce sat on their horses with hats in their hands and reflected upon their blessings on the tenth day of the trail on a Sunday morning. "Man never made a church as beautiful as God made this" about said all that needed to be said. The sense of reverence held by most men of the outdoors could well be summed up, more as a feeling of awe and God fearing, than as a function of conscious formal worship. Paying homage through the expression of words or ceremony might be a difficult enactment, but the failure to find words or to mingle in a congregational gathering made a cowboy no less respectful, nor less grateful in his silent, solitary vigils. In his prayer, the cowboy acknowledges that others find their Maker in the light that filters through stained glass windows, while he walks closer to his Lord under the quiet starlight on the open prairie. It is with a statement of case, without thought of apology or the need, even, for apology, that the cowboy makes the concession he has never lived where churches grow. He finds his cathedral to be God's creation as it stood naturally from the beginning and feels himself a part of it.

The cowboy gives thanks for his station in life and for the freedom he feels. He appreciates that his is not a life bound by time clocks nor walls and streets, and asks only for work that is in the open, and to be a partner of the wind and sun. He asks that he may continue his life humbly as he began and wishes not for a life of ease nor of excess. He wishes to be fair and considerate to the man less fortunate than he may be, and asks for help in being generous and square with others. The cowboy admits to being careless, at times, when he's in town, but shuns meanness and petty smallness. He asks to be as honest as the horse he rides and as big and open as the country he is privileged to gaze across from his saddle. He prays to be as clean as the wind that follows the rains, and free as the hawk, hanging suspended, high above him on unseen zephyrs.

The cowboy asks forgiveness for when he's forgetful, and is thankful for understanding in dealing with vexations, large and small. He acknowledges that the Lord knows him better than did his own mother, and prays that a watch be kept on all that is said and done. He asks to be kept straight if he should waver and prays for guidance as he follows his final trail reaching for that last horizon. A cowboy's prayer is beautiful in its simplicity and freedom from pretense. The cowboy and the man of the range tend to look for good in every challenge, and as they behold the wonder of their environment, they are leaders in their willingness to do their part to maintain and sustain it. The extra effort of stewardship is accepted as a given responsibility and it is highly motivating. The person in tune with the land appreciates the specialness of his world. He senses the vastness and purpose of all that has been created, and takes more time to become acquainted with the places, plants, animals and people he encounters, and finds there is something to appreciate about each.

While not entirely of a religious connotation, this appreciation has, more or less, evolved into certain standards of conduct pertaining to range life. These standards are, in large measure, what set ranch life and life-style apart in a unique unwritten system of ethics. Some of these standards have passed down as follows: Be soft-spoken, listen rather than say much and keep your eyes open to the smallest of details. Be self sufficient and able to depend only upon yourself, but be always ready to lend a helping hand to a neighbor. Give the stranger and his horse shelter and food and don't mind his business. Don't disagree with the ramrod–if he's made a

– Endless Tracks Across Centuries

mistake he'll know soon enough. Avoid government handouts–they're like giving yourself a transfusion from the left arm over to the right arm, and spilling half the blood on the way! Don't look too hard at the brand on a strange horse, but tally it. Take care of your neighbor's critters as you would your own–he'll be doing the same for you. Don't turn grass root-side up–it's a contagion that scars and corrupts the land for a long, long time. Women come in two kinds–the ones like your mother, and the ones behind lace curtains–you don't talk about either kind. If paper and pen aren't handy, back your word as you would your signature.

The cowboy gives thanks for his life as it is and for the freedom he feels.

– Endless Tracks Across Centuries

EPIC TRAILS —

MONDAY, AUGUST 21, 1989. ELEVEN DAYS ON THE TRAIL —

UP AT 6:02. ELEVENTH DAY TRAILING. THIS IS THE LONGEST I HAVE EVER TRAILED. BACK IN JUNE, 1969, MARGIE AND THE KIDS AND I TRAILED 152 COWS AND THEIR CALVES FROM NEAR HAVRE TO THEIR NEW RANGE AT THE RANCH ON FRENCHMAN CREEK. TEN DAYS ON THE TRAIL THAT TIME. LOTS OF WAYS, SEEMS LIKE IT WAS ONLY YESTERDAY, AND OTHER TIMES, SEEMS A HUNDRED YEARS AGO. GOOD TO THINK BACK ON THOSE TIMES.

TRAILED TO CHARLIE SCHWENKE'S CORRELS ALONG HIWAY 191. GOT THERE ABOUT 1:30 P.M. WILL MAKE THIS THE DISTANCE FOR TODAY AND CAMP HERE FOR THE NIGHT.

LARRY AND I TOOK 2 HORSES AND WENT BACK TO DON ROBINSON'S TO LOOK FOR TENDER FOOTED COW WHICH HAD DROPPED BEHIND BECAUSE SHE WAS GETTING LAME. DID NOT FIND HER. SHE MUST BE BRUSHED UP SOME WHERE HIDING. HAVE TO LOOK AGAIN LATER FOR HER. THIS MAKES OUR COUNT 112 HEAD.

WENT TO ZORTMAN FOR SUPPER AND TO GET FUEL. OLD TIME TRAIL HANDS DID NOT HAVE CHOICE OF PICKUP NOR TRAILER TO GO BACK FOR CRIPPLED STOCK, OR FOR ~~RECORN REKO~~ 'REKONISANS' — YOU KNOW — SCOUT NEW TERRITORY! LOTS OF TIMES A HAND WHO HAD BEEN WITH A TRAIL HERD BEFORE GOT THAT JOB OF SCOUTING FOR LATER HERDS. THOSE OLD TIME COWBOYS WOULD THINK WE WERE SURE A BUNCH OF 'GREENERS'. I THINK I'D HAVE LIKED THEIR WAYS BETTER.

—ENDLESS TRACKS ACROSS CENTURIES

EPIC TRAILS—

Went back to camp after supper. Every one thinking about tomorrow and wondering how crossing will go. It was short day today, maybe too much time to think! Only made 6 miles so have 92 miles left to Roundup.

Margie came to camp about 11:00 p.m. Nice night. Big moon. Still wondering about tomorrow.

Beautiful morning... man never made a church as beautiful as God made this.

Chapter 11
THE EARLY YEARS

Eleven days on the trail and tomorrow should see them reaching the wide Missouri River. Connie had hoped that it would be possible to ford the river, but this would not be possible. The mud banks on either side of the water level would prove too treacherous due to water level draw down that had gone on consistently through the dry years leading up through 1988. Bureaucratic red tape regarding access seemed even more formidable. The herd would just have to be trailed across the Missouri on the Robinson Bridge at the Highway 191 crossing and they were having to follow the highway right of way in the area anyway because of the Charles M. Russell National Wildlife Refuge extending up both sides of the river to well west of the bridge. It had surely been beautiful trailing across country to this point. There were places from which it seemed you could see just about to the end of the earth! Connie and his drovers were feeling more and more exhilaration as the trek progressed and today was a milestone. While he had trailed from summer country to winter range each Fall and back again in the Spring there had been no drives until now as long as that one Connie and his family had undertaken a bit over 20 years before when moving their herd from the Wild Horse Lake country to the Frenchman Creek ranch.

Connie and Margie had continued to operate the home place near Wild Horse Lake through the '70s on a commuting basis and put in a lot of miles along the High Line, back and forth between Malta and Havre, during those years. But the Frenchman Creek ranch was home now and definitely home to the children and their livestock. The ups and downs of the cattle economy and of the general agricultural picture through the '70s made the continued operation of both ranches very stressful at times and getting ahead was tenuous at best. All three children were developing into good hands during the early '70s as evidenced by the Kids Barrel Racing and Kids Calf Roping standings in the annual Northern Rodeo Association listings. Connie was concentrating his rodeo efforts on the timed events, too, so was spending time with all three children in teaching them to team rope and hauling them down the road to rodeos.

Connie and his family held their First Annual Cox Ranch Team Roping in 1973. That same year is when the team of Connie and son, Casey, then 15 years old, won the Ten Head Roping at Lewistown. There were over 100 teams entered in this competition and many of them very tough ropers, all capable of consistent fast times. It is no wonder that Connie looks back at times such as that with happy reflection and a bit of pride. The Annual Cox Ranch Team Ropings have continued but weren't all fun and games. They took a lot of work and organization. There had to be adequate stock for the contestants to draw. Teams were coming from a wide areas and maintaining the annual dates for the event needed to be consistent so the teams entering could plan their schedule with other rodeos and team ropings and effectively work out travel routing. Mother Nature sometimes really cooperated and at other times she completely turned her back on them. The arena at the homestead on Frenchman Creek could be very remote and even totally inaccessible because of the gumbo mud if it rained or snowed, and on occasion it did! Or one could plan on staying at the ranch a few extra days if the weather started out nice but a quick Spring storm caught you before you could climb the narrow switchback road out to the top and get the 30 miles to Whitewater. Sometimes the ropings had to be moved in to Malta and in recent years they have been held at the Whitewater arena, but they have grown consistently and many people enjoy them and look forward to the reunion they represent.

Connie Cox hurrying to beat the flag at Roundup, Montana, in 1969.

Photo courtesy of Margie Cox.

– Endless Tracks Across Centuries

Connie and Casey, Team Roping in 1974 at the home ranch.

Casey, age 16, and Clinton, age 15, Team Roping, 1974.

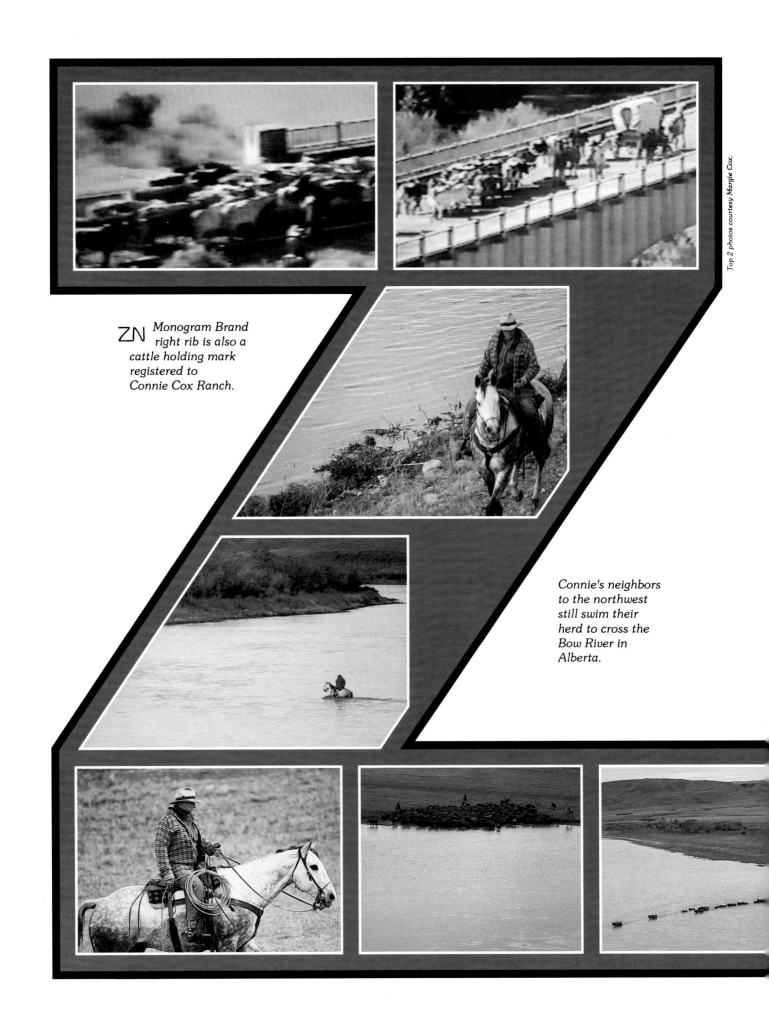

ZN Monogram Brand right rib is also a cattle holding mark registered to Connie Cox Ranch.

Connie's neighbors to the northwest still swim their herd to cross the Bow River in Alberta.

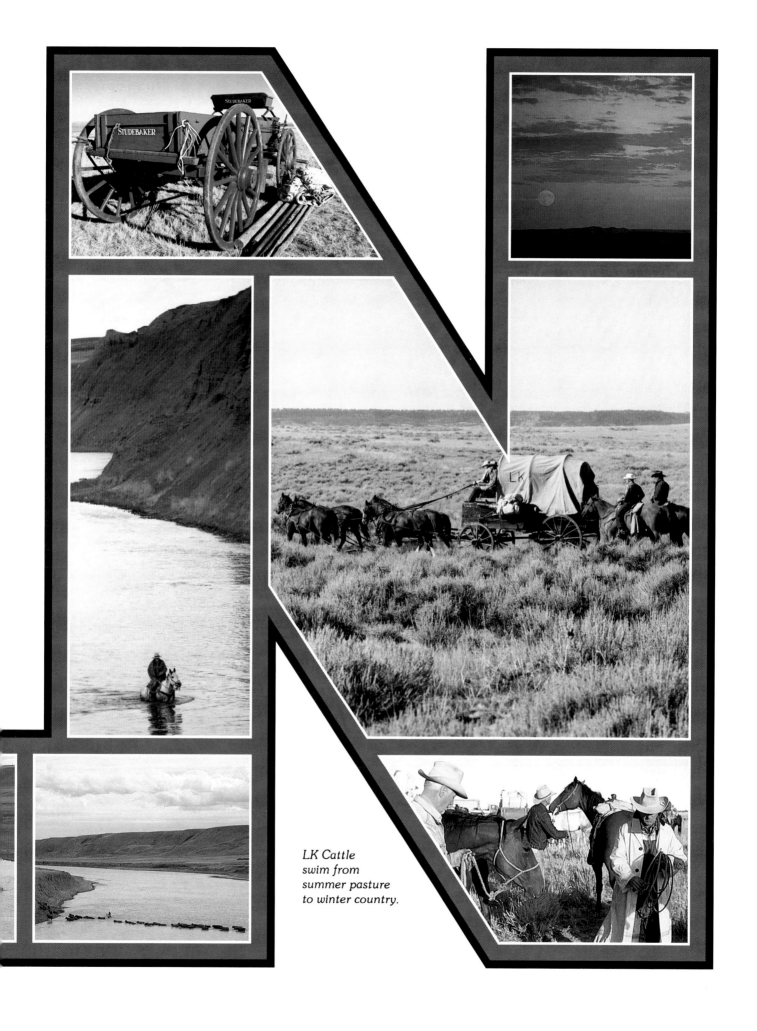

*LK Cattle
swim from
summer pasture
to winter country.*

EPIC TRAILS—

TUESDAY, AUGUST 22, 1989. A DOZEN DAYS OUT—

Up at 2:50 A.M. Could't sleep. Try to make Missouri River by 8:00 A.M. Got cows off bed ground and trailed them by myself for 3 miles. Rest of crew came along about 6:30 A.M. Margie went on with pickup to flag traffic coming from south of river.

Made it to Robinson Bridge on Missouri by 9:00 A.M. All riders are nervous after Milk River Bridge crossing. Larry went ahead with team and wagon. The loose horses followed him and cows followed and they went right across. You sometimes never know. Cows weren't nervous — just us!

Sure was a pretty sight with the wagon, saddle stock and cattle all strung out coming down the hill and crossing the bridge. Smooth as our crossing went compared to what we expected it could have been, sure made me think how relieved those old timers must have been when they had had to swim their stock or get through bogs or quicksand before finally safely making a crossing. Times some of them didn't make it. For many, their only monument to have been a drover on one of those historic early drives, was a lonesome grave with a crude wooden marker along the banks of the North Platte, Canadian, Yellowstone or some other river like the Missouri which claimed them.

Will Rasmussen rode with us this morning to help

—ENDLESS TRACKS ACROSS CENTURIES

WITH THE RIVER CROSSING. AFTER GETTING ON THE SOUTH SIDE OF THE MISSOURI WE STOPPED ABOUT 10:00 A.M. AND FIXED BREAKFAST AND TO LET THE COWS REST. WILL AND HIS WIFE, 'HONEY,' ATE WITH US. DICK MARSHALL, LARRY JORDAN, SR., 'SPEED' KAMORACK AND AMOS CHARBONEAU STOPPED BY OUR CAMP AND HAD COFFEE WITH US.

I LOADED 4 HEAD OF FOOT SORE COWS INTO TRAILER AND TOOK THEM AHEAD TO ROUNDUP FEEDLOT. WE TRAILED ANOTHER 3 MILES IN THE EVENING AND CAMPED AT A GRAZING ASSOCIATION CORRALS. SAM WEBB AND DELORES HELPED FLAG TRAFFIC ALONG THE WAY THIS EVENING AND STAYED TO HAVE SUPPER WITH US. MARGIE COOKED SUPPER AND THEN LEFT TO GO HOME TO RANCH. SHE TOOK 'BLAZE' WITH HER BUT 'KILLER' IS MISSING AGAIN. DOGS HAVE BEEN GOOD HELP. HOPE WE FIND 'KILLER' OR HE FINDS US AGAIN.

WEATHER TURNED REAL HOT WITH NO WIND THIS AFTERNOON. WE MADE 12 MILES TODAY. EIGHTY LEFT TO ROUNDUP.

Like a schooner at sea, many are the storms that've been weathered – and many the seasons. Fire, pests, wind and drought. Blizzards, hail and floods – depressions and the whims and foibles of bureaucratic 'Do-Gooders'... But it hasn't all blown away. We've seen 'er all and still able to roll – reckon this'll always be 'Next Year' country!

Chapter 12

TOUGH TIMES

The worry and sleepless night wondering how the Longhorns would consider the high bridge across the Missouri River was most fortunately all for naught. This did not upset Connie nor the rest of the riders a bit and they were happy with their luck at how the cows had strung out across the bridge. Larry's team and wagon went right down the middle of the deck and it was interesting to watch how the loose horses and cattle almost seemed to flow into a single file as they followed. This was the only indication at this crossing that the Longhorns might be leery of anything at all about the bridge. They strung out almost as if they seemed to believe the only place they were supposed to step was on the yellow dividing line between traffic lanes. It was obvious they had no intention of going close to the bannister edge. The team, King and Maggie, hardly flicked an ear when pigeons flew out from underneath the bridge. The loose horses and cattle appeared oblivious to any distraction, intent only on the yellow paint strip before their noses.

It was always nice to have some good luck and Connie was thankful for it. The river crossing behind, it was good to let the cows have a rest while the crew stopped for breakfast. It was pleasant to visit with the people who had driven out to watch the crossing. With the interest being shown in his effort, Connie couldn't help but become more optimistic that the Big Drive was actually going to happen. There was great enthusiasm for it among those stopping at his camp, and this made for a good feeling. This whole ranching and cattle industry could stand some good luck. To be sure, much of Montana had had some decent moisture for a change and the grass was as good this year as Connie could remember it. Calf prices were looking good for a change, but it would take more than one or two good years to begin to make up for the past eight or ten. The drought of several years running, the fires of '85 and worse in '88, the grasshoppers, a run of not too good prices and the high interest rates in the early '80s had done a number of outfits in and the memories came back vividly.

It had got to the point for Connie and his family of having to decide where to cut and tuck so that there might be something left to "keep a whippin' and spurrin'." It was a bitter and soul rending pill, but in order to keep the Frenchman Creek place and to be able to continue operating, they had to let the old home place at Wild Horse Lake go. Interest rates had got to 18% and worse and there was just no way to keep everything going with calf prices lower than the cost of production and grass never getting more than "a bit and a half high, and then the old cow better hurry before the wind wore it off and blew it away." The '80s then were spent as a period of recovery as well as just hanging on. The share cows had helped because numbers were important, especially to the banker. Quality of numbers was also important if the ranch was going to be able to beat the cost of production and have any return. Herd health management and herd reproductive efficiency would prove more cost effective than dealing with problems after the fact, but it was difficult to reconcile laying any dollars out in advance to head off problems, when for years the practice had been to treat problems case by case, and then often with too little and too late!

It was fairly difficult, also, to convince the banker to let you budget in the costs of management programs, or to be able to pay a little bit more for performance proven bulls, or invest in an artificial insemination program, when "any old sales ring bull 'would settle' your cows." There has been quite a bit of improvement in this mentality in recent years, but unfortunately it still persists too frequently among those who would advise the rancher with management questions. Some interesting things happened during the tough years while some banks and insurance companies were becoming owner-operators of failed family operations. Marginal lands which had had the grass plowed up in large scale "sod-busting" endeavors, for purposes of grain production, were blowing away. Many of these properties had been leveraged into an "improved" book value only to be also taken over by the

– Endless Tracks Across Centuries

banks and insurance companies. The government, always ready to "help," established the Conservation Reserve Program, or "acreage set-aside," to take these marginal and eroding soils out of production, and to get them back into grass cover. In some areas it was a bit difficult to get the grass to grow because of the drying, burning winds and no moisture. Tumbleweed could make it though, and it was not uncommon at times to see snow removal equipment out in the Summer and early Fall clearing the highways of these drifting weeds.

Cow numbers declined in Montana and across the country by one-fourth to one-third, as the drought and other conditions, both natural and man wrought, persisted. Cash flows declined with the cow numbers. There was a "whole herd buy out" program for dairy cows, also instituted by action of the government to deal with milk and dairy product surpluses, and while it was denied that there was any "dumping" effect against the beef market by

the liquidation of the participating dairy herds, it certainly was not helpful. One quite positive factor which evolved out of all this, however, has been a more rapid turnover of cattle inventory all the way through the "chain" or "pipeline," and a resulting leaner end product, genetically trimmed as opposed to having excess "fed on" fat having to be trimmed at the meat cutting counter. This has resulted in a maintenance of supply of red meat at the retail level within a few percentage points of levels previously available from a mother cow herd nationwide consisting of a fourth to a third more cows. How this might shake out to help ranchers like Connie in this time of recovery is a question which seems to have no simple answer. Getting all the facets to fit together and headed down the trail in the right direction is about like trying to get the chuck wagon to camp with the tongue broke out of it. It'll pull but won't go in the right track or may run over something on the way!

Yup it's broke all right – we're adrift!

– Endless Tracks Across Centuries

EPIC TRAILS—

WEDNESDAY, AUGUST 23, 1989. THIRTEENTH DAY ON THE TRAIL —

Up EARLY. AMOS CHARBONEAU WRANGLING THIS MORNING. HAD TO GO AFTER HORSES. THEY GOT OUT DURING NIGHT SO HAD TO HUNT FOR THEM. COWS GOT OUT TOO AND DRIFTED AWAY IN THE NIGHT. DIDN'T GET ON THE TRAIL UNTIL 10:00 A.M. WE TRAILED SOUTHEAST ACROSS THE GRAZING ASSOCIATION RANGE. WE MADE CAMP TO HAVE A BITE AND TO LET CATTLE REST ABOUT 2:30 P.M. RESTED 'TIL 6:00. THEN WE TRAILED ON TO SWEN HOLLAND'S CORRALS AND CAMPED FOR THE NIGHT.

AFTER A HOT AFTERNOON YESTERDAY, THE WEATHER WAS NICE AND COOL TODAY. WIND WAS AT OUR BACKS OUT OF THE NORTHWEST AND IT RAINED ABOUT A TENTH. KEPT THE DUST SETTLED. DAYS BECOMING NOTICEABLY SHORTER AND MORNINGS REAL CRISP. WE TRAILED 11 MILES TODAY. ANOTHER 69 MILES WILL SEE US ON THE EDGE OF ROUNDUP. WONDER HOW PLANS FOR THE BIG DRIVE ARE SHAPING UP? KNOW ITS GOTTA BE A REAL BIG CHORE WITH A LOT OF HEADACHES. MUST BE A LOT OF RED TAPE, TOO, THAT THE OLD TIME TRAIL BOSSES PROBABLY DIDN'T WORRY ABOUT. THEY PROBABLY WOULD HAVE TRADED SOME OF THEIR WORRIES THOUGH, IF THEY COULD HAVE FORESEEN. I WONDER ?

-ENDLESS TRACKS ACROSS CENTURIES

Chapter 13

BETTER TIMES

It was slow getting on the trail today. After reflecting on what had been a period of not too much fun in the cow business, Connie figured the stock just naturally had to rub it in a bit, so had got out during the night just for good measure. Maybe it served him right, but it had been a time of trial, and it was good that it was past. With the cows finally on the trail by midmorning, he decided it would be a good idea to think on things as they had begun to shape up this year. There was no clear light at the end of the tunnel and this thing had always been cyclical. Trouble was, in the past the pendulum seemed to swing a lot further one way than the other. Might it be, that for a change, it would go out into better times for a period of more than just a year or so? Some of the positive things to ponder included the prospects of expanded markets, both at home and for export. His north fence line, the 49th parallel, was the longest, friendliest border in the world, and Canada had always been a good trading partner of the U.S. With this new free trade agreement between these neighbors there should be some stabilizing influence on the cow business for both sides. The prospects of teaming up to pursue other foreign markets as partners, rather than as competitors, seemed a good idea to Connie. To take the entire decade of the '90s to enact the free trade agreement seemed a bit long.

Connie's thoughts turned to how things were hopefully shaping up for "The Great Montana Centennial Cattle Drive" and how it would celebrate a hundred years of Montana's history, and especially how the emphasis would be upon the grassroots aspects of the cattle business. It made him feel sure that this was a positive thing he was doing to try being a part of this event, and in so doing, to maybe help provide more opportunity for Montanans like his children and grandchildren here at home. He wanted to be able to do something that would help people remember this epic event and the reason for it for years and years to come. The start was positive and each day on the trail, passers-by indicated there was growing enthusiasm. He could tell there was growing excitement for it to happen each time he took some footweary cows to Roundup, too. Opportunity; yep, that's what it was all about!

Opportunity for the people of Montana, and especially for future generations; that's what this Centennial celebration is all about!

EPIC TRAILS—

Thursday, August 24, 1989. Fourteen Days—

    Gathered horses at 6:30 a.m. Fixed breakfast and started the cows down trail by 8 o'clock. I took 4 more foot-sore cows to Roundup while crew trailed. Herd made it to Lester and Carol Sluggett's place at 5:30 p.m. They invited us in for supper. Larry had stopped to grease the wagon at Ed and Mickey Styer's. We had a good rain — seven-tenths inch so got plenty wet.

    Didn't try to go beyond Sluggett's after supper due to rain. Slept in their garage so had dry bedrolls which were welcome. Even with the rain we made 14 miles today. Only 55 miles left to Roundup.

Chapter 14

GETTING THEM STARTED

Today makes two weeks on the trail to Roundup. The weather has turned cool and rainy so the crew trailed right along through midday after getting a bit later start following breakfast. With the stop to grease the wagon, and with the rain, everyone was happy to make the evening camp a little early and even happier at the prospects of a home cooked supper and dry place to roll out beds at Lester and Carol Sluggett's place. It seems each day on the trail has been sort of like a chapter out of Connie's life. He guessed while the rainy days were much fewer in number over the years than the dry windy ones, they still were the ones that gave one a chance to stop for a moment and do some thinking back. There was a soothing and easy feeling with the rain that was missing on the all too frequent days of bracing against the wind. The wind built a tension that seemed to affect all living things. To be convinced of this requires merely a look at the way trees grow in Montana anywhere east of the Rocky Mountains. Or, possibly, it would be more correct to observe the way trees try to survive, rather than really grow, in these challenging elements. The trunks all tend to lean toward the northeast away from the prevailing southwesterly winds and the branches give the impression of reaching out in the same direction as the trunk leans; reaching either for help, or reaching as if to break a fall, should the tree lean too far. Animals and men alike turn their backs or tails to the winds, trying to protect their faces and eyes, and trying to keep their breath from being taken away.

The rare exception among all living things innate to this land is the buffalo or North American Bison. The shaggy mane of thick, wool-like hair, the massive hump and heavy forequarters of these animals combined to give them the ability to face into the winds rather than away. They faced the storm as they faced predatory danger. The buffalo has been called nature's snow plow. Many an animal of lesser strength could find a bite of grass or twig of browse after the buffalo had broken through the drifts. Antelope and rabbits and upland birds had the better of it if they shared a range in wintertime with the buffalo.

Thinking on these things as the rain dripped off his hat brim and ran down the creases of his old yellow slicker to splash off the stirrups, Connie brought his thoughts back closer to the present. He reckoned he and Margie had been fortunate to raise their children in what he felt was a good way of life even if there were times when one might question whether or not it was a good living. He had taken the kids everywhere with him when they were little, in preparation for the training and rodeo competition they all enjoyed when they got a bit bigger. Sometimes they might not have thought a given chore was that much fun and he knew there were times when he got dark looks for being a hard task maker. This was especially so when it had been an extra long cold morning on the feed wagon or when one of them had been bumped and jolted around by an unruly colt or by an ornery old cow. He knew there had been times when he probably should have granted a little more sympathetic response to a childhood emotional moment. Understanding when compassion should overrule sternness was sometimes easier to feel within than it was to express or demonstrate outwardly. This conflict and the wanting ache that came to the throat because of it was no different a feeling in adulthood and parenthood than it had been a generation ago when the adult had been the child. Connie perceived that this communication impasse, so common between generations, had not prevented his children from developing quite adequate self images. He sensed that, as young adults starting their own families, they appeared ready to deal with any generation gap they might encounter in a pretty straightforward manner.

In reality, he thought, you only had a fairly short time in which to get them started. In his own mind, it somehow added up to about three periods of approximately two to five years each to do this, or to get the proper impression made. The first stage, or formative years he'd heard it called, probably was closer to two years than five. You loved them a lot, played with them probably not as much as you would have liked to have had time to, and corrected them more than you liked to. The next stage, the preschool and early school years, it seemed although it wasn't necessarily so, that they were their mother's and the teachers' charges and dad didn't get much of a handle on them. Then in the third stage, somewhere between about eight and twelve to thirteen or fourteen years of age, all of a sudden little children became small to middle sized real people capable of doing all sorts of amazing things. You wanted God to grant you lots of patience, but you needed Him to do it right now! The sobering thing about all this was you hoped it went right the first time because getting them started was about all the chance you got; barely green broke!

– Endless Tracks Across Centuries

EPIC TRAILS —

FRIDAY, AUGUST 25, 1989. THIRD WEEK BEGINS —

DIDN'T GET UP 'TIL 6:00 A.M. HAD BREAKFAST AT CAROL AND LESTER'S. SAT AROUND AND VISITED 'TIL 8:30. REAL MUDDY FOLLOWING YESTERDAY'S RAIN SO ROAD WILL BE SLOW GOING FOR A WHILE. WE COUNTED THE COWS OUT OF THE PASTURE GETTIN' READY TO TRAIL AND I GET 103 WHILE ANDY ONLY GETS 102 IN HIS COUNT. 'COURSE ANDY COUNTS LEGS AND DIVIDES BY FOUR IN GERMAN AND ALWAYS COMES UP WITH ONE HEAD LESS THAN ME!

LEVI AND LES SLUGGETT HELPED US TRAIL TO DICK DELANEY'S RANCH. A COUPLE MILES BEFORE WE REACHED THE RANCH, DICK MARSHALL AND HIS TWO BOYS, BRETT AND BRAD, CAME TO RIDE. AMOS CHARBONEAU LEFT US TO GO HOME. HE'S A GOOD HAND — KNOWS COWS AND HORSES AND SURE GOOD HELP. LEVI AND LES HAD A LITTLE EXCITEMENT WHEN THEY SAW 2 RATTLESNAKES!

WHEN WE MADE CAMP AT DICK DELANEY'S RANCH, GEORGIA DELANEY FIXED SUPPER FOR US. CAROL SLUGGETT AND JAN MARSHALL HELPED HER AND THEY SURE FED US GOOD. IT'S BEEN A COLD, WINDY DAY AND TRYING TO RAIN. ONLY MADE 9 MILES TODAY. LEAVES 46 MILES LEFT TO ROUNDUP.

-ENDLESS TRACKS ACROSS CENTURIES

Chapter 15
THE FAMILY THAT RODEOS TOGETHER . . . . .

Everyone has heard the adage, "the family that prays together stays together," or has used it at one time or another. It may not be a legitimate metaphor to make the denotation that, "the family that rodeos together does a lot of other things in life pretty well, too." Nevertheless, the comparison seems fair when looking at a number of families who have followed the rodeo circuits over a period of years and over a span of two and sometimes three or more generations. Besides family names already mentioned in chapter 3, such as Gee, Jacobsen and Nelson, there are numerous others which may be recognized in several walks of life outside the rodeo arena. Names like Cremer, Pauley, Greenough, Johnson, Gladstone, Simon, Skelton, Butterfield, Knight, Buetler and many more come to mind. Connie Cox and his family are not an exception. To be sure, other sports besides rodeo have their Junior Leagues, their amateur and professional categories, their Senior Divisions, and their Men's and Women's classifications. Rodeo, however, will, time and time again, see more family members, spanning more generations, competing at the same time than will be found anywhere else in the sports world.

You may see members of the same family in any or most of the recognized events in a given rodeo, but competing primarily within specific age divisions in keeping with concerns for safety and a sense of fairness related to the attainment of experience in the performance of the event. Youngsters can get started in Little Britches, Junior or Kids Rodeo, High School Rodeo and graduate to College Rodeo while their parents may be competing in regional Amateur or Professional competition. The kids may see a grandfather or grandmother performing in any number of events sanctioned by the National Old Timers' Rodeo Association. Standard events generally recognized include Calf Roping, Team Roping, Steer Wrestling, Saddle Bronc Riding, Bareback Bronc Riding, Bull Riding and Ladies' Barrel Racing. Depending on age categories, gender and the particular organization, additional events may include Break-away Roping, Ribbon Roping, Steer or Wild Cow Riding, Steer Roping, Pole Bending, Wild Cow Milking, Wild Horse Racing, Mutton Busting, Kids' Barrel Racing or mixed age and gender roping events, such as Century Team Roping. Ranch Rodeos are becoming popular with Team Penning, Cutting Horse Competiton and other ranch work related events.

In between practicing, training horses and competing, a family which is busy at rodeoing usually is found giving time to committee work and other community affairs. Family members are almost always the "extra hands" to do the needed work at home and to help the neighbors when they are short of help. Connie and Margie's three children developed early self sufficiencies that have enabled them to go about finding their own opportunities and careers with self confidence and self images eager to look beyond the status quo. As one friend summed up the situation when talking about a rodeo family in general; "Yep, if they'd 'a had Ladies' Barrel Racin' in Great Grandma's day, yuh might not have been able to talk her into wearin' jeans but yuh wouldn't have been able to keep her outa' the arena! She would have stayed lady-like but she would have been tough even if she never rode anythin' but side saddle!"

... And the next Barrel Racer is...? ? "GRANDMA, WHO ???"

The family that rodeos together...
...does a lot of other things in life
pretty well, too.

The top left and 3 lower photos courtesy of Margie Cox.

EPIC TRAILS —

SATURDAY, AUGUST 26, 1989. SIXTEEN DAYS TRAILING —

UP AT 6:00 A.M. AND HAD BREAKFAST IN HOUSE AT DELANEY'S. ANDY REALLY FILLED UP ON A LOT OF PANCAKES. I ASKED HIM, "HOW COME YOU EATING SO MANY PANCAKES WHEN YOU ONLY EAT ONE WHEN I COOK?" ANDY SAID, "IT WASN'T SO MUCH THE PANCAKES AS IT WAS THE COLOR OF THE PANCAKES." HE THOUGHT PANCAKES WHEN I COOK ON THE TRAIL ONLY CAME IN ONE COLOR. "BLACK."

TRAILING BY 7:00 O'CLOCK. LOTS OF HELP TODAY — J.J. DELANEY, BARB DELANEY, TACOMA DELANEY, MONA LINDLEY, OF ROUNDUP, CAL AND RANDY NUNN OF WINNETT, AND DICK, BRAD AND BRETT MARSHALL. BEAUTIFUL WEATHER TODAY.

WE CAMPED 9 MILES FROM DELANEY'S RANCH AND WENT INTO WINNETT TO HAVE SUPPER. DECIDED TO STAY FOR SATURDAY NIGHT DANCE. DIDN'T GET BACK TO CAMP 'TIL 3:00 A.M. HAD A GOOD DAY AND FUN NIGHT. WON'T TAKE LONG TO STAY ALL NIGHT BETWEEN NOW AND DAYLIGHT! COOL BREEZE. HAVE 37 MILES LEFT TO ROUNDUP.

-ENDLESS TRACKS ACROSS CENTURIES

Chapter 16
A NEED TO DIVERSIFY

Saturday again and another beautiful day with one more "40 hour week" put away. The hospitality shown to Connie's drovers all along the way had been so heartwarming. The way Andy Mueller had filled up at the Delaney's breakfast table had been the cause of some good natured chiding and Connie had received a very matter of fact response in the critiquing of his chuck wagon culinary efforts. The question was raised whether people here would be so friendly and hospitable if they lived closer together? Connie couldn't feature people like they'd been visiting being any way but the way they were. He could remember when he'd traveled to the Midwest to rodeo in the '60s that people who lived just doorways apart sometimes appeared too busy in their own little worlds to know their neighbor. Often, though, these same people would be very kind to a stranger such as himself. He was reasonably certain that a little of the cowboy code as he defined it could do a lot of good in a lot of places. Without pointing an accusing finger at anyone, he acknowledged that different circumstances drove people to act in ways sometimes that to an outsider might be viewed as self-serving when in actuality such action was more survivalistic or self-preserving.

Urban dwellers or people living closer to civilization than the ranch on Frenchman Creek would or could get a second job to help make ends meet if their survivalist problems were similar to some he had experienced. Living as remotely as Connie and some of his neighbors did made such a plan more than a little bit impractical so they had to turn such problems into opportunity by learning to diversify. Over the years, the diversifications Connie had initiated had been varied enough to keep things darned interesting even if the idea at a given moment may not have helped to balance the budget. Being serious about rodeo when he was "hitting a lick" was just one such example. As early as 1970, he had dealt with another problem and turned it into opportunity by devising a plan to lead hunters who frequented his ranch into being more thoughtful and considerate as they swarmed in to enjoy themselves. Many were already of such a frame of mind, but others could at times be very thoughtless and indifferent. These latter types could make a rancher fighting mad. Gates would be left open and stock could be mixed or lost. Unauthorized vehicles would leave tracks all over and sometimes valuable animals would be left dead without a trace of the killers.

In order to deal with this problem Connie invited a number of his town friends, who enjoyed coming to the ranch to hunt, out for a pre-season visit. He challenged them to work together with him to preserve the enjoyment for all by asking each to carry a card stating simply: "HUNTER–Please don't drive on grass, leave gates open, nor throw beer bottles or garbage on ground. If you see anyone else doing these things please let me know." At the bottom was his name and phone number. Beyond this simple effort, he asked that if anyone were foolish or unlucky enough to shoot one of his cattle, that it be properly cared for and reported to him and paid for at the going price for beef. He also wanted a report if there had been a successful hunt. If you were found on his ranch, you'd better have your card! By getting people to reciprocate a little common courtesy, Connie helped to make landowners and hunters better friends. The Phillips County Wildlife Association recognized Connie for this effort in 1971. He has continued to accommodate courteous sportsmen since that time.

In more recent years, Connie's efforts at diversification have included joining forces with Don Jacobs, a Montana Rodeo Producer, to raise bucking horses, and in the interests of improving livestock nutrition for his cattle ranching neighbors, Connie handles a quality supplemental feed as a dealer for the MoorMan's® Co. In the effort to produced quality rodeo bucking stock, a band of brood mares with some known rodeo history is run loose in the breaks on the ranch and bred to stallions which also have some history of rodeo capability. The offspring are handled only minimally until two years of age, at which time Jacobs Rodeo tries them out to see what inclination they have to buck a rider off. If the result appears satisfactory, these horses go back to the ranch to mature without further handling for another year or so. At the age of 4 or 5 they are allowed to perform and if results are still positive, they go to a PRCA stock contractor, Mike Cervi. In 1989, four such horses, "Roan Angel," "Hilda Blue," "Billy Blue," and "T22-Frenchie" qualified for the PRCA National Finals at Las Vegas. "Hilda Blue" was runner-up Saddle Bronc of the year. In 1990, an additional horse, "Connie's Pet," has qualified for the PRCA National Finals. Connie's efforts to diversify have truly been interesting.

If a rancher is a proper steward of land and water he can hope to grow a little grass. If the grass is managed right, it'll provide some beefsteak to feed the hungry.

It'll also make feed and habitat to benefit wildlife and to benefit those who look to wildlife for enjoyment, recreation and revitalization...

... At the ZN Ranch some of the grazing is diversified to produce additional recreational livestock in the form of some very athletic bucking horses and good roping cattle.

EPIC TRAILS—

SUNDAY, AUGUST 27, 1989. THE SEVENTEENTH DAY —

MORNIN' COMES AWFUL EARLY SOMETIMES. REAL SHORT NIGHT. UP AT 6:30 A.M. BIG HEAD! DON'T FEEL TOO GOOD — BUT HAD FUN LAST NIGHT.

GLAD FOR THE HELP AGAIN OF DICK AND BRETT MARSHALL. THEY RODE AND TRAILED WITH US 'TIL 11:00 A.M. WE CAMPED FOR A COUPLE HOURS, HAD DINNER AND LET THE STOCK REST. 'COURSE WE DIDN'T NEED ANY REST OURSELVES AFTER THE GOOD NIGHT'S SLEEP WE HAD LAST NIGHT! IN THE AFTERNOON WE TRAILED ON TO THE JOE DELANEY RANCH. WHEN WE CAMPED FOR THE NIGHT WE WERE ON ROY OLSEN'S RANCH.

WEATHER WAS REAL NICE IN THE MORNING BUT TURNED COLD AND RAINED IN THE AFTERNOON. MOTHER NATURE IS A BEAUTIFUL LADY MOST OF THE TIME AND REAL GOOD TO US BUT ONCE IN A WHILE SHE CAN BE A REAL BITCH AND CAN MAKE LIFE MISERABLE WHEN SHE CHOOSES TO! SOMETIMES SHE DOESN'T WANT TO GIVE YOU MUCH WARNING WHEN SHE DECIDES TO THROW ONE OF HER TEMPER TANTRUMS EITHER.

HAD SUPPER ABOUT 7:00 P.M. CAL SORENSON CAME FROM LIVINGSTON TO TRAVEL WITH US AND TAKE PICTURES. HE DROVE FROM THE WIND RIVER RESERVATION IN WYOMING WHERE HE HAS BEEN DOING A PHOTOGRAPHIC STUDY AS PART OF A SERIES HE IS PREPARING ABOUT THE MYTHS AND LEGENDS OF THE PLAINS INDIANS. HE HIT OUR TRAIL JUST IN TIME TO GET IN ON THE COLD RAIN AND TO GET GOOD AND STUCK IN THE MUD.

WE MADE 10 MILES TODAY, 27 MORE TO ROUNDUP.

—ENDLESS TRACKS ACROSS CENTURIES

Chapter 17

MOTHER NATURE

With nearly a month of summer supposedly left on the calendar there was no question that this day would certainly feel much longer than the night which had just preceded it. By afternoon it felt as if summer had zoomed right on past the autumnal equinox as a chill settled in with the rain. A person could experience snow any month of the year in Montana, but this trail crew could surely do without it right now. Mother Nature was being plenty whimsical just to keep them reminded how unpredictable she could really be. Except for the discomfort of the cold, the rain was welcome just about any time, and Connie was thinking how these showers would allay some of the prairie fire danger that was always a concern. This had been an exceptionally good grass year and fires on the plains could be just as devastating as in the forests. Man could try being extra careful but he was helpless against the capricious ways of nature if she decided to put on one of her "fiery and snuffy" displays of awesome power and grandeur in the form of a dry lightning storm. It was no wonder that the trail drovers of a hundred years ago had such a dread of any sudden weather change.

Thinking on the lighter side for a moment, Connie couldn't help but laugh when he thought of some of the music of the dance band last night, or at least someone had called it music, and he thought of how it might have caused a stampede rather then helped prevent one! He wondered at how some of the old ballads of "Teddy Blue" Abbott's time had come about as the trail herders and the night guards improvised and made the lyrics up while they rode their slow circle. It would be interesting some time to try finding out the history of some of those songs, particularly of those which probably had not been written down. Many, he was sure, were lost with the demise of the old cowboys of that era. How many of those early day cowboys taking their turn at night watch had made up verses out of boredom? How many wondered, out of nervous apprehension, if hopefully by singing they might keep the cattle from spooking at other strange night sounds? And how many lines had come about as the result of a lonesome rider's outright fear of nature's unsettled ways? He may have seen the flicker of distant lightning and hoped he could maintain the night's solitude by quietly singing to still his own racing heartbeat as he prayed that neither he nor the herd would hear the inevitable rumble of the thunder that was to follow?

Now, as then, people who worked with the land and cattle to wrest their livelihood could find Mother Nature a friendly companion and helper one moment, only to have her turn into an unforgiving and mean mistress without warning, at the next turn. It was good that providence and Mother Nature seemed to team up to control one's destiny more often for the better than for the worse, but like the lonesome night herder of old, that jumpy feeling never quite would go away. Connie felt that one of the things that made the rancher a usually good steward of his resources was his constant striving for a balance which made him work in a conciliatory partnership with nature as much as possible, rather than trying to oppose her. Whether they realized it or not, and whether they had a name for it or not most good ranch managers practiced a somewhat holistic approach in the stewardship of the environment and resources available to them. It was more than a little disconcerting to have self proclaimed experts constantly finding fault and criticizing the animal agriculturists and other food producers under the guise of consumer advocatism or environmentalism while they ignored the fact that the targets of their disdain had to live in harmony with the environment in order to survive. It took a lot of willingness on the part of the Good Lord and Mother Nature, both, for the rancher to have the renewability, annually, of all the parts necessary to keep his operation viable and vital. And it took a lot of hard work, blood, sweat and tears, in cooperation with that willingness, to be able to stay hitched to your operation when the forces dictated you'd have to get by or get ahead on two or three average to good years out of eight or ten.

Connie had been absorbed in these thoughts many times and knew he would have to remain engrossed in this vigil many times in the future in order to keep that balance that Mother Nature demanded. All in all, he'd have to give her credit for being a pretty nice partner, but she sure could cuff you about the head and ears and skin up your nose and chin if you got out of line with her much! There was nothing like having a snap of Saint Elmo's fire run down your slicker buttons and off your saddle horn to the hardware on your horse's bridle to get you paying real good attention to what Mother Nature might be trying to tell you!

– Endless Tracks Across Centuries

*Th' 'Fiery'
'N 'Snuffy'
are rarin'
to go.*

EPIC TRAILS—

MONDAY, AUGUST 28, 1989. EIGHTEEN DAYS SOUTH—

VERY COOL THIS MORNING. CAMP VERY MUDDY. CAN'T MOVE. COWS RELUCTANT TO GET UP FROM SPOT THEY'VE WARMED ON THE WET GROUND FOR THEIR BEDS. CAN REALLY SEE THE STEAM OF THEIR BREATHING IN THE CHILLY DAWN AIR. HORSES AND CREW ALL STANDING AROUND WITH HUMP IN THEIR BACKS AND SHIVERING TO WARM UP. WILL EAT BREAKFAST EARLY WHILE WE WAIT FOR MUD TO DRY ENOUGH TO BREAK CAMP. BRUCE IS COOK THIS MORNING. WARMED US UP GOOD WITH COFFEE, BACON, EGGS, POTATOES WITH ONIONS AND BREAD. FINALLY GOT ALL THE KINKS OUT AND GOT COWS TO TRAILING ABOUT TEN AFTER 9 A.M.

AFTER CATTLE GOT GOING GOOD I WENT BACK TO CAMP, THEN RODE UP ABOUT HALF A MILE TO WHERE CAL SORENSON HAD GOT STUCK IN MUD LAST NIGHT. CAL POURED ANOTHER CUP OF COFFEE AND WE HAD A GOOD VISIT. MUD DRIED ENOUGH SO HE COULD DRIVE OUT AT LAST AND WE CAUGHT UP WITH CATTLE AND CREW WHERE THEY CAMPED FOR LUNCH AT 2:20 P.M. LET CATTLE AND HORSES REST 'TIL 4 P.M., THEN STARTED THEM ON TRAIL TO HUGHES' CORRALS ALONG SIDE OF HIGHWAY #244

MET THE MARSHALLS AGAIN ALONG THE ROAD, DICK, JAN AND BRETT, AND VISITED WITH THEM. CAL AND I RODE OUT THEN TO MEET CATTLE ON THE TRAIL BUT DIDN'T FIND THEM. WE RODE BACK AND CREW ALREADY HAD THEM TO THE CORRALS AND WERE MAKING CAMP. ATE SUPPER AT 8:00 P.M. THEN CAL TOOK SOME NIGHT PICTURES STARTING ABOUT 10:00 P.M. KEPT US UP 'TIL AFTER MIDNIGHT. CAL LIKES TO JUST GET GOING ABOUT THE SAME TIME OF DAY I'D LIKE TO BE FINISHING UP. SEE IF CAN ADJUST !?

—ENDLESS TRACKS ACROSS CENTURIES

EPIC TRAILS—

Even without our photographer friend stirring everything up this evening, it was busy around camp. J.J. and Tacoma Delaney had trailed with us all day and their folks came to pick them up about supper time. My daughter, Charlene Coleman, arrived with Tia, my 4 year old grand-daughter, who is going to ride on into Roundup with us. It made for a wonderful day. The cool - near cold, of the damp morning had turned nice and warm in the afternoon. Night's beautiful - about 40 degrees with no wind. Feel of fall is in the air.

We made 8 miles today leaving 19 miles to Roundup.

—Endless Tracks Across Centuries

Chapter 18

THE BIG OPEN

One of Montana's abundant natural resources is gumbo mud. After the rain this mess has a very slick, waxy or soapy consistency while still quite wet on the surface. As it dries, it becomes very sticky and tenacious, fastening itself to just about anything which comes in contact with it. When completely dry, its silt-like close particulate characteristic makes it rock hard so that a large wad or chunk of it which may have accumulated on a wagon wheel and then got peeled off may very well break the next wheel which jolts over it. It is almost impossible to travel across while still mud and rougher than the most jagged of lava-like rock for animals to walk over when sunbaked. If possible, it is best left undisturbed when wet so that the worst discomfort experienced while traveling across it dry is the talc fine dust that rises with each footstep to sandpaper the eyes, nose and throat! Gumbo, in its various forms, must really be experienced to be appreciated!

The same could be said about much of Eastern Montana, or maybe of Montana generally. The "Big Sky" openness and vastness of the Missouri Plateau almost defies description with words but both can unquestionably be "felt."

It may be difficult for the first time traveler to Montana, or for the person who has never traveled here, to believe just how expansively boundless it seems from border to border. Its greatest east-west distance is a bit over 550 miles, and the greatest north-south distance is over 320 miles in the west and is 280 miles in the eastern end of the state. In a questionnaire reportedly sent out by the Montana Department of Commerce for purposes of garnering tourism data, officials were surprised and dismayed to learn that many visitors to the "Big Sky" country gave affirmative answers when asked, "Have you ever visited Yellowstone National Park?" and, "Have you ever visited Glacier National Park?" but responded in the negative to the query in the same questionnaire, "Have you ever visited Montana?" Similarly, there are those who think that all Montana consists of is mountains, and this can possibly be excused because the name, Montana, comes from a Latin word meaning "mountainous regions." To be sure, Montana is the largest of the Rocky Mountain states, and has many ranges of mountains, but the eastern three-fifths of the state is made up by the part of the Great Plains known as the Missouri Plateau.

Yep, this must be Eastern Montana – sure looks like a lot of "BIG OPEN" to me!

– Endless Tracks Across Centuries

Before the Expedition of Lewis and Clark, in 1805, few white men had been to the territory that now makes up the state of Montana. There is no telling how long the region would have continued to be considered of little value had gold not been discovered at Gold Creek in 1858. The Native American inhabitants of the land were little disturbed except by a few fur trappers and Indian traders those years in between. The eastern nearly two thirds of the state continued to be considered part of the Great American Desert and virtually worthless by learned and official persons on the banks of the Potomac right up to and including the time of the homesteading efforts enacted to entice settlers to the area. The cowboys who had come up the trail with the great herds of the late 1800s and had stayed knew this grassland was more precious than the gold and other treasures attracting fortune hunters westward, but it took that innate generosity of governmental mind and spirit, more commonly termed largess, to start real settlement of this land. It is interesting to note how little this "spirit" of governmental "help" has changed since that time. Now, generations later, some learned folk have apparently returned to the "Great American Desert" ways and days of thinking and have dreamed up a new, yet, similar term, "The Big Open."

Since it is covered only by acres of grass or wheat and barley and not by "mountain scenery" it can't be worth much, so why not turn it all back to a wild and empty "big open" space? Do you suppose then that the tourists and recreationalists who didn't even know they were in Montana the last time they visited the "mountainous regions" would come back and enjoy the "Big Open" and maybe even know where they were? It tends to make those who "live" there and depend upon making their living there ponder as they enjoy a beautiful sunrise on a morning the wind isn't blowing, or as they share the fretfulness of a herd of mama cows bawling for their calves at weaning time. It tends to make them also deeply appreciate a kind note from the visitor who went back home to city streets "knowing" where they'd been as they shared a glimpse of the same sunrise and found a place in their heart for a part of Montana that would beckon them back again and again! Fortunately, it would be this visitor who would be remembered rather than the questionnaire respondent or the do-gooder, "I'm here to help (change your life forever) agent of bureaucratic process." The remembrance that would come back to the mind of the inhabitant of "The Big Open" would be one of kind regard for a true "neighbor."

Where else but in "THE BIG OPEN" could a cowboy get the gumbo out from between his toes
and shed some Alkali while sharing the bath with his horse?

– Endless Tracks Across Centuries

EPIC TRAILS—

TUESDAY, AUGUST 29, 1989. NINETEEN DAYS ON THE TRAIL —

Up at 6:15 THIS MORNING. PUT COFFEE ON AND WRANGLED HORSES. THIS WAS GREAT PLACE TO CAMP - TWO SMALL FIELDS. HAD TO WAIT HOUR AND A HALF FOR BREAKFAST. GUESS SHORT NIGHT MAKES CREW LOSE TRACK WHO'S GOIN' TO BE FIRST UP OR WHO GETS LEFT WITH JOB OF COOKING. AFTER NEARLY 3 WEEKS I FIGURE THE REST OF THE BUNCH WOULD BE FALLING ALL OVER EACH OTHERS BEDROLLS TO BE FIRST IN LINE AT COOK FIRE SO AS TO NOT HAVE TO EAT MY BURNT OFFERINGS, ANYHOW. SHOULD HAVE STARTED TO TRAIL RIGHT AT DAYBREAK.

AFTER THE LATE START WE HAD TROUBLE AT A BRIDGE ON CREEK. COWS WERE SPOOKED BY SOMETHING ABOUT IT AND WOULDN'T CROSS. HAD TO TAKE THEM INTO ANOTHER FIELD TO FIND PLACE THEY WOULD CROSS. GOT 3 MORE MILES SOUTH AND DID NOT KNOW WHICH WAY WE COULD GO. TALKED WITH HUTTERITE BY NAME OF KEN STAHL AND HE FIRST SAID, "DON'T THINK YA CAN GET TO ROUNDUP FROM HERE WITH YOUR CATTLE."

I ASKED HIM IF THERE WASN'T SOME WAY AROUND A COUPLE OF MORE TIMES AND KEPT GETTING SAME REPLY, "THERE'S JUST NO WAY FROM HERE YA CAN DRIVE NO CATTLE ON A TRAIL TO ROUNDUP — NO WAY YOU CAN GET THERE!"

YOU SHOULDA' SEEN HIM GRIN AND HIS EYES LIGHT UP WHEN I ASKED HIM ONE MORE TIME AND JUST HAPPENED TO LET HIM GET A BIT OF A GLIMPSE OF A TWENTY I'D PULLED FROM MY POCKET! "OH, YAH,- YAH, I THINK YA CAN GET FROM HERE TO ROUNDUP WITH YOUR COWS,

-ENDLESS TRACKS ACROSS CENTURIES

ALL RIGHT!" HE THEN PROCEEDED TO GIVE DETAILED DIRECTIONS WHICH WAY TO GO. "YA GOTTA TURN HALF A MILE EAST - DEN 3 MILES 'SOUT' AND HIT 'TA COUNTY ROAD 'T GOES EAST 'N' WEST. YA GO 2 MORE MILES BACK T'DA WEST 'N'T ROAD WILL TAKE YA SOUT' AGIN — OKAY?"

WE FOLLOWED HIS DIRECTIONS AND CAMPED TO EAT AND REST THE STOCK WHEN WE HIT THE EAST AND WEST ROAD. WE CAMPED 'TIL 4:00 P.M, THEN TRAILED THE 2 MILES WEST AS STAHL HAD DIRECTED AND THE ROAD DID AGAIN TURN 'SOUT'. THIS TOOK US PAST THE FLATWILLOW CHRISTIAN COMMUNITY, A COLONY OF HUTTERIAN SECT OR BRETHREN WHERE THE MEMBERS AND THEIR FAMILIES LIVE IN A GROUP OR COMMUNAL SETTING AND HOLD PROPERTY IN COMMON.

THE HUTTERITES TREATED US GREAT JUST AS EVERYONE ELSE HAS ALONG THIS TRAIL. THEY GAVE US FRESH COLD WATER, COFFEE AND FRESH BAKED ROLLS. WHAT GREAT COUNTRY WE HAVE PASSED THROUGH AND WHAT FINE WONDERFUL PEOPLE WE HAVE VISITED WITH.

RED KNUDSEN FROM WINNETT JOINED US TO TRAIL ON INTO ROUNDUP. FULLER LAUGERMAN CAME BY AND SHARED SODA POP AND A COLD BEER. WE TRAILED ON TO HOLLIDAY'S CORRALS WHERE WE CAMPED FOR OVERNIGHT. I HAULED INTO ROUNDUP FEEDYARD WITH TRAILER AND 3 MORE FOOTSORE COWS. HAD FLAT TIRE BEFORE GETTING BACK FOR SUPPER. WEATHER WARM AGAIN. JILL SUNDBY AND LARRY MAYER WITH THE BILLINGS GAZETTE CAME OUT TO ASK QUESTIONS AND TAKE PICTURES. THEY CAMPED WITH US OVERNIGHT HOPING TO GET SOME MORNING PICTURES.

WE MADE 9 MILES TODAY. JUST OVER 10 MORE TO ROUNDUP.

-ENDLESS TRACKS ACROSS CENTURIES

Chapter 19

WALK IN ANOTHER'S TRACKS

What a cross section of personalities had been encountered thus far on this trek! Yet, to a person, all had expressed enthusiasm, support and cooperation regarding the effort. Each visit along the way had provided some sort of heartening interlude that seemed to make the decision the more worthwhile. Here they were only one more day from reaching Roundup, and were actually about a day ahead of schedule. It was refreshing to be able to enjoy the fellowship of friends and passersby and even a group such as the Flatwillow Christian Community which they'd come by this afternoon, and have each be not only nonjudgmental, but also genuinely thrilled to share in what was becoming more and more a determined endeavor.

It would be a mistake to think these people were impassive or unresponsive to what might excite normal interest or emotion. They were truly caught up in the magnetism of what appeared to them to be no less than a great adventure. They gathered around Connie as he shared moments out of his journal with them. One elderly gentleman Connie believed was the religious leader of the colony showed off with pride the replicas of stagecoaches he had created in miniature to celebrate the Centennial. They would not hear of the trail drovers going on until they had been served refreshments which included a generous sampling of their home baking and canning. An acappella choir of the women apologized for their group not all being present, but entertained the crew beautifully with a number of songs. They happily responded to a request from Connie for "The Old Rugged Cross," among others.

In thinking about people and presumed differences, Connie was reminded of the admonishment he'd grown up with of not pointing an accusing finger because of the other three which automatically pointed back at the accuser. He thought of his good friend, Joe Big Knife, and his people's gentle counsel against finding fault with another, "until you had walked several days in the other man's moccasins." A lot of what had been going through Connie's mind these days and nights on the trail, he summed up, could be boiled down to one word. Appreciation. Yes, appreciation was what his senses were trying to grasp. Without realizing it was happening, or just how or when, there was an awareness that he was taking time to become acquainted with the specialness of people and his world around him. The vistas he could see, the freedom of spirit he felt, the animals and the plants, the sounds of life around him, the smell of the sage and the primrose; all became discoveries he knew were there, but wondered if he'd really fully appreciated before? He realized he had preferences, with favorite friends, foods and so on, and he was sure appreciation varied, but somehow, as he looked across this Flatwillow basin, he sensed a greater purpose and responsibility of being a part of it.

In a way, it made him think of a mirage, as the vastness shimmered around the distant horizon, but unlike a mirage, the sensation did not seem unattainable. He knew this one moment of realization or appreciation was worth the whole trip if he didn't go one step further. Accepting the possibility of a greater purpose and the responsibility of increased appreciation would require giving time to new ideas. Connie hoped there would be some way he might be able to share the feeling he had right then with his family and with people who would not have the opportunity, for one reason or another, to view these same horizons. He was really thankful for the happiness, health and sense of well being he was experiencing, and to put the boot on the other foot, so to speak, made the wish that others would be able to walk in his tracks!

A positive outlook made all the difference in the world. Opportunity seemed to exist today where none could be seen yesterday. The weather was warm again and Connie reflected upon how the tracks of the wagon had looked as if they would reach clear to infinity on the rain dampened trail earlier. He decided his hopes and dreams were as long as those wagon tracks and that they should roll on forever. It was a good feeling as they trailed on to Holliday's corrals where they would camp for the night. He was looking forward to riding with Red Knudsen tomorrow. If the wagon tracks seemed to reach toward infinity, the experience lines at the corners of Red's eyes reached past infinity, individualizing a character of notable traits. The weathered features, Connie was sure, were reminiscent of memorable trails and experiences which might be reflected as they rode along.

Features reminiscent of memorable trails.

Tracks across the Flatwillow prairies.

101

EPIC TRAILS-

WEDNESDAY, AUGUST 30, 1989. 'THE TWENTIETH DAY —

Up EARLY. LARRY AND I DECIDED TO GET TO TRAILING AT DAYLIGHT WHILE IT'S COOL LIKE WE DID THE FIRST DOZEN DAYS ON THE TRAIL. IF ANYONE WANTS COFFEE OR BREAKFAST THEY ARE ON THEIR OWN 'TIL 10:00 OR 11:00 O'CLOCK. JILL AND LARRY OF THE GAZETTE LEFT FOR BILLINGS AT 9:45 A.M. WE GOT TO GARY AND DIANE WACKER'S AT 11:25 A.M. AND THEY HAD US IN FOR BREAKFAST. WE CAMPED AND LET CATTLE REST THERE 'TIL 3:00 P.M.

TRAILED ON DOWN TO BOB AND MARGARET LIND'S PASTURE TO SET UP CAMP FOR THE NIGHT. WEATHER WAS WARM DURING DAY AND COWS GLAD FOR THE STOP. COOLING OFF GOOD TONIGHT AND TRYING TO RAIN A LITTLE. MARGIE CAME FROM RANCH AND WILL STAY 'TIL AFTER WE HAVE COW SALE AT LEAST.

COVERED 10 MILES TODAY AND ROUNDUP IS JUST OVER THE RISE SOUTH OF OUR CAMP.

-ENDLESS TRACKS ACROSS CENTURIES

Chapter 20

ON THEIR OWN

"We'll reach the rimrock bench overlooking Roundup today," Connie and Larry said aloud as they agreed with each other, "and we won't worry about who's goin' to be camp cookie this mornin'." It was warming up pretty well when they stopped at Wacker's so the cows were happy for the rest and the crew lucked into another home cooked breakfast. Having Tia along made Connie think back to when Tia's mother and the boys were little, and how it seemed to take no time for them to grow up and be out on their own. He sort of hoped grandchildren didn't grow quite so fast but was sure such thinking was mostly wishful. Seemed like Tia and Cash were growing like little weeds. Casey and Diane's little girl, Cassidy, was hardly half a year old and Connie knew she'd change a lot between times they'd get to see her since they lived so far away in Georgia. Tia, at 4 years, and Cash, at 2 years of age, were close enough, with their folks living at Cutbank, for he and Margie to get some pretty good "spoiling" in on them, but they were still quite a ways away.

Casey, Clinton and Charlene were all close enough in age so that it seemed the empty nest happened just about over night. They were all doing school things and summertime rodeo competition one minute and then were out of high school and off to college it seemed like the next minute. Casey had gone rodeoing the summer he was 15. That was in '73 and only four years later, in '77, he and Mike Beers were Collegiate Champion Team Ropers. All three have continued to rodeo since high school days. Casey and Clinton both Team Rope and also rope calves some. Charlene heels some in the Team Roping and competes in Ladies Barrel Racing.

Casey and his wife, Diane, and daughter, Cassidy, live in Georgia, where Casey works as an Independent Distributor and National Sales Director with National Safety Associates, headquartered in Memphis, Tennessee. The firm is a leading company in the manufacture and sales of water and air filtration equipment, both high priority environmental concerns in our society and the world today. Casey continues to rodeo professionally, competing in PRCA Team Roping. He qualified for the PRCA National Finals Rodeo competition at Las Vegas, Nevada, in 1988. Casey attended Blue Mountain College at Pendleton, Oregon.

Clinton, and his wife, Denise, live and ranch in the Whitewater community, not too far distant from Connie and Margie on Frenchman Creek. Clinton attended Dawson Community College, at Glendive, Montana, for a short time before deciding to take up ranching. Denise is a Saskatchewan native. Besides working at ranching, Clinton does some custom haying and this is a welcome help to Connie. Clinton also maintains cattle for Team Roping competitions and assists Connie and Margie in putting on the Annual Cox Ranch Team Roping each Spring. Clinton will continue with the Annual Team Roping, Connie hopes.

Charlene is married to Tip Coleman and they and Tia and Cash live near Cutbank. Charlene attended Eastern Montana College in Billings and she and Tip farm and ranch, including sheep and wool production. Charlene is also an Independent Distributor and Sales Coordinator with National Safety Associates. Charlene and Tip compete regionally some in Team Roping and find time to help with the Annual Cox Ranch Team Roping as well. Charlene competes in regional Ladies Barrel Racing, and she and Tip give both their children guidance and encouragement in getting them off to the right start with horses.

With diversification being a strong factor in Connie's ranching operations, it is not difficult to understand his children with their initiative, enthusiasm and work ethics. Connie says, "They are all very independent and had to learn from an early age about responsibility. We know they are free spirits and only hoped we could help them have their feet on the ground and their heads pointed in the right direction when they got out of school. They had plenty of space to grow and they were active enough to use most of it! We probably don't know how to say it right or say it often enough, but we are very proud of them all and know they are good citizens. No parent rears children without some anxious moments, but God has been good to us with our family and we are thankful."

Charlene and Casey are both active in helping with training at the local, regional, and the national level, in their association with National Safety Associates. They also work to introduce people to the business opportunities the company offers.

"Free Spirits"
They need clear, happy tracks to follow,
and bright horizons soon to look beyond.
Give them roots, yet plenty space to grow;
with wings to try – quickly, on their own!

–2

Oh, Lord, they've gone – North, South, East and West,
    Trailing across new horizons and away from home.
Now on their own – You helped us try our very best;
    In You we trust – and know they'll not be alone.
Thanks and Amen.

EPIC TRAILS—

THURSDAY, AUGUST 31, 1989. END OF THE THIRD WEEK ON THE TRAIL —

EVERYONE RELAXING TODAY — NO TRAILING. HORSES, CATTLE AND CREW, I'M SURE ARE HAPPY FOR A BREAK. RED KNUDSON LEFT THIS MORNING TO GO HOME. WHAT A GREAT COWBOY! HE SAID HE'LL NEVER TRAIL AGAIN — GLAD HE COULD TAKE PART IN WHAT COULD BE ONE OF THE LAST LONG TRAIL DRIVES. REST OF THE HANDS ARE PONDERING WHAT ALL MAY GO ON IN NEXT FEW DAYS AS THESE COWS OF OURS GET IN WITH THE BIG DROVE THAT IS BEING THROWN TOGETHER FROM ALL OVER THE STATE OF MONTANA FOR THE BIG PUSH FROM ROUNDUP TO BILLINGS?

IT'S REALLY SOMETHING TO THINK ABOUT AND SURE LOOKS AS IF THE 'BIG DRIVE OF '89' IS GOING TO ACTUALLY HAPPEN. HAVE SEEN A LOT OF EXCITEMENT GOING ON AS HORSES ARE STARTING TO ARRIVE AT WALT COLLINS' FEEDYARD AND LEACHMAN'S LEAD HERD OF BIG HORNED CATTLE ARE BEING PENNED THERE ALSO TO BE READY TO LEAD THE WAGON TRAIN AND ALL THE PARADE OUT ON LABOR DAY MORNING. TRUCKLOAD AFTER TRUCKLOAD OF CATTLE ARE COMING TO ALFRED ADOLPH'S RANCH ACROSS ON THE SOUTH SIDE OF THE MUSSELSHELL RIVER THIS WEEK-END WHERE THE MAIN BIG HERD OF CATTLE IS BEING PUT TOGETHER. ALFRED AND DORIS ADOLPH'S SON, DARREL, IS MANAGER AT WALT COLLINS' ROUNDUP FEEDYARD. BOTH OF THESE MEN HAVE BEEN REAL GOOD TO WORK WITH AS I'VE BEEN TAKING OUR FEW FOOT-WEARY COWS IN TO THEIR LOT AND THEY WILL HAVE A PEN READY FOR OUR MAIN BUNCH OF COWS WHEN WE TRAIL ON IN TOMORROW MORNING.

WENT IN TO WATCH THE RODEO IN ROUNDUP IN AFTERNOON.

ENDLESS TRACKS ACROSS CENTURIES

*... Are they
ever busy
little people!*

*If I'd known
grandkids
could be so
much fun...*

108

EPIC TRAILS—

GOT TO SEE A NUMBER OF COWBOYS I HAVEN'T SEEN FOR QUITE A WHILE. IT WAS SURE GOOD TO TALK WITH THEM. WEATHER IS NICE FOR THE RODEO AND LOTS OF PEOPLE ARE BEGINNING TO GATHER FOR THE 'BIG DRIVE' INTO BILLINGS.

THE BILLINGS GAZETTE HAD A NICE WRITE UP IN THEIR PAPER THIS MORNING. FROM LOOKS OF MY PICTURE IT APPEARS I'VE SHRUNK A LITTLE SINCE WE LEFT HOME. FOUND A SCALE AND WEIGHED. WEIGHT— 174 POUNDS. HAVE LOST 14 POUNDS ON TRAIL SO FAR. MY HORSE, 'BLUE', IS LOOKING A LITTLE LIKE A GREYHOUND TOO.

BEING AS WE'VE TAKEN OFF FOR THE DAY WE WENT INTO THE MAVERICK BAR AFTER THE RODEO TO VISIT AND SEE IF WE CAN'T WASH SOME OF THE TRAIL DUST DOWN. DIDN'T MAKE IT BACK TO CAMP 'TIL 3:15 A.M. AMOS CHARBONEAU FROM FORESTGROVE IS CAMPING WITH US AND WILL HELP US TRAIL ON INTO ROUNDUP FEEDYARD.

-ENDLESS TRACKS ACROSS CENTURIES

Chapter 21

IF I HAD KNOWN GRANDKIDS WERE SO MUCH FUN

Connie Cox was reported to have said something to the effect; "If had known grandkids were so much fun, I might not have had kids!" Not wishing to take anything Connie may have said out of context, it is appropriate here to throw additional light on the coherence of this comment if it was stated as reported. Knowing of Connie's love for his own children, and his aforementioned pride in their accomplishments, and respect for their individuality, it should go without saying that any such comment would be only possible to categorize as just one more "Connieism" out of "Cox's Old Cowboy Dictionary." As with most other "Connieisms" from this unwritten tally of references, the listener would have to pay just as close attention to what was not said or inferred and do a little reading between the lines. We will have to leave the supposed comment at that.

A fact that is for certain is that Connie and Margie really enjoy the children of their children, "the Grandkids," and are doing for and with them as they did their own. They are no different than any other loving (and maybe just a bit indulgent) grandparents in this regard. Possibly, like so many other families, they are finding time with grandchildren to be less harried now that they are seasoned grandparents than the time they were able to share as young parents with their own little ones. This is one of the lovely things about grandparenting. It is intended, I think, to be sort of an extension of parenting, only with a little seasoning added, and just the right touch of delicious spices! Fortunate, indeed, are the grandchildren who really get to know and share time with loving grandparents, and a most wonderful elixir of extended family life is that tasted by the children lucky enough to share time with great-grandparents. Elixir is used here in the dual sense that as "The Philosophers' Stone" it was supposedly a substance held capable of changing base metals into gold; and as a sweetened liquid, usually laced with spirits, it was used as a carrier for medicinal agents. What better medicine than to turn the twilight times of parents' parents or parents' parents' parents into golden moments of learning and experiences for little ones? And what more precious memories for all than by such blessed sharing?

The stories told, Great-grandpa's collection of ancient tools and other wonderful relics, named and unnamed, Great-grandma's special tea parties, with tiny swirly sugar and cinnamon pie-crust cookies or short bread, made auspicious treasures for the children. It was a fair trade, for the wide-eyed wonderment and delighted small voices quickened the hearts, and, for a moment at least, erased the ache in old joints of the elders. For them, these interludes were like mirrors through which they could reflect back, and for an instant, see the diaphanous vision of one, two, perhaps three generations from some poignant prior memory. For some, grandparenting is that second chance that time and circumstances and Providence for whatever reason did not allow. It is an opportunity which parents with loving hearts and ways who become grandparents seldom take lightly. They may not have missed the first chance – just found it way too short in time and substance – so are thankful for the second chance. Grandpa, Connie "PaPa" Cox, and Grandma, Margie, aren't asking questions. They are just taking advantage of the opportunity God has granted them to be grandparents and are enjoying the experiences. So are their grandkids!

There is another thing about grandparenting. The saying that history repeats itself because we weren't listening the first time is in many instances justified. The person who does things because "That's the way my dad did it and the way my granddad did it, so it's good enough for me and mine!" still lives out there. He isn't, however, limited in his range to the prairies or mountainous regions of Montana, or to Appalachia, or even just to rural America. He may be found on Main Street, or Fifth Avenue, or 711 Civic Circle, or 1989 Wonder Way. A number of his kind seem to end up entrenched in the vicinity of the Banks of the Potomac! These latter ones (talk about history repeating itself?) appear bent on only one purpose in life; the architecture, design, manufacture and then zealous custodianship of things known as "pork barrels." Fortunately some traditions may be kept and heritage preserved, although change that is dynamic and unavoidable is possible. Reduced back to the private world of one family or a few families, grandparenting may be observed to include little touches of all of this. Seasoned with love, concern and some sage wisdom and experience, it luckily translates into something which "works" for lots of grandchildren.

There is a parallel between Connie's philosophy as a grandparent, reasons for "The Great Montana Centennial Cattle Drive of 1989" and the purpose of the Montana Rural Development Fund. This parallel has to do with Connie's reflections back to the early years, the tough times and then the better times. It has to do with getting them started and opportunity. It has to do with what this trek, and "EPIC TRAILS - Endless Tracks Across Centuries" and the spirit of Montana's Statehood Centennial remembrances are all about. The Montana Rural Development Fund within the framework of the Montana Community Foundation is all about opportunity, too. While drifting his Longhorns along the trail these past weeks, and particularly being able to watch Tia ride with the wind blowing through her pretty hair, Connie could see the sky blue and cloud and sage silver pieces of a big jigsaw puzzle fitting together. The meandering tracks of the cows defining the edges of brown and gold and grass yellow or green with blacks and whites and brindles and roan colored pieces in the foreground picture would all fit in their proper place with some vision and nudging. His lariat which had been dragging behind Blue suddenly flicked out and the honda end sent a big ol' horse fly sailing off the hide of a speckled cow. "Hah, hah, yuh black hearted ol' devil, yuh'll have to find yer own spot to fit in this here puzzle – if yuh ever land! Ol' cow never felt a thing – just glad to be rid of that tormentin' pest!" Tia had been worried about that old ugly fly biting and hurting that nice cow and she was impressed when "PaPa" Connie's rope deftly sent the insect "zinging" off into space.

"The Great Montana Centennial Cattle Drive" would be a celebration of one hundred years of Montana's history, and in the process, it would create a history of its own. The Drive's lasting legacy will be a permanent endowment fund that will benefit many for years to come. The purpose of the Montana Rural Development Fund would be to further the healthy development, education, and welfare of rural Montana's citizens, the viability of Montana's rural communities, and the development of Montana's rural economy.

A continuing Advisory Committee of Montana rural residents and the Montana Community Foundation Board of Directors would work together to identify unmet rural needs that might benefit from fund assistance. It has been hoped that programs benefiting rural Montanans would encourage and help families continue their lives here and encourage their children to remain in Montana also. "Rural" as used with reference to the Montana Rural Development Fund would be intended to be broad in meaning, not meant to exclude benefits to people in urban communities since even the largest of these communities is closely related to rural Montana. The emphasis of the fund, however, would be to provide help to people in areas that may have greater need due to the lack of charitable systems more prevalent in urban communities.

For example, The ARCO Foundation established a fund within the Rural Development Fund for the Bitterroot, Gold, and Mountain Regions only.

Anyone could participate in building the Montana Rural Development Fund by making a gift, or through estate planning by use of will, trust, or remainder interest. Individuals would be memorialized by establishing a named fund trust within this fund or gifts might be made anonymously.

The "Cattle Drive" legacy would create a wonderful opportunity for people involved in Montana heritage to make a permanent and lasting gift to Montana's rural people and to that heritage! Connie liked the idea as his reflections centered on his own life and the lives of his children and their children. Maybe he hadn't lived a hundred years too late, after all. Might be a way to give a hand up to the old timers he thought about, too, whom he knew would really get a kick out of seeing the "Big Drive of '89" but for one reason or another were down on their luck and would miss it.

A little about the overall purpose of the Montana Community Foundation, may be summed up from the "Mission Statement" appearing in the 1989 First Annual Report of the Montana Community Foundation, and included here with their permission:

– Mission Statement –

"The Montana Community Foundation is a steward through which private assets entrusted to us by donors are invested to meet the challenges of contemporary life. We are committed to respecting the trust and intent of our donors, while maintaining our integrity and responsiveness as a community foundation.

"We seek to protect and enhance the unique resources of Montana–its people and their needs, its diversity of culture, its richness of artistic creation and appreciation, and the beauty of its land, air and water–so that these resources may be enjoyed now and in the future.

"We are committed to equality of opportunity and justice for all Montanans. We seek to enhance human dignity by providing support for community members to participate actively in determining the course of their lives and the life of the community.

"We seek to establish mutual trust, respect and communication between the Foundation, its grantees and the communities they serve. We will respond to creative ideas of organizations and individuals as they address the opportunities and challenges of changing community needs.

"We are committed to using the resources entrusted to us for funding the highest quality projects throughout Montana, recognizing that issues often are complex, interdependent and changing. We will seek out new and creative approaches to solving problems as well as methods that are tried and effective.

"We recognize that the process of change and enhancement involves cooperation among individuals, groups and institutions. We will be a catalyst in this process as a leader in the Montana Philanthropic community"

As Tia and "PaPa" Connie rode along, Grandpa Cox thought, "Yeh, this trail drive and wagon train into Billings will really be something the people of Montana can take a holt of and get their teeth into. It should be somethin', all right. Really would put the bite on things!"

Bite on the wrap!

EPIC TRAILS —

FRIDAY, SEPTEMBER 1, 1989. 'TWENTY-TWO DAYS —

    UP AT DAYBREAK. SURE DIDN'T TAKE LONG TO ROLL INTO ONE SIDE OF BEDROLL AND OUT THE OTHER SIDE. PROBABLY WOULD HAVE BEEN JUST AS WELL TO HAVE TRADED OUR BEDS FOR A BARN LANTERN LAST NIGHT. AMOS AND I WRANGLED HORSES AND STARTED COWS TO FEEDYARD. LOTS OF HELP TODAY. OVER 15 RIDERS, 6 OF THEM FROM THE FLATWILLOW COLONY. WE'LL JUST LEAVE OUR CAMP SET UP FOR NIGHTS AT ROBERT AND MARGARET LIND'S RANCH 'TIL WE HEAD FOR BILLINGS ON MONDAY. WE TRAILED ACROSS AND DOWN A SORT OF STEEP ROCKY RIM AND CAME INTO COLLINS CORRALS FROM THE NORTH ON THE BACK SIDE OF THE FEEDYARD.

    WE WEIGHED THE COWS ACROSS WALT'S SCALE AND THEY HAVE GAINED 19 POUNDS PER HEAD DURING THE THREE WEEKS ON THE TRAIL — NEARLY A POUND A DAY. AFTER WEIGHING THE COWS AND SEEING THEY FOUND HAY AND WATER WHERE WE PENNED THEM WE WENT TO THE ROUNDUP FAIRGROUNDS TO THE OLD TIMERS' RODEO. I ROPED TERRIBLE BUT SAW MORE OLD FRIENDS.

    MORE PEOPLE, HORSES, WAGONS AND CAMPERS COMING TO TOWN. MORE CATTLE COMING FROM ALL OVER. BRAND INSPECTORS, VETERINARIANS, DROVERS AND CHUTE CREW WORKING FULL TIME THROUGH THE NEXT FEW DAYS PROCESSING CATTLE AS THEY COME OFF TRUCKS. THE MAIN HERD IS REALLY GROWING AS THEY TURN THE CATTLE TO THE MEADOWS BELOW ADOLPH'S RANCH. LOOKS LIKE THE DRIVE IS GOING TO BE A BIG SUCCESS. WEATHER IS BEAUTIFUL. OUR DAUGHTER, CHARLENE, AND LITTLE GRANDSON,

-ENDLESS TRACKS ACROSS CENTURIES

EPIC TRAILS-

CASH COLEMAN, CAME DOWN FROM CUTBANK. CHARLENE WILL HELP
US WITH THE AUCTION SALE OF COWS TOMORROW. CASH IS JUST BIG
ENOUGH TO BE 'LOTS OF HELP' EVERYWHERE! HAVE SURE ENJOYED
HAVING HIS SISTER, TIA, RIDING WITH US THESE LAST DAYS.
NOBODY COULD HAVE TOLD ME ONLY A FEW SHORT YEARS AGO HOW
MUCH FUN GRANDKIDS' CAN BE. TOMORROW WILL BE A BUSY DAY.

- ENDLESS TRACKS ACROSS CENTURIES

Chapter 22

WHEN COWBOYS COME TO TOWN

Having spent last evening visiting with old friends at the Maverick in Roundup, Connie was looking forward to getting the cows trailed on into Walt Collins' pens so they'd be settled and have a day to rest before sorting them into sale lots early tomorrow morning. He was also looking forward to seeing more of his old rodeo cowboy buddies this afternoon at the Old Timers' Rodeo to be held at the Roundup Fairgrounds Arena. He'd entered the Team Roping competition in the 50 to 60 year old age group. The chance to see these cowboys and swap yarns with them was bringing back recollections of lots of fun times when Connie was flying to rodeos, and besides paying entry fees and keeping gas in his fuel tanks there wasn't much else to go on but the fun and practical jokes they played on one another. Harlow Skelton, who team ropes now in the Old Timers' Rodeo Association rodeos, had been one of those cowboys and a tough competitor, Connie remembered, in the Steer Wrestling when they were younger. Harlow and Norma live at Sun River, Montana, and Connie always got tickled at a favorite saying of Harlow's, "Never say whoa in the middle of a mud hole!" It sort of summed up those good times.

Harlow was talking recently to another acquaintance and allowed, very prosaically, "You know, I used to go to all those rodeos and I knew everybody at all of 'em. Nowadays,

I go to a regular everyday rodeo and all the cowboys are young guys an' I don't know any of 'em, hardly, 'cept for what I read in the point standin's. But, I go to all these Old Timers' rodeos an' I still know ever'body – I just can't remember their names!"

Another friend of Connie's tells of a time in Lewistown and they were having a little "re-ride" get-together at the Bar 19 after a roping. Connie had hauled a load of roping steers to the event and had his trailer loaded and ready to go home afterward. It was parked close by to this "pass-time" establishment when a couple of the hands who'd probably partaken of a little too much "who-hit-John?" happened to notice it as they were leaving the place. These happy fellows just naturally had a bright light come on inside the place they wear their hats so proceeded to back Connie's pickup and trailer to the back door of the lounge and unloaded the roping cattle into the interior. Needless to say, these men knew they would be personas non grata when the "roundup" commenced among the tables, dancers and barstools, so they went on about their way. The excitement inside was handled with some loss of composure, but it was only temporary and just a little out of the ordinary for what could be expected when cowboys come to town!

Roped terrible – They say new bifocals will really mess up your golf swing too!

EPIC TRAILS—

Saturday, September 2, 1989. 'Twenty-Third Day —

Up early to work cows for sale. Larry Klinger has 31 Longhorns which he is putting in the sale with our cows. We sorted cows into pairs and threes to make up sale lots. Our son, Clinton Cox and his wife, Denise, came down from Whitewater to help with sale. Several people, some from out-of-state, expressing interest in buying "just one cow" so they will have their own "critter" to go in the 'Big Drive'. Good crowd gathered for sale. Auction started at 11:00 A.M. and we were done by 1:40 P.M. Cows averaged bringing a per head price of $692.00. Twenty-three head didn't sell so will take them to auction in Billings after 'Big Drive'.

Ray ("Rainbow") Hillman and Clinton worked the cattle back after each lot was sold and "Shorty" Bertolino worked corral gate all day. All real good hands. We've sure had good help with this venture all along. Charlene's husband, Tip Coleman, came down from Cutbank to help today, too, and to join the celebration. They've asked us from Latigo to put our bunch of cattle back together since they are trail-wise to help lead the wagon train and people riding in the parade through Roundup Monday morning. We won't go right in with those big horned big steers of Leachman's Lead Herd but will drop our cows in right behind them.

Weather was real nice in morning but turned hot and windy in afternoon. Had a downpour in the evening so should

Endless Tracks Across Centuries

Countin' 'em in.

Who'll bid 600? Bid-A-Dollar;
Bid-A-Dollar; Bid-A-Dollar, Now 700!

Fresh off grass.

Lookin' back.

Good gate hoss.

Pennin' them back.

Auction Day at Roundup M̄89 Trailhead.

117

SETTLE THE DUST. LOTS OF PEOPLE STILL COMING INTO TOWN. LOOKS GREAT. COLLINS' FEEDYARD IS FILLING UP WITH TEAMS AND PEOPLE'S SADDLE HORSES. ACROSS THE RIVER ON ALFRED ADOLPH'S MEADOWS THE MAIN HERD IS REALLY COLORFUL AS IT TAKES ON SIZE. PEOPLE WITH CAMERAS EVERYWHERE.

WATCHING THE PEOPLE AS THEY REACT AND TAKE THIS ALL IN IS REAL INTERESTING. THERE'S GREAT INTEREST IN THE LONGHORNS AND ACROSS THE ROAD AT THE STAGING GROUNDS FOR THE WAGON CIRCLES WHERE EVERY STYLE WOODEN WHEELED IRON TIRED WAGON IMAGINABLE IS SETTING UP CAMP. EVEN HAVE ARTISTS SETTING UP ALONG SIDE OF PENS IN THE DRIVE ALLEYS TO WORK ON WAX MODELS FROM LIFE AS THEY LOOK AT SOME OF THE FINE SETS OF HORNS ON MANY OF THE LEAD HERD CATTLE.

WOULD SURE BE NICE IF OUR SON, CASEY AND HIS WIFE, DIANNE, AND OUR LITTLEST GRANDCHILD, THEIR DAUGHTER, CASSIDY COULD BE HERE WITH US FROM GEORGIA. WOULD ABOUT MAKE THE DAY AS COMPLETE AS IT COULD BE.

IT'S BEEN A BUSY ONE. BEAUTIFUL RAINBOW OVER CAMP.

—ENDLESS TRACKS ACROSS CENTURIES

Chapter 23

AUCTION DAY IN ROUNDUP

"Big brown bug bit a big brown bear–bid a dollar here, bid a dollar there!" It takes a nimble tongue and a quick eye to practice the auction chant and catch the bidder's nod. Connie had tried to demonstrate for Tia and Cash how the Auctioneer would sell the Longhorns. He and they laughed at his efforts and he was pretty sure he'd never have any honorific title of "Colonel Connie Cox" as a silver tongued agent of the auction market. The grandkids were excited and were they ever busy! It took just about as much crew to keep those two corralled as it did to sort the cows into lots for the sale. There was plenty of help, though, and good help as they grouped the cows into pairs and threes according to color, size and other similarities. With the addition of Larry Klinger's 31 head they had a nice offering as the crowd looked them all over prior to the start of the bidding. The cows from Frenchman Creek were slicking up nicely, having gained nearly a pound a day as they grazed their way the past three weeks to Roundup. Olsen's big dun steer had weighed in on Walt Collins' scales at over a ton and Connie had won a little wager with a man who'd declared, "He's dum shore big, but he's too tall–that daylight 'neath him don't weigh much–he won't go much over 1900 pounds!"

It took a bit over two and a half hours to complete the auction and Connie had hoped for a $700.00 average on the Longhorn cows. He was pleased that they did come very close to this figure. It was pretty much in line with the general market and except for the Cattle Drive fever, if there were any affect from it, the prices were just a good solid commercial value for a bred stock cow. Connie would just "throw in the pretty horns, the rainbow colored hides, the centuries old genetics and mostly docile dispositions as an added bonus for those who wished to have an honest to goodness trail wise Centennial cow in the Big Drive." Buyers from out of state, as well as Montanans, had advantage of this offering. Ed Brecke, Jr. from as far away as Stetsonville, Wisconsin, was among the successful bidders, and he and his associates really enjoyed themselves with their own Montana $\frac{M}{89}$ branded critters as they joined the trail on to Billings.

It was good to have Clinton and Denise and Tip and Charlene there helping with the sale. Margie was going a mile a minute keeping track of Tia and Cash, with Denise's help. It would have been about a near perfect day if Casey,

Diane and Cassidy could have been there too, but Cassidy was still pretty tiny for all this. Each lot was carefully penned back after they had gone through the auction ring and the "sold" hammer had fallen. They would be reassembled, after sorting them up as to number brands and recording all the buyer information tomorrow morning, because the Latigo people had asked that Connie might give them the benefit of having the stabilizing influence of these now trail-wise cattle to help lead the parade through the streets of Roundup. It would be fun and Connie knew he'd have no trouble hand picking some quiet reliable drovers to handle them past the crowd. To be asked was an honor, and he knew for certain, "it would not happen again for at least another 100 years."

The Leachman lead herd of beautiful big old big horned steers were being assembled just down the way in some south pens at Collins' lot and they were the center of a lot of attention as people stopped to photograph them and there were even artists set up having the advantage of captive live models to view. Steve Lilligard from Stanford, Montana, was set up in an alley next to one pen doing a sculpture of a particular specimen of the Longhorn breed. He just bent his head and squinted his eyes as the day turned hot and the wind came up; there would be intervals when his model would lay down or another animal would jostle in front of him, but Steve was patient, knowing the work of today was just a start. He'd have a lot more time and effort in before the piece was finished and he would be able to cast it in his foundry into the consummate bronze and patina he envisioned in a limited edition. Connie wondered at the wealth of fine art this Centennial celebration was stimulating.

Jay Contway of Great Falls had done a beautiful sculpture of a brush popping 1880s cowboy with running Longhorn steers as the official Commemorative Bronze for Great Montana Centennial Cattle Drive of 1989. He'd entitled it "Turning Them North" and Connie knew there were only 100 to be cast in the Commemorative Limited Edition. Another noted cowboy artist Connie knew, Jim Dye, of Windham, near Stanford, had done a great piece for the Judith Basin Century Roundup and Branding and another he called "Quiet Day In Utica" for a Commemorative to that settlement of Charlie Russell's Montana beginnings. This was really going to be a 100th Birthday Celebration to remember!

Lower 4 photos courtesy Don Boyer.

The cattle drive roundup gathers at 'Roundup' settlement on the Musselshell River.

This Great American Desert used to be an ocean bottom – really!

First you drink - then I wash up - then I cook grub for this outfit!

A harbinger of good for this 'Big Drive of '89.

121

EPIC TRAILS—

SUNDAY, SEPTEMBER 3, 1989. 'AN EVEN TWO DOZEN DAYS' —

Up early. Fall is in the air and while it always seems the coldest just before dawn, the break of this Sunday morning promises a beautiful day. Lots of dew on bedroll this morning and bones a little creaky as crawl out and shiver around trying to get coffee to heat up.

Went to work at 7:45 a.m. to sort sale cattle from yesterday's auction. Number brands bit hard to read so took a lot of time. Didn't finish up 'til 5:10 p.m. Tip and Charlene helped all day. Tia and Cash took turns riding with me. They like to ride with "Pa-Pa". Grandad has to admit he enjoys it a lot, too.

The feedyard is buzzing. Lots of people and horses still coming in. Wagons from Alberta and Saskatchewan, a beautiful Concord Stagecoach from Texas, and many, many more arriving to join the colorful circles of wagons coming from counties across Montana and surrounding states. Traffic is backed up all along the roads by the registration tents and across to the river by the Big Red and White "Busch" tent on the corner past the wagon circles. Loaded cattle liners line up to cross the bridge over the river to go over and unload main herd cattle at the Adolph Ranch while empties of every description from ranch rigs to 18 wheelers wait to cross back over going back through town. The day stayed beautiful as promised.

-Endless Tracks Across Centuries

Chapter 24

ANTICIPATION

It is a beautiful Sunday morning and the place is like a beehive. People are lined up everywhere as this last day of processing them and their animals in for the Big Drive goes on. All the wagons for the train are pretty well set up over at the staging area and it is a colorful sight. Looks like about nine or ten camps or circles with from 20 to maybe 30 wagons each. The wagon circles are color coded so that people assigned to a given portion of the wagon train for the ride into Billings will be able to keep coordinated with their place each day in the drive. Wally McRae, Montana's favorite cowboy poet and declaimer of epic verse, was heard discussing the color coding of the wagon circles with Baxter Black, veterinarian from Colorado turned raconteur and cowboy poet of wide acclaim. "Just look at these wagon circles, yellow, red, green, purple, orange and all, but there doesn't seem to be any color code for any wagons from California in case there are any wagons here from there and some lost California soul should need to find their camp," Wally was thought to have said, somewhat in dismay.

"And may I be so naive as to implore what color wagon circle someone from California ought to be in search of?" Baxter inquired. "Why, mauve, of course," Wally replied.

As colorful and entertaining as an exchange between these two friendly bards could be, it was only a part of the color and excitement of this last day of frenzied preparation for tomorrow, the day everyone was anticipating. The rain of last night and the beautiful rainbow that arced over the staging area just at sunset had set a delightful tone for all that was going on this last day and it presaged the most keen of expectations for the trek to be embarked upon tomorrow. A stop by the chuckwagon camp for the drovers with the main herd only whetted the appetite for the days yet to come even more. The main herd was reaching numbers approaching 3000 head of cattle and the number of colorful Longhorn type cattle being assembled would have made the drovers of 100 years ago proud of how the breed had survived and indeed one could think was flourishing again in Montana. There were certainly others too, making a dramatic representation of the cattle industry, so much the foundation of Montana's economy. There were Herefords, Angus, Shorthorns, Charolais, Limousin, Gelbvieh, Simmental, Red Angus, Bramha, Salers, Brown Swiss, Tarentais, Pinzgauer, Holstein, Ayrshire, Galloway, Scotch Highland, and others along with the every cross-breed imaginable. More were steadily being processed through the receiving area as the day drew on. The remuda of loose saddle horses around the chuckwagon camp sported some of the finest blooded stock that could be found anywhere. The wranglers with the drovers' camp were busy maneuvering new additions through the pecking order to rapidly establish a social element in this horse herd that would be most interesting to watch through the days to come.

Teams of every description were evident. Big matched spans of the heavy draft breeds, including Percheron, Belgian and Clydesdale were massive, yet pranced with a lightness of foot that belied their great size. Light to medium hitches of Morgan or Quarter Horse origin were prevalent, as were many that appeared to trace back to the three way natives with some touch of Thoroughbred in their background that Connie could remember were the mainstay of the northern Montana and southern Canadian prairies of his boyhood and before. And there were mules, mules of every description. One interesting 4 horse hitch that was interesting to watch had not been obviously a 4 up set of two spans before arriving at the drovers' camp. They were just in the process of learning to work together, but learning they were, and quick, too. They were with Neil McKinnon's LK chuckwagon from Alberta and Bob Hale was putting them through their paces driving them harnessed, but unhitched from his saddle horse. When asked why he was riding one horse and deftly maneuvering the two spans in front of him, Bob simply replied, "Sure beats driving them from afoot!"

That evening, the LK chuckwagon cook, Buck Draper, treated his drovers to a fresh seafood supper of baked Salmon and Dungeness cracked crab, hand carried the day before from Camano Island, Washington. When queried about the incongruity of such fare in a cattle drive camp, Dr. Draper replied, "I'm just starting you out right. The drovers of old wanted eggs and oysters when they got off a long trail. You're in the middle of the Great American Desert aren't you? Some old cowboy is going to be riding along here maybe in another 100 years and he'll look down, see these crab shells and say, 'By heck, this really was the bottom of an ocean once, wasn't it!?'" Who'd argue that this wasn't the wind-up to a perfect day of anticipation?

Anticipation of an 'Epic' happening!

EPIC TRAILS—

MONDAY, SEPTEMBER 4, 1989. "FIRST DAY OF THE BIG DRIVE - OUR 25TH —

Up early! The biggest day in the history of Roundup is about to begin. About the biggest day in history ever far as I'm concerned and know plenty of folks around here feel the same way I do this morning. Wranglers have been jingling horses from Collins' pens since hours before daylight. Everybody gettin' their wagons hitched up. Drovers across the river have main herd bunching and moving toward south end of field where they'll start them out on the trail. Cavalry outfit is all trim and ready for parade. You can see 'Old Glory' lots of places — riders carryin' her and Stars and Stripes flying from several wagons. Makes it kinda hard to swallow — keep having to wipe dust or something out of eyes.

About 2700 head of cattle in main herd, some 300 more to lead wagon train of more than 200 wagons and some 3500 saddle horses and riders out of Roundup. Somebody figured 678 heavy and light draft horses and mules making up teams. Pack horses and mules and at least one jerk-line hitch of I think 12 or 14 in the team pulling a string of 4 covered wagons.

Main herd on trail up through breaks and trees south of river shortly after daybreak. They'll miss town and come into trail behind where wagon train will pull off for tonight's camp. Parade started for Roundup at 10:45

—ENDLESS TRACKS ACROSS CENTURIES

EPIC TRAILS—

A.M. LEACHMAN'S LEAD HERD OF BIG HORNED CATTLE GO FIRST. OUR LONGHORN COWS FOLLOW 30 MINUTES LATER, THEN THE WAGONS START TO ROLL. THOUSANDS OF PEOPLE LINED UP TO SEE PARADE GO THROUGH TOWN. BOTH SIDES STREET ARE PACKED AND THERE ARE PEOPLE ON ROOF TOPS AND HANGING OUT OF WINDOWS FROM UPPER FLOORS EVERYWHERE YOU LOOK.

LEAD HERD SEEMED LITTLE DIFFICULT TO HOLD UP AHEAD OF US. HEARD LOTS OF SHOUTING AND HOORRAHIN' AS THEY WENT WEST AROUND THE CORNER FROM MAIN STREET. HOPE THEY KEEP THEM CHECKED AND DON'T SPILL THEM. DARREL ADOLPH, AMOS CHARBONEAU AND MYSELF MOVED OUT IN FRONT OF OUR COWS AND THEY HELD NICELY AS THEY TRAILED THROUGH THAT CANYON OF SPECTATORS LINING THE STREET. WE HAD ABOUT 20 OTHER COWBOYS AND A COWGIRL RIDING ALONG TO FLANK THE SIDES AND FOLLOW BEHIND TO KEEP COWS TOGETHER. THIS CREW MADE ME PROUD IN SPIRIT WITH THEIR QUIET, ASSURED CAPABILITY AS WE MOVED AHEAD OF THE WAGON TRAIN AND BIG MOB OF RIDERS. STILL HAVING PROBLEM WITH DUST GETTIN' IN EYES.

THE WAGON CIRCLES MOVED OUT ONE-BY-ONE WITH PROBABLY SOME 200 TO 300 CATTLE DRIVE PARTICIPANTS A HORSEBACK WITH EACH 20 TO 25 WAGONS AND THEIR OUT-RIDERS. LOOKING BEHIND US THEY STRUNG OUT FARTHER THAN WE COULD SEE AS THEY BEGAN TO ROLL. I'LL HAVE TO LEAVE IT TO THOSE WE RODE BY AS TO WHAT THE PARADE OF THE 'GREAT MONTANA CENTENNIAL CATTLE DRIVE OF 1989' LOOKED LIKE. ALL I KNOW IS IF I LIVE TO BE A HUNDRED YEARS

—ENDLESS TRACKS ACROSS CENTURIES

EPIC TRAILS—

OLD I'LL NEVER BE FULLY ABLE TO DESCRIBE THE FEELINGS THAT ARE DEEP INSIDE. WHAT A GREAT DAY! AND IT IS ACTUALLY TAKING PLACE. IT'S HAPPENING!

WE MADE CAMP AT A SPOT 10 MILES SOUTH OF ROUNDUP. JAY STOVALL, TRAIL BOSS FOR THE MAIN HERD, AND HIS DROVERS, A HAND PICKED GROUP OF SOME 100 PLUS GOOD COWBOYS AND COWGIRLS TRAILED THEIR HERD OF SOME 2700 CATTLE ACROSS THE HILLS FROM SOUTHEAST OF ROUNDUP TO A CAMP SITE AND BED GROUND A BIT SOUTH OF THE CAMPSITE OF THE WAGON TRAIN. WE PUT OUR COWS IN WITH THIS MAIN BUNCH FOR THE REST OF THE DRIVE INTO BILLINGS. WHAT A SIGHT TO SEE SO MANY CATTLE POUR INTO THE FIELD THAT WILL BE THEIR BED GROUND FOR TONIGHT.

GLAD TO BE A SMALL PART OF ALL THIS.

—ENDLESS TRACKS ACROSS CENTURIES

Chapter 25

THE BIG DRIVE OF '89 IS A SHARED HAPPENING

Shared was the only way to describe what was happening this morning. Every person involved was contributing a portion to what was truly going to become an epic event. The Latigo people, their committees, volunteers, and sponsors had to breathe a little easier albeit none appeared to have any time to do so as everything seemed to smoothly get underway. The parade through Roundup was thrilling. The contribution shared by all the participants who had planned so long to be a part of it was as a part of themselves and those who came to watch picked up on the feeling. They reciprocated in the spirit of what was happening. The timing of departure of each segment of the drive had to be very precise – not too early and not too late, because all traffic on major intersections leading from anywhere into the town of Roundup had to be stopped and rerouted in order to get the drive out of town and on its first day's route – then off that route to the first night's campsites so that normal flow of transportation to and through Roundup could be resumed for the night. This precision timing would have to be repeated the second day, also because of routing requirements. Following the second day the trail would lead through open country but logistics of traffic control would still be extremely critical on the main artery from Roundup to Billings because of the viewing public.

And the viewing public were just as much apart of the "Big Drive of '89" as all those who were making it happen. One person from Billings was heard to say, "I know nothing of horses or cattle or the livestock industry and have never been in a walk of life where I had to be any closer to the basic needs I take for granted than my supermarket shelves. However, when I knew The Great Montana Centennial Cattle Drive of 1989 was really coming my way, I knew I not only had to see it – I had to touch it – and I had to have it touch me!"

The main herd was beautiful as it flowed through the hills and trees. There were exciting moments and there would be more throughout the week. As Connie's Longhorns resumed the trail and moved through Roundup, he had a feeling which he knew was a once in a lifetime experience. The only way to try to explain it was to look around and see the same outpouring reflected on faces and cheeks which had a glisten not readily seen on weathered countenances used to masking feelings more readily than being visages of pictured emotion. Not so today – people were completely caught up in this epic event.

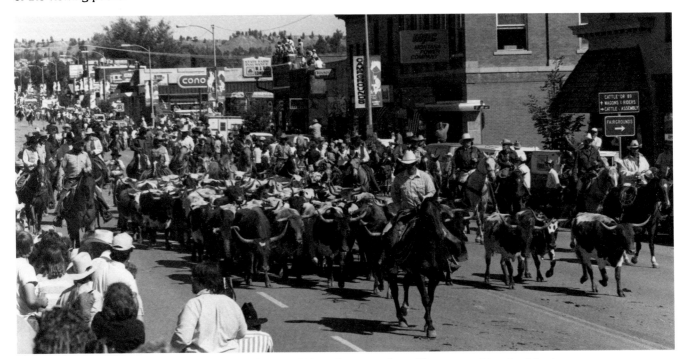

Connie's Longhorns parade out of Roundup on a day of history making for Montana.

– Endless Tracks Across Centuries

EPIC TRAILS—

Tuesday, September 5, 1989. Day Two of The Big Drive—Make it 26 Days
Trailing for Our Outfit—

Pace seems different depending on where you look. Some people starting to harness teams and hitch up early. Others just taking time with coffee and camp chores. Wranglers busy bringing loose horses and catching them from rope corral for people. Several people have kept their teams tied right at camp to the wheels of their wagons but most horses either picketed in rows to long picket lines or loose herded in pasture by night wranglers.

Quite a variety of excitement around the wagon camp through the night. Most of the wagon circles had nice central campfire and lots of story tellin' and yarn swappin' going on, as well as, singing and cowboy poets telling their stuff. Big Red and White Budweiser tent had music and dancing. A bunch of loose wrangle horses broke away and decided to run away. Those horses decided to head back for Roundup since back tracking I guess was the only territory they were familiar with. Lynn Taylor, head wrangler for the Big Drive, and some of his good help including, Spud Cremer and Gary Crowder, managed to catch and rope some of them as they tried to escape through the pine trees on the rimrocks or down the highway. A few horses did get clear back to Roundup and were brought back from Collins' feedyard today.

Also heard that one of the chuckwagon cooks with the

MAIN HERD DROVERS' CAMP HAD HIS HORSE REAR OVER BACKWARDS WITH HIM AS THEY WERE JUST PULLING OUT YESTERDAY MORNING FROM ALFRED ADOLPH'S RANCH. FELLER BY NAME OF BUCK DRAPER COOKING FOR THE L K CANADIAN CHUCKWAGON WHICH IS ONE OF 6 CHUCKWAGONS WITH THE MAIN HERD AND DOING MEALS FOR ALL THE DROVERS AND THEIR SUPPORT CREWS AND A LOT OF PRESS PEOPLE TRAVELING WITH THAT CAMP. BUCK CAME OVER FROM THE COAST IN WASHINGTON JUST TO BE THE COOK ON THE L K CHUCKWAGON. REPORT THIS MORNING SAID HE WAS TAKEN FROM ROUNDUP TO BILLINGS BY HELICOPTOR FOR CARE OF A DISLOCATED HIP AND FRACTURES OF HIS LEG AND PELVIS.

HEARD OF COUPLE OF OTHER PEOPLE THROWN OR FALLING FROM HORSES THE FIRST DAY BUT NO OTHER MORE SERIOUS MISHAPS THAN BUCK'S AND KNOW HE'D A LOT RATHER FINISHED THE DRIVE ON THE TRAIL AS HAVING TO HEAR ABOUT IT FROM A HOSPITAL BED. HE SERVED UP PRETTY GOOD CHUCK, TOO, INCLUDING A BIT OF FRESH SEAFOOD HE'D BROUGHT WITH HIM FROM THE COAST. THINK HALF THE PEOPLE IN DROVERS' CAMP WERE STOPPING BY HIS FIRE SUNDAY NIGHT. CHUCKWAGON GOOD COOKS AREN'T THAT EASY TO COME BY EITHER BUT THE LK WAGON GOT HOLD OF ONE OF DR. SCOTT'S VETERINARY SUPPORT STAFF HELPERS NAME OF "RADAR" AND THEY 'VOLUNTEERED' HIM TO BE THEIR COOK. DON'T KNOW WHY THEY DIDN'T COME TO ME FOR EMERGENCY HELP? GUESS ANDY MUST HAVE TIPPED THEM OFF 'BOUT MY FAMOUS 'BLACK' PANCAKES. THEY PROBABLY DON'T WANT ANY COWBOYS STARVING ALONG THE TRAIL IS HOW COME ANDY NOT TO RECOMMEND MY CAMP COOKING ABILITIES.

MAIN HERD GOT MOVING EARLY SOUTH ALONG HIGHWAY 87

—ENDLESS TRACKS ACROSS CENTURIES

EPIC TRAILS—

AND WAGON CIRCLES BREAKING CAMP LOOK LIKE A NOT SO SMALL EARLY FRONTIER TOWN PACKING UP TO MOVE. WAGONS ROLLING OUT BEHIND LEACHMAN'S LEAD STEERS BY 10:45 A.M. GLAD OUR COWS ARE GOING TO TRAIL THE REST OF THE WAY INTO BILLINGS AS PART OF THE MAIN HERD. KINDA LEAVES THE COX RANCH CREW AS SORTA' FREE AGENTS. LARRY'S TEAM AND WAGON AND THE REST OF US I THINK WILL FIND IT PLENTY ENJOYABLE JUST TRAILING ALONG THE REST OF THE WAY WATCHIN' ALL THE PEOPLE AND GOIN'S ON AND VISITIN'. ANDY'S SHORE RELIEVED I DON'T GET A STEADY JOB AS A COOK AND I'M NOT LOSIN' MUCH SLEEP OVER IT EITHER.

LEAD HERD SORTA WARMED UP AND NEEDING TO TAKE A REST IN THE AFTERNOON GOING UP NORTH SLOPE OF THE BULL MOUNTAINS. SO WAGON TRAIN DETOURED AROUND THEM ON AN OLD ROUTE WHICH CAME IN JUST PAST THE TUMBLEWEED SALOON WHERE TONIGHT'S WAGON CIRCLE CAMP WILL BE AT 'THIRTY-MILE' RANCH. MAIN HERD AND DROVERS' CHUCKWAGON CAMP IS A COUPLE MILES FURTHUR SOUTH JUST OFF TO WEST OF THE ROAD. THE TRAIL WILL GO OUT ACROSS OPEN COUNTRY STARTING IN THE MORNING AND PEOPLE ARE LOOKING FORWARD TO THAT.

BEEN A FEW MORE WRECKS TODAY BUT NONE APPEAR TO SOUND TOO SERIOUS. ONE GIRL WAS HURT WHEN HER HORSE FELL. DON BOYCE'S WORK TEAM ACTED UP AND ONE HORSE GOT BALKY AND REARED UP BREAKING TONGUE OF DON'S WAGON. DON'S WAGON IS WITH THE HAVRE BUNCH WITH THE BROWN WAGON CIRCLE. HAVING THESE WAGONS AND THE RIDERS AND ALL THEIR HORSES

-ENDLESS TRACKS ACROSS CENTURIES

EPIC TRAILS—

ASSIGNED COUNTY BY COUNTY AND AREA BY AREA TO COLOR CODED WAGON CIRCLES FOR THEIR LOCATION AT NIGHT CAMPS AND THEIR ORDER IN THE TRAIN ON THE TRAIL SURE SEEMS TO CUT DOWN ON WHAT COULD HAVE BEEN A LOT OF CONFUSION.

BY TIME WE GOT TO THE TUMBLEWEED AND THIRTY MILE RANCH AND CAMPED MY TRAILING BAG IS MISSING OR I LOST IT SOMEWHERE. GOOD THING MY HEAD IS SCREWED ON OR I MIGHT LOSE IT TOO. IT GOT VERY HOT THIS AFTERNOON AND A STRONG WIND CAME UP AS PEOPLE TRYING TO GET WAGONS CIRCLED, HORSES PICKETED AND TENTS SET UP. LOTS OF DUST BLOWING. THIS TIME OF YEAR COULD SEE AN ABRUPT WEATHER CHANGE. WIND HAS TURNED COLD AND TRYING TO RAIN A LITTLE TONITE. HOPE IT DOESN'T DO TOO MUCH OR MAYBE TRY AND SNOW. I'LL WISH I HAD MY TRAIL BAG AND A FEW MORE DRY GOODS THAN WHAT I'VE GOT ON IF IT DOES.

—ENDLESS TRACKS ACROSS CENTURIES

From peaceful quiet on the prairie ...

The lead herd coach 'dances' out of Roundup.

... To pandemonium parading out of Roundup.

Connie's Longhorn cows resume the trail.

Lead steers come down Main Street.

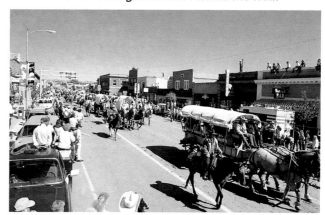

People even on rooftops – and wagons, wagons, wagons.

Centennial shadows silhouetted.

Jerkline hitch with 4 covered wagons!

133

Chapter 26

CIRCLING THE WAGONS AT "THIRTY MILE" CAMP

The trail happenings on the first day out of Roundup, for the most part, equalled or surpassed nearly everyone's greatest expectations. There were some mishaps, but emergency services personnel seemed almost like mythical multiple personages in being able to get to problem areas with dispatch and to start rendering assistance. The planning and hard work of a lot of dedicated people was realized time and again as problems were met and dealt with. Latigo Corporation and all involved with them, plus the people of Roundup, and Montanans, generally, were showing their state and the rest of the world, it appeared, that they were equal to the task they'd set out to perform. The "Big Drive of '89" would truly be a legacy in its own right while making its page in history. The first night's campsites had to be reached by following the main highway between Roundup and Billings and there had been concern the terrain at the wagon camp wouldn't be spacious enough. The leaders of each wagon circle had proven themselves capable of adapting and all the people in their respective portions of the wagon train had pitched in and they simply worked things out to make everything fit. The ingredient which Latigo had worried a lot about, but really couldn't predict or place a handle on, came through with innovative, spontaneous efficiency. That ingredient was the grass roots spirit embodied in practical "can do" capability. More importantly, everyone was having a good time getting the job done!

A lot of the people involved with getting the wagon train and parade moving on schedule missed getting to see the main herd move out. It resembled a living sea of color and flashing horns in Monday's early morning light. It was a sight to behold as the drovers paced the cattle, and allowed the social order, which had formed over the past few days during the assembly of the herd, to dictate an orderly stringing out movement after an initial and expected first run. By midafternoon when the herd reached the highway behind the wagon train they were becoming used to trailing and many of the people who had missed seeing their early morning start were treated to a spectacular sight as nearly 3000 cattle literally poured into the bedground. Connie's cows seemed happy enough being put in with the main herd but obviously intended to stay grouped comfortably amongst their own familiar sisterhood or "cow sorority."

"... And then I says to this other old nag..."

– Endless Tracks Across Centuries

The horses and cattle almost would give the appearance of visiting or communicating enjoyment in the occasion with one another the same as their human counterparts were. It was interesting to watch some of the individual animal personalities assert themselves. Some were evidently clowns, others were eccentric cranks, and in the case of some of the remuda horses when jingling along in the loose bunch, a person didn't have to use much imagination to actually form the notion a given horse might be an accomplished practical joker. If some of the seasoned wranglers were asked, they'd tell you the joke was quite often on one of the human animals rather than pulled on a fellow cayuse! A game often observed among the cattle would be a version of "king of the mountain" wherein a few head would rush up on top of a little rise along the trail and either start pawing up dirt in a challenge to others, or make a big to-do over rubbing their heads on the ground and "fighting" with the smallest of erosion cuts or prairie dog mounds. Naturally, others would consider this bustle a challenge, so there would have to be some head knocking and a swift butt to some vulnerable ribs before the capricious critters were put back on the trail.

By the time the drive had passed the crest of the Bull Mountains on the second day, the drovers and wranglers were pretty familiar with these various idiosyncrasies of a number of their respective equine and bovine charges. The wagon teamsters knew the balky and otherwise temperamental members of their various hitches. A lot of people, unaccustomed to serious horseback riding, or bouncing along on wagon seats which often didn't have much bounce, were becoming acquainted with tender spots on their anatomies with which they had not been properly introduced before! There had been only a few instances of serious misunderstanding between man and beast, the most unpleasant having occurred early yesterday morning when Buck Draper's horse had reared over backwards, pinning Buck beneath and causing him a dislocated hip and fractures of the pelvis, leg and some ribs. Dr. Draper was flown by helicopter to Billings where his injuries were surgically repaired. If people though he was cranky around the chuckwagon and cook tent they should have visited him after a week and a half in the hospital. One little nurse was sure D.V.M. stood for "Durned Violent Man" rather than Doctor of Veterinary Medicine!

Ed Kirby of Great Falls got drafted from Dr. Scott's emergency animal ambulance veterinary support crew to do double duty as chuckwagon cook for Neil McKinnon's LK wagon. He did a great job and quickly picked up the nickname, "Radar II" from our Canadian friends and the drovers, press people, and others eating at the LK wagon. "Radar" did not disappoint any of the cowboys who had already sampled Buck Draper's camp cook wares and ways. They found "Radar's" coffee stout, his grub good and his demeanor every bit as grouchy! When the big blow came up as the wagons circled into camp at "Thirty Mile" many folks were really beginning to feel right "at home." Would there be snow on the ground in the morning?

Good Morning, Yahoos – This is your friendly wake up call!

– Endless Tracks Across Centuries

135

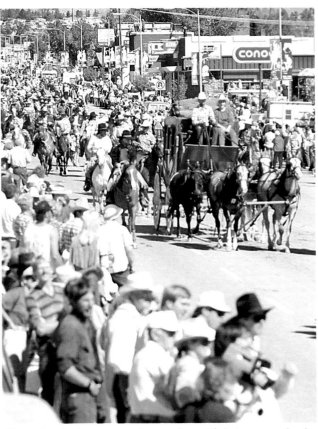

*More wagons – and 'Old Glory' –
This is what it's all about!*

Every kind of wagon and some beautiful stage coaches!

*Oops, was everybody at
'The Maverick' last night?*

Wagon train in the 'Bull Mountains

Big horned cattle in 'Big Sky' country.

Back on nature's road, headed for camp.

Some settlement, this wagon 'circle'?

Pickin' and Grinnin' by wagon camp fire.

Our neighbor's old chuck wagon and rope corral _ been from the 'Powder' to the "Red Deer' and headin' to the Yellowstone.

Prairie 'Sentinel' marks turn of wagon trail into open country for rest of drive.

Wagons trek under the rim.

137

EPIC TRAILS—

WEDNESDAY, SEPTEMBER 6, 1989. DAY THREE AND TWENTY-SEVEN—

WELL IT LOOKS LIKE THIS MORNIN' MOTHER NATURE IS FEELIN' REAL LADYLIKE AGAIN. THE BIG BLOW FROM LAST NIGHT WENT OUT OF HERE LIKE IT CAME IN — IN A HURRY! DAWN IS HEAVY WITH HAZE OF DUST MAKING UP SOME CLOUDINESS AND IT'S REAL COOL. BUT LOOKS LIKE IT'LL CLEAR OFF AND WARM UP NICE. IT DIDN'T RAIN ENOUGH IN NIGHT TO EVEN BEGIN TO SETTLE THE DUST THE WIND STIRRED UP SO WILL BE REAL DUSTY AND GRITTY TRAILIN' TODAY.

COULDN'T GET JOB BEING CHUCKWAGON COOK BUT DICK WALKER WHO'S PRESIDENT OF THIS LATIGO OUTFIT THAT HAS DONE ALL THE PLANNIN' AND COORDINATIN' OF THIS BIG DRIVE THINKS I MIGHT STILL MAKE SOME SORT OF 'HAND' SO AFTER WRANGLING OUR HORSES I LOPED ALONG TO THE SOUTHWEST WITH DICK AS WE LEFT CAMP. HE DIDN'T TELL ME HE WAS GOING TO MAKE ME A 'HAND' AT OPENIN' GATES AND LETTING DOWN WIRE FENCES AHEAD OF THE WAGON TRAIN. OH, WELL, MY HORSE 'BLUE' DOESN'T SEEM TO MIND AND IN FACT IS LOOKIN ALL AROUND AND I THINK ACTUALLY REALLY ENJOYING HIMSELF — SORT OF CAREFREE TAKIN THIS POINT OUT AHEAD OF ALL THESE WAGONS AND THOUSANDS OF PEOPLE INSTEAD OF JUST HAVIN' TO PUSH HIS OWN BUNCH OF OLD COWS ALONG THE TRAIL. SEEMS TO THINK HE'S A REAL PROUD OL' HORSE AND I'D BE THE LAST TO TRY TELLING HIM ANYTHING DIFFERENT. EVERYBODY'S GOT TO BE SOMEWHERE AND WALKER AND I GET THE CHANCE

-ENDLESS TRACKS ACROSS CENTURIES

EPIC TRAILS—

TO HAVE A GOOD VISIT AS OUR HORSES LOPE ALONG AND AS WE STOP TO OPEN GATES AND FENCES. LATIGO HAS REGULAR CREW OF 'VOLUNTEER COWBOYS' LIKE MYSELF WHO'LL FOLLOW ALONG AND CLOSE ALL THESE GATES AND FIX THE FENCES AFTER THE WAGONS AND ALL THE DRIVE PASSES THROUGH EACH PART OF THE TRAIL.

WAGONS ROLLING ALONG SHORTLY AFTER 10:45 A.M. AND EVERYBODY SEEMS IN GOOD SPIRITS AS THE DRIVE HEADS INTO OPEN COUNTRY AND AWAY FROM ROADS. COUNTRY TODAY HAS SOME RUGGED PLACES TO GO THROUGH AND IS PRETTY HILLY IN PLACES AS WE MOVE AWAY FROM THE BULL MOUNTAINS AND THE SHELHAMER'S THIRTY-MILE RANCH CAMPSITE. IT'S QUITE A SIGHT TO LOOK BACK FROM OUR LEAD VANTAGE POINTS ON A RIDGE AND SEE THE WAGONS STRUNG OUT AND A BIG CLOUD OF DUST MARKING THEIR WAY. AND AHEAD ANOTHER DUST CLOUD HANGS ALONG THE TRAIL WHERE JAY STOVALL AND HIS DROVERS AND WAGONS HAVE GONE WITH THE MAIN HERD AND REMUDA OF LOOSE HORSES.

TODAY ISN'T WITHOUT ITS SHARE OF EXCITEMENT. AT 12:40 P.M. LEACHMAN'S 4 HORSE HITCH WERE GOING AT A PRETTY GOOD LOPE WITH THEIR SHINEY RED STAGECOACH LOADED WITH PEOPLE AND THEY HIT A RUT AND UPSET THE COACH. IT LANDED ON ITS SIDE AND SHOOK THE PASSENGERS UP PRETTY GOOD. ONE GUY APPEARS HURT, POSSIBLY SERIOUS, SO DICK WALKER CALLS FOR MEDICAL AID AND ALSO A HELICOPTER ON A HAND CARRIED RADIO-PHONE HE'S PACKIN'

-ENDLESS TRACKS ACROSS CENTURIES

Turnin' 'em out of the trail.

Some worked today – some just played!

A snappy "4 Up" full of vim and vinegar!

Up hill – downhill - in a cloud of dust.

Giddyup, mules – hang on, Ma!

ON HIS HORSE. THIS AGAIN IS A CONVENIENCE OF MODERN MEANS AND WAYS THAT, LIKE THE 'CHOPPERS' AND PICKUPS AND TRAILERS, THE OLD TIME DROVERS AND TRAIL BOSSES IN TEDDY 'BLUE' ABBOTT'S OR CHISOLM OR GOODNIGHT'S TIMES DIDN'T HAVE BENEFIT OF. SEVERAL OTHER KEY PEOPLE HAVE THESE HAND RADIOS, TOO, SO HELP GETS ON ITS WAY PRETTY QUICK AND THE INJURED MAN IS MADE STABLE AND COMFORTED RIGHT ON THE SPOT AND THEN AIR LIFTED TO HOSPITAL IN BILLINGS JUST TO BE SURE HE'S OUT OF HARM'S WAY.

THEIR OVERTURNED COACH IS RIGHTED AND IT, WITH ITS 4 HORSE HITCH, DRIVER AND REST OF PASSENGERS SEEMING NO WORSE FOR WEAR, HEADS ON FOR CAMP. OTHER HELP THAT RESPONDED TO THE RADIO CALL INCLUDED THE HEAD WAGON BOSS AND BECAUSE IT IS SO HILLY IN THIS AREA A LITTLE CONFUSION DEVELOPED WHEN SOME WAGONS GOT INTO SOME STEEP GOING TRYING TO FIGURE OUT WHERE IT WAS THE WAGON BOSS HAD DISAPPEARED TO. OTHERS WENT A DIFFERENT DIRECTION AND IT TOOK SOME EXPERIENCED HANDS HELPING OUT BY HITCHING ON WITH SADDLE HORSES AND THROW ROPES TO GET SOME WAGONS AND TEAMS STRAIGHTENED AROUND AND GOING THE RIGHT WAY AGAIN.

WHEN ASKED WHAT HAD CAUSED THE COACH TO WRECK, ONE OLD COWBOY OBSERVED, "HECK, 'PEARS TO ME THEY WUZ DOIN' 'BOUT 70 IN A 10 MILE A HOUR SPEED ZONE SO THEY JIST NATUR'LLY UPSET IN THAT CHUCK HOLE!"

—ENDLESS TRACKS ACROSS CENTURIES

EPIC TRAILS—

WHEN RESPONDING TO WALKER'S CALL FOR ASSISTANCE AND ASKING FOR DIRECTIONS TO THE SCENE OF THE UPSET STAGECOACH, WE HEARD ONE GUY GIVING TYPICAL COWBOY DIRECTIONS IN REPLY. "JIST LOOK FOR THIS OL' 'BANDON'D SHACK OVER HERE TO LEFT OF YONDER HILL AND IT'S DOWN THIS HERE DRAW RUNNIN' OFF A GOOD SIZE COULEE — NO WAY YUH KIN MISS 'ER!" THE DOCTOR AND EMERGENCY MEDICAL TREATMENT UNIT AND CHOPPER ALL FOUND THEIR WAY IN SPITE OF THIS 'HELPFUL' TRAVEL GUIDE.

WE GOT TO THE NEXT CAMPSITE BY ABOUT 3:00 P.M. BUT IT WAS ABOUT DARK BEFORE SOME OF THE LAST FEW WAGONS STRAGGLED IN AND GOT TO SETTIN' UP CAMP WITH THEIR CIRCLES. I THINK SOME PEOPLE ARE SLOWING DOWN A BIT AND BEGINNIN' TO GET A FEW SADDLE SORES AND BUMPED BEHINDS OFF THE WAGON SEATS. HEARD TALK OF, "THOUGHT I LEFT THAT JUG O' LINIMENT RIGHT HERE IN MY TRAIL SACK — NOW WHERE TH' DICKENS DID IT DISAPPEAR TO?" "MUST'VE 'VAPORATED!" "JUG AN' ALL?"

I DIDN'T GET BY TOO GOOD MYSELF. BESIDES THE DISAPPEARANCE OF MY TRAIL BAG AND SPARE DUDS YESTERDAY, MY BEDROLL IS NOW MISSING. THE ONLY THINGS I'VE GOT LEFT TO LOSE BEFORE WE GET TO BILLINGS ARE MY GOOD HORSE, 'BLUE', AND MY SADDLE.

GOT PRETTY WARM THIS AFTERNOON AND VERY DUSTY.

— ENDLESS TRACKS ACROSS CENTURIES

Chapter 27

THE LATIGO OUTFIT HEADS 'EM UP AND MOVES 'EM OUT

There was no snow on the ground when Connie peeked out of his bedroll on the dawn of the third day for the "Big Drive." In fact there were not any real clouds of the storm which had threatened last evening; it was more a heavy haze of dust hanging in the gray damp dawn air. Every step people and animals were taking stirred up a white powdery fog of the stuff and there were quite a few steps being taken as the sun broke through the coolest moments between darkness and daylight. It was necessary to shuffle about trying to warm up a bit. There would be lots of neck scarves draped over noses and mouths as people moved along the trail today. This morning the drive would move into open country and the conditions of the environment were not diminishing the spirits and anticipation of the people as they broke camp and prepared to move out across the prairie. The wranglers were taking the dust conditions as a matter of course as they caught horses and helped people get their mounts haltered and led away to be saddled.

Jay Stovall's drovers had the main herd up and beginning to move and some of the men were holding any sore footed animals off to the side as the rest struck the trail. The support crew would pick any lame animals up in trailers and give them a lift. Dr. Brent Thompson, veterinarian riding with the main herd, was being especially watchful for any signs of respiratory problems in cattle or horses that might result from the increased dusty conditions. The emergency animal ambulance was busy taking calls from other practitioners who were with the wagon train. People were able to quickly locate help if they had a concern for their animal because wagons with a big "V" on their canvas were located with several of the wagon circles. If additional care to that capable of being administered right on the spot were needed the patient would be loaded and taken to a waiting veterinary clinic in Roundup or Billings. The owner or rider had no trouble hitching a ride temporarily with a friendly wagon teamster.

The enthusiastic call and feeling of "head 'em up–move 'em out" could be heard and felt all along the column as the drive moved past a rustic windmill standing in the dusty morning light. The windmill appeared like a prairie "sentinel" marking the turn for the wagons as they embarked on the day's trek. We would be remiss if we did not describe

something of The Latigo Outfit and its organization, and the mission of the Great Montana Centennial Cattle Drive of 1989 for the reader and give credit for the benefit of future generations to those who worked so hard to bring this epic happening to a reality.

The overall mission of the Great Montana Centennial Cattle Drive of 1989 would be to create a participant/spectator event centered on the movement of several thousand head of cattle from Roundup, Montana, to Billings, Montana. Latigo Corporation established three basic objectives to this mission:

First, to celebrate Montana's Statehood Centennial through recognition of the state's Western heritage and commemoration of the 19th Century livestock industry in Montana.

Second, to promote the modern day beef industry in Montana. This objective would be realized through provision of media and spectator opportunity and participation, increased public awareness of the livestock industry and the nutritional value of beef in the diet, the provision of a regional social opportunity for ranch oriented people, and the creation of a beef marketing opportunity for owners of livestock which would take part in the cattle drive.

Third, to establish a perpetual endowment for the benefit of Montana ranch families and Montana rural communities.

The historical background behind Latigo's adoption of this mission was prepared as part of the introduction for Latigo's operational plan which was researched and written by J. K. Kuzara of Roundup, a member of Latigo's Board of Directors. We deeply appreciate the help and permission of Mr. Kuzara and Latigo for allowing us to convey this information, and most especially to Mr. Kuzara for sharing additional time and effort on behalf of Latigo, their sponsors, their committees and staff and their many volunteers so that some acknowledgment and thanks might be extended to all who worked so hard to make the "Big Drive of '89" a reality.

Referring specifically to the historical background furnished by Mr. Kuzara, the conceptual development of the cattle drive would be based on similar activities in which

Montana was an essential element during the latter half of the 19th Century. During that period, hundreds of thousands of cattle were trailed to Montana from other beef producing areas, some as far away as Mexico and southern California, as well as the many drives originating out of Texas. These early day drives formed the foundation of Montana's cattle industry, an industry which has since had a most significant impact on the state's development.

As an industry, cattle ranching had its roots in the southwestern portion of the United States where numerous "cattle kings" held sway over large tracts of land and herds of animals. As a food staple, beef replaced the buffalo or American Bison upon the wanton decimation of that species. Like the buffalo, cattle thrived on the early Springs and green grasses of the southern climes and naturally drifted north toward cooler temperatures and more lush pastures as summer heat dried up sources of water and surrounding rangelands.

By Fall, hundreds of thousands of cattle could be found grazing in Montana and Wyoming. A typical trail drive from Texas to Montana would proceed at a leisurely pace and require upwards of five months to complete. During that time the stock would be allowed to graze endless rangelands found in the present day states of Texas, New Mexico, Oklahoma, Arizona, Nevada, Utah, Kansas, Colorado, Nebraska, South Dakota and Wyoming. Reports and logs have indicated that in 1871 alone, more than 500,000 cattle were trailed to Montana.

Disposition of the huge beef herds would typically involve additional trail drives extending hundreds of miles to various railhead shipping points and finally to Chicago or other mid-western packing plants and commission firms which became the backbone of the great central markets which were established at points like Kansas City, Omaha, Denver, Sioux City and Minneapolis-St. Paul. Many animals and cowboys, however, remained in Montana and it was they who formed the basis of the state's cattle industry.

While the huge trail drives only lasted for a period of about a decade, cattle operations within the state itself were hardly of less magnitude and surrounded by no less visions of romance. In 1884, for example, about 850,000 cattle were to be found on Montana ranges. By this time, over three-fourths of these cattle were being raised here, the balance still having been driven up the long trails into the state.

Cattle belonging to numerous owners, some no less colorful than their predecessor "cattle barons" of the Southwest, were now ordinarily roaming and grazing loose on the vast ranges of Montana. When market time arrived, cowboys working for all owners would round up the stock, separate animals belonging to the outfits for whom they "repped" and assemble them into herds which were to be sold and begin the drives to shipping points. Similar round ups took place in the Spring when calves were branded to identify ownership according to the brands found on their mothers. The "rep" would again be present to tally the new crop head count for the owners of those respective cows and brands.

Places where feed, water and natural barriers, such as cutbanks or bluffs against which a herd could be easily held, were found and became popular places to hold round ups. Such was the case of the present site of the City of Roundup; thus the origin of the settlement and the town's name.

It was from that period of Montana's history and its influence on the Montana of today that the idea of a huge modern day cattle drive was born. A conversation between three friends across the dusty hood of a pickup truck parked in front of a small town saloon was where and how the idea originated. These three friends were Barry McWilliams, Stan Lynde and Jim Wempner. Their idea and diagrams drawn in the dust on that pickup truck hood since had grown into one of the largest and necessarily complex efforts to be put forth in the planned celebration of Montana's past 100 years. But beyond Montana, the cattle drive concept also would recognize the contribution of many other states and peoples to the development of the American West.

Organization of the Great Montana Centennial Cattle Drive of 1989 and its related events was the purpose behind formation of Latigo Corporation. Incorporated as a Montana non-profit entity in December 1987, Latigo Corporation would be governed by a fifteen member Board of Directors selected for their interest in the event, expertise in particular aspects necessary to the success of the cattle drive, and willingness to devote considerable amounts of volunteer time to accomplish the cattle drive mission. From their number, the Directors elected officers and named and staffed several committees whose purposes would be to plan and execute the event. And now it was happening!

Following is a listing of the Board of Directors of Latigo Corporation, together with a brief biographical sketch of each:

ALFRED ADOLPH

Alfred Adolph was born and raised in the Roundup area of Montana. He graduated from Roundup High School. As a youngster, Adolph worked as a cowboy on several ranches in the Roundup community and also gained experience with horse-drawn vehicles and horse-drawn farm equipment. Prior to World War II, he worked as a welder in the Seattle-Tacoma (Washington) Ship Building Corporation, and worked as a cow puncher for the Miller Land & Livestock Company of Parkham, Wyoming. That firm supplied up to 25,000 head of Mexican steers under a U.S. Government Beef Contract at the time. Adolph then served with the U.S. Army in the European Theater during World War II.

Following the war, Alfred Adolph leased a cattle and grain operation and went on to manage a 500 head cow-calf operation. He later worked more than 5 years as a motor operator in Roundup area underground coal mines, and spent a season working military construction in Tule, Greenland.

Prior to his Farmers Union retirement in 1981, Adolph spent 29 years as manager of the Roundup Farmers Union Oil Company, a supplier of fuels, petroleum products, and a broad range of livestock feed and equipment.

During his years with the firm, he regularly served as Rodeo and Parade Chairman of the Annual Musselshell Valley Chamber of Commerce July 3-4 Rodeo and instructed Roundup area youngsters in Bronc Riding, Bull Dogging (Steer Wrestling), Roping, and Barrel Racing rodeo events.

Mr. Adolph continues to manage his own cattle ranching operation east of Roundup and rides at the 13,000 head capacity Roundup Feedlot for Walt Collins during its October-April feed cycle.

DAVID L. AUER

David L. Auer was born and raised in the Central Montana area near Comanche. He graduated from Broadview, Montana, High School and earned his B.S. Degree from the University of Montana. Mr. Auer is a Certified Public Accountant and serves as President of Wyo-Ben, Inc., a supplier of down-hole drilling materials. He is on the Board of Directors of the First Interstate Bank of Billings.

Auer has an extensive history of community involvement. He is currently Chairman of the Board of the Montana Community Foundation and Chairman of the Community Development Foundation. He is a past president of the Deaconess Medical Center Board and the Rimrock Foundation, currently serving the latter as a Board member.

Mr. Auer is a past president of the Wyoming Mining Association and a past president of the Yellowstone Kiwanis Club. He also served as a member of the Billings School District #2 Board of Trustees.

PATRICK K. GOGGINS

Patrick K. Goggins is the owner-manager of the Public Auction Yards of Billings, Montana, one of the state's largest livestock marketing facilities. In conjunction with the yards, Goggins is president of Western Livestock Reporter, Inc., a firm which publishes the regional *Western Livestock Reporter* and *The Agri-News*. He also owns and operates the Vermilion Ranch near Billings, a substantial purebred and commercial cattle and farming entity.

Goggins has lived in Montana nearly all his life and was raised in the Fromberg area. He is a graduate of Montana State University and has served as herdsman on several Montana ranches. Mr. Goggins also gained experience working as a field editor and sales representative for several livestock publications, including *The Western Livestock Journal*, out of Denver.

Mr. Goggins is a well-known livestock auctioneer and enjoys a widespread reputation as a spokesman and authority on livestock matters throughout the United States.

N. C. (PETE) HINSON, JR.

Born in Odessa, Texas, Pete Hinson lived with his parents on a ranch which his father managed near there. At age 10, the family moved to Ashland, Kansas, where Pete's father was partner-manager of another cow-calf-yearling cattle operation consisting of a base herd of 600 cows and some 3500 to 4000 yearlings. Hinson graduated from Ashland High School and attended Kansas State College for two years on a full-ride track scholarship. He then transferred to Kansas State University where he earned his B.S. Degree in Animal Science with a minor in Business in 1967.

Hinson worked eight years for Oppenheimer Industries as an Assistant Vice-President and Chief of the firm's Ranch Management Division where his duties involved managing absentee owner properties held as investments. He then joined Metropolitan Life Insurance Company as a consultant responsible for a five state area where he evaluated and initiated agricultural loans on farms and ranches.

Between June, 1982, and December, 1986, Mr. Hinson was involved in the Metropolitan life insurance Company Agricultural Investments program. Since that time, he has been Treasurer and Operations Manager for Transmountain Land & Livestock Company, a Metropolitan subsidiary which own and operates several ranches which together maintain some 40,000 head of cattle and over 150 employees.

GAY HOLLIDAY

Gay Holliday was born and raised in Billings, Montana, and has lived in Musselshell County for the past 35 years with her husband, Frank, ranching near Roundup.

Gay served as the Montana Charter President of Women Involved in Farm Economics (W.I.F.E.), representing agriculture on the Governor's Economic Advisory Council, and served on the Board of Directors of Rural Area Women and the National Family Farm Coalition in Washington, D.C.

Gay served four terms in the Montana House of Representatives before retiring as a Legislator.

Mrs. Holliday is a Charter Member of the Montana Simmental Association, and belongs to O.E.S., Past Matron, P.E.O., V.F.W. Auxiliary, Roundup Women's Bowling Association and Pine Ridge Golf Club. She was recently named to the community Board of Directors of the Montana State Bank.

Gay currently serves as the Executive Secretary of the National Old Timers Rodeo Association, which she helped to Charter and which sanctions over 50 rodeos each year in the United States and Canada.

JOSEPH K. (KIM) KUZARA

J.K. Kuzara was born and raised in Roundup, Montana, graduated from Roundup High School, and attended Eastern Montana College in Billings before enlisting in the United States Air Force during the Vietnam War. His military duties involved collecting, analyzing, documenting and reporting Strategic Air Combat and strategic wartime capabilities.

Kuzara has more than two decades experience in newspaper journalism and advertising. A member of the Montana Air National Guard, Kuzara has served on the State Adjutant General's Air Staff for six years where he is involved in the planning, coordinating and controlling of Montana Air National Guard activities.

He was a member of the Musselshell County Planning Board for 13 years and served in the capacity of Chairman of that body for 11 years. During that period, he was involved in the assembly of the county's master plan and he researched, wrote and published a county coal impact study for the Farmers Home Administration.

Mr. Kuzara owns and operates a small livestock and grain operation. For ten years he was involved in the ownership and operation of an engineering and land survey business which undertook various land subdivisions, road, dam, waterway and airport projects. Kuzara served as a Director of Faunco, Inc., owner of a 13,000 head feedlot and grain elevator complex.

He was a Director of the Musselshell County Chamber of Commerce for 12 years and served as its president for 8 years.

STAN LYNDE

Noted western artist, Stan Lynde was raised on his family's ranch near Lodge Grass, Montana, on the Crow Indian Reservation. He created the comic strip *Rick O'Shay* in 1957 and for nearly 20 years wrote and illustrated that feature. In 1978, Lynde created the comic strip *Latigo* for the Field Newspaper Syndicate (now News America Syndicate) and produced that feature until 1983. He then created the cartoon series *Grass Roots* in 1984 as a self-syndicated feature for weekly newspapers throughout the United States.

Mr. Lynde is the co-founder of New Inspirations, a company devoted to the production and sale of Christian art prints, cards and books. Mr. Lynde calls himself "a Westerner by birth and inclination" and his work with *Rick O'Shay, Latigo,* and *Grass Roots* aptly reflects his life-long interest in the history, lore and legend of the American West. Stan has recently published a book entitled *Rick O'Shay, Hipshot and Me,* an autobiographical sketch.

Lynde is listed in Who's Who in American Art, and Great Britain's Men of Achievement, and is a recipient of the Inkpot Award for Achievement in the Comic Arts. He has also received the Montana Governor's Award for The Arts.

GWEN McKITTRICK

Mr. Gwen McKittrick has spent 60 years feeding, handling, and managing cattle and horses. Much of this time involved driving teams of horses and mules hitched to wagons and other farm machinery. For three decades, Mr. McKittrick was occupied with resource management work, mostly dealing with grass and rangeland.

MIKE MURPHY

Mike Murphy was raised on his family's ranch south of Musselshell, Montana, and graduated from Melstone High School in 1976. He attended Montana State University and later founded Bull Mountain Outfitters, a firm that caters to big game hunters and recreationists throughout Montana. Murphy has also been involved in Farm/Ranch real estate acquisition and sales, and has done consulting work for energy and utility companies on right-of-way acquisition. He has worked extensively with outdoor film companies producing wildlife, hunting, and outdoor activity films where his guiding expertise, wagon management and outfitting experience have been necessary and invaluable. Murphy has been featured in several domestic and foreign outdoor publications.

Mr. Murphy is a past Director of Custer Country, a regional tourism and promotion organization with nationwide markets. He remains associated with his father on the family ranch south of Musselshell and continues operation of Bull Mountain Outfitters.

EARL ROSELLE

Born in San Diego, California, Mr. Earl Roselle, the son of a long-time Navy family, joined the United States Navy the day after Pearl Harbor. After World War II, he attended Northern Arizona University and earned a Degree in Business in 1954. Shortly thereafter, Mr. Roselle moved to Montana where he has owned and operated a cattle, horse and buffalo operation near Billings on Pryor Creek. Roselle has also spent 33 years with Bankers Life of Des Moines, as a sales agent.

In addition, since World War II, he has been involved in the film industry as a contact-liaison between filmmakers and local interests. His work has involved finding locations casting, providing Native American participants for films, and providing horses, tack and other requirements for such productions as *Little Big Man, Missouri Breaks,* and *Legend of Walks Far Woman.* Mr. Roselle has also been deeply involved with Billings area civic and service organizations.

JAMES R. SCOTT

Jim Scott was born and raised in Sheridan and Dayton, Wyoming. He spent much of his early years on the Padlock Ranch in northern Wyoming and southern Montana. Jim attended the University of Denver and the University of Wyoming.

Since 1976, Scott has been associated with First Interstate BancSystem of Montana, holding numerous positions. Currently, Jim is vice chairman of First Interstate BancSystem of Montana and president of First Interstate BancSystem of Montana Foundation.

Jim has been involved with numerous community and state organizations, including Montana Community Foundation, Alberta Bair Theatre, Montana Ambassadors and Montana Nature Conservancy.

JAY STOVALL

Mr. Jay Stovall has spent his life on the family ranch near Billings, Montana. A graduate of Billings Senior High School, Mr. Stovall has, for the past 40 years, trailed several thousand cattle a distance of about 40 miles twice annually as a routine part of his family ranch operations.

Stovall is a past school board member, a member of the Montana Stock Growers Association, the National Cattlemen's Association, the NILE 200 Club and the Shriners' Black Horse Patrol where he serves as Captain (leader).

Mr. Stovall hails from a long tradition of Montanans and Montana heritage. His great grandfather arrived in the state with famed explorer/citizen John Bozeman in 1864. Mr. Stovall is an enrolled member of the Crow Indian Tribe.

RICHARD E. WALKER

Originally from Cody, Wyoming, Mr. Walker moved with his family to a ranch south of Musselshell, Montana, as a youngster. He still owns and operates the ranch with a son, Brian. Walker graduated from high school at Musselshell and earned a Degree in Mathematics from Montana State University. He attended graduate school at that university.

Walker taught Mathematics and Physics for 11 years prior to taking over the family ranch. He served for 11 years as a school trustee and served 4 years as a Musselshell County Commissioner. In that capacity, Walker was a member of the Montana Association of Counties Economic Development Board and its Agricultural Committee, the Central Montana Health Board, the Musselshell County Hospital Board, and the Roundup Centennial Cattle Drive Committee (a quasi-government organization formed as a result of an inter-local agreement).

Mr. Walker served on the Musselshell-Golden Valley A.S.C.S. Committee and is a past Director of the Musselshell-Golden Valley Stock Growers Association.

JAMES A. WEMPNER

Born in Plainview, Minnesota, Mr. James Wempner graduated from the University of Minnesota with a Degree in Agricultural Economics and a Minor in Animal Husbandry. He was employed by a bank in Cavalier, North Dakota from 1948 to 1951, after which he moved to Billings, Montana to a position with the Midland National Bank (now First Bank of Billings). Mr. Wempner retired from banking in 1981 as Vice President of First Bank's Agricultural Department. He currently pursues farming and ranching interests he has in Big Horn, Yellowstone and Sweetgrass Counties.

CAL WINSLOW

Cal Winslow was born and raised at Deer Lodge, Montana, and attended Montana State University in Bozeman, Montana, after graduation from high school. He received a B.S. Degree in Education in 1971 from Eastern Montana College in Billings, Montana. Mr. Winslow is a graduate of the National Planned Giving Institute of Memphis, Tennessee and has pursued Continuing Education endeavor in various marketing, estate planning and fund raising instructional courses.

Winslow has served as Coordinator of Events, Yellowstone Boys and Girls Ranch, Billings, Montana, where he was full-time lodge parent, teacher, activities director and supervisor of work program. He was District Director of the Muscular Dystrophy Association of Billings where he established telethon network, patient services programs, medical clinic and summer camp programs. He then became District Director of the Tucson, Arizona Muscular Dystrophy Association, working in fund raising and patient services.

In 1977, Winslow became Director of Community Relations for St. Vincent Hospital, Billings, Montana. In 1977-78 Winslow was Campaign Finance Director for Congressman Ron Marlenee. He also served as Business Development Manager for Midland National Bank in Billings in 1978 and 1979. From 1979 to 1982, Winslow was Director of Development and Public Relations, Deaconess Medical Center, Billings, Montana, serving as Administrator of marketing, public relations, volunteer services and fund development. He has served as President of the Deaconess Foundation, Billings, from 1982 to the present.

From 1980 to 1988, Winslow served as a State Legislator in the Montana House of Representatives, representing House District 89. During that time Winslow's political involvement included: Chairman, Coal Tax Oversight Committee, Vice Chairman, Legislative Human Services Committee, National Vice Chairman, Committee on Human Services at the National Conference of State Legislatures in 1983, and from 1983 to 1988 he served on the Legislative Finance Committee. In 1985 and 1987 Winslow chaired the Appropriation Sub-committee on Human Services, and served on the Governor's Council on Cost Containment in 1985, as well as the WICHE Committee on Junior Colleges. In 1987-1988, Winslow was a Republican Candidate for Governor of Montana.

Winslow has served on numerous other local, regional, state and national civic committees, and with a vast array of professional and community organizations, including Eastern Montana College Task Force, National Association of Hospital Development, Billings Chamber of Commerce, Campaign Chairman for Boy Scouts of America and many, many others.

Of the Latigo Outfit, this dedicated Board of Directors and all who worked to make the "Big Drive of '89" happen, United States Senator from Montana, Max Baucus, had the following comments for EPIC TRAILS - Endless Tracks Across Centuries:

"HEAD 'EM UP, MOVE 'EM OUT! That's what we did for six days on the Montana Centennial Cattle Drive. What some thought impossible was accomplished in splendid fashion for the whole world to see. Only Montana could re-create with authenticity such an event which was the backbone of our statehood a hundred years ago. Although cattle drives were commonplace in the history of America's heartland, to reproduce one between Roundup and Billings was an historical event enjoyed by thousands from all parts of our state, nation, and several other countries.

"From the beginning in Roundup, it was exhilarating to be a part of this once-in-a -lifetime adventure. As a drover, not only did I have the advantage of sharing the responsibility of herding hundreds of Longhorns, but also the opportunity to view the breathtaking scenery of our state. Working with Jim Leachman's lead herd, we did everything possible to give the drive a genuine look. This meant jeans without zippers, no bright colored clothing, authentic tack and canvas tents.

"There was a sense of long-range commitment after being only an hour out on the trail, and this was invigorating. We were off! My emotions were soaring!

"Being able to move around the campsites at the end of the day is one of my best memories. The evenings were a special time, sitting with companions and swapping tales of

... Proud to be a Montanan.

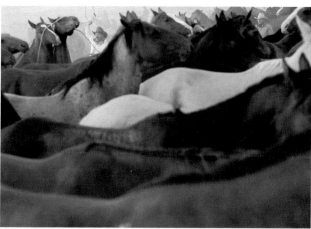

Catching up early morning mounts out of rope corral for drovers.

Head 'em up – Move 'em out.

Drovers ready to go for the day.

Catered cow oasis.

Connie Cox's Longhorn cows are put in with main herd for the remainder of the drive into Billings.

Roundup camp kitchen on wheels packed up and ready to roll.

The 'Hoolihan' Throw.

Hey, wait for me, 'Blue' – my boss has lost his trail bag and bed roll. Sure hope he hasn't lost me!

Change of weather coming?

'Designer' mules, all dressed up in fly nets.

Takin' a little snooze.

A snappy, 'six-up' matched team.

151

The Great Montana Centennial Cattle Drive of 1989.

Don't even think about it!

We're all ears, boss!

Oh, Boy! Nice place for a roll and dustin' off.

Veterinarian riding with the main herd.

Jinglin' the loose hosses.

Veterinarian's wagon with wagon train.

A century and a half in the saddle reflecting on ranges, roundups, rope corrals and good horses they've known.

"Four-Up" Hitch and the trail ahead from seat of the Chuckwagon.

Drovers' camp loaded up, harnessed, ready to hitch teams and move out.

A few of today's working cowboys plan the day.

One-two-three loops... who gets the yellow horse?

Wagon circle camp with tents, short tipis ...

Another day begins.

... And tall wigwams.

On the trail again and eating miles,...

You don't say? – How'll you know or less you try?

... Eating some dust, too!

156

CACTUS, YUCCAS AND ROCKS

A cowboy's life is simple, his possessions–few–
   Some duds–hat–saddle–boots–spurs–rope and socks,
His tack must be in order, as from the corral–
   He tops the broncs the boss has led.
And from which he must mold a top cow pony, trusted and true–
   One, with which he'll have to share life's hard knocks;
He finds no soft pillow of eiderdown or feather ticking,
   Upon which to rest his tired head.
       . . . .There's only–Cactus, Yuccas and Rocks.

From his tarp and bedroll he'll strectch and yawn;
   As, in from the remuda rides the dusky nighthawk,
To take his turn at dawn's damp, dewy sleep–
   While day hands saddle up and lope out; the herd to the trail, led.
His chuck he takes at the wagon, from dutch-oven and tin cup–
   From testy ol' camp cook with iron skillet, pewter spoon and crock.
And he dreams a ballad to softly hum or sweetly play,
   On his harmonica–to restless critters as they bed–
      . . . . Amongst–Cactus, Yuccas and Rocks.

A cowboy's rewards are few–he loves the range and herd–
   A night in town–a game of cards–a drink to toss.
His lonely summer's pay, he'll gladly squander on silver spurs,
   Or inlaid bit–jack o' diamonds or ace-high stakes.
He might die at a crossing or in a fall–or for tender touch or smile,
   But on his grave, doubtful even a simple wooden cross;
As on the starlit prairie, with only the wind and coyote,
   to wail and mourn–his final resting place he takes–
      . . . . Marked simply by–Cactus, Yuccas and Rock.

– Endless Tracks Across Centuries

our day's experiences. Friendships were made quickly because of our mutual experiences – aches, pains, and, of course, a few saddle sores, which we knew were all a part of the adventure. More seasoned cowboys gave us greenhorns sympathy and often times a good natured ribbing. Our campfires, replete with music, dancing, stories and jokes, were highlights that sustained us. We kept our goal in sight, just as our great grandfathers did 100 years ago. We knew Billings was just over the horizon.

"Our Centennial Year in Montana was filled with adventures – I was lucky to share some of them. But I have to admit, 'The Great Montana Centennial Cattle Drive of 1989' tops my list of memories. I tip my hat to those who made it a success. They are just one more reason I'm proud to be a Montanan!"

Senator Baucus's comments reflected the spirit shared by everyone involved, and the memories, which will be recalled time and again, will be enhanced by the authenticity which inspired those comments. From the clothing and rawhide tree of the old 1880s vintage "A fork" saddle which the Senator rode (see page 149), to most of the wagons, harness, other tack and equipment, right down to brass hooked lace-up boots and ladies' frontier bonnets depicted on many of these pages, the genuineness of the scenes which unfolded was remarkable.

With all the excitement which had taken place, this day had been a long one and many on the wagon train were faced with setting up their camps in the dark. Hats, faces, clothes and teams were cloaked with the fine dust from the trail. If there were any lagging spirits, they seemed to rekindle as the campfires began to glow at each wagon circle and the fiddles and guitars began to tune up. The tiredness which prevailed was a happy one and there would be a deep sleep for many of the weary travelers tonight.

Having now even lost his bedroll, Connie decided to gravitate close to the cookfires by the chuckwagons at the drovers' camp. He figured he could trade one night's comfort for lots of hot black coffee and the visiting that would go on around some of these fires just about all night long anyway. A couple of the camp cooks in particular seemed to get their last stragglers and the night watch cowboys coffeed up barely in time in the wee hours after midnight to stoke up the cookfire in preparation for getting tomorrow's (or Connie guessed it was already today's) breakfast started!

Be ready to set the brakes, Pard – they're gonna need a breather!

– Endless Tracks Across Centuries

*Not to worry –
They've been a
lotta miles and
they know how
to hit a
lick on a
little grade
like this!*

*Waiting
to help
at the
crossing.*

Just keep your bonnet on Mama – the rider's got the brake!

Rollin' along on easy ground again.

160

EPIC TRAILS—

THURSDAY, SEPTEMBER 7, 1989. 'FOURTH DAY — TWO TO GO —

AFTER THE LONG DUSTY DAY YESTERDAY IT SEEMED LIKE LOTS OF FOLKS WERE MORE INTERESTED IN THE LONG LINE-UP GOING TO PORTABLE SHOWERS SET UP BY LATIGO THAN IN THE LINE-UP TO THE CATERERS' CHUCK. I AM A LITTLE STIFF IN THE JOINTS MYSELF THIS MORNING. MISSED THE GRUBLINE AND DIDN'T FIGURE SHOWER WOULD DO MUCH UNTIL I GET ANOTHER CHANGE OF DUDS. DIDN'T MIND MISSING THE SHOWER LINE NOR GRUBLINE BUT SURE COULD'VE USED MY BEDROLL.

CAMP BREAKING UP ABOUT 10:30 A.M. I GET TO TRAIL ALONG WITH WRANGLING CREW TODAY. THEY JINGLE THE LOOSE HORSES ALONG AT A FASTER CLIP THAN THE REST. RODE ALONG WITH RAY ('RAINBOW') HILLMAN FOR A WHILE AND HAD A GOOD VISIT ABOUT OUR RODEO DAYS YEARS AGO. IT'S WARMING UP GOOD AND I SEE A TREE ABOUT 2 MILES OFF TO THE SOUTHWEST. LOOKS LIKE A GOOD PLACE FOR ME TO EASE OVER AND SHADE UP TO MAYBE CATCH UP ON A LITTLE SHUT-EYE THAT I MISSED LAST NIGHT.

I STARTED TO RIDE OVER TOWARD THAT TREE BY MYSELF BUT RAN INTO A FENCE SO TURNED AND WENT STRAIGHT SOUTH LOOKING FOR A PLACE TO GET THROUGH. SEEIN' I'M GOING TO MISS GETTIN' TO MY TREE I SPY A CUT-BANK AHEAD THAT HAS A LITTLE SHADE SO SIZES IT UP AS JUST AS GOOD A PLACE FOR A LITTLE NAP. I GOT OFF MY HORSE AND UNSADDLED, PUT A HALTER ON 'BLUE' SO

ENDLESS TRACKS ACROSS CENTURIES

EPIC TRAILS—

HE CAN GRAZE AND FILL UP A LITTLE WHILE I NAP. ANYHOW NEED SADDLE BLANKET FOR BED TO DULL SOME OF THE CACTUS AN'ROCKS AND SADDLE MAKES GOOD PILLOW. THINKIN' NIGHTS'RE GETTIN' SHORTER OR I'M RUNNIN' DOWN AND I'M BARELY STARTIN' TO ENJOY MY NAP, HORSE HAIR, SWEAT AND ALL, WHEN ANY DREAMS I MIGHT 'A BEEN PLANNIN' ON ARE INTERRUPTED BY SOMEBODY HOLLERIN'. "HEY, YOU HURT, 'ER NEEDIN' HELP?"

I SLIDES MY HAT OFF MY EYES AN'SQUINTS AROUND TO SEE WHO'S DOIN' THE HOLLERIN' AND MESSIN' UP MY NAP. I'M HALF ASLEEP AND DON'T SEE ANYBODY AT FIRST. THEN I LOOK BACK OVER MY HEAD AND THERE'S A HORSE STANDIN' RIGHT ABOVE ME ON THE CLIFF WITH A COWBOY LEANING OVER, PEERING DOWN. "NO, I'M OKAY — WHO IS IT?" I ASK.

"DOUG MARTIN." HE SAYS. DARN, I HAVEN'T SEEN DOUG, I GUESS, IN 10 YEARS. SMALL WORLD. HE'S HECK'UVA GOOD HAND AND WE HAVE A GOOD VISIT WHILE I CATCH AND SADDLE "BLUE". THEN DOUG RIDES ON TO CATCH DROVERS AND HERD. "BLUE" AND I LOPE EASY, ON TO WHERE NEXT WAGON CAMP WILL BE. JUST TIE UP AND LOOSEN CINCHES BY BIG RED AND WHITE 'BUSCH' TENT AND WATER "BLUE". "BLUE'S BEEN WATCHIN' THE BIG TENT SINCE WE LEFT ROUNDUP MONDAY AND HE THINKS IT'S THE 'BARN' ANYWAY! GOOD PLACE TO CUT DUST.

CAMP BUSIER THAN USUAL AS PEOPLE GETTIN' READY TO HOST THE PUBLIC TONIGHT. TWENTY THOUSAND OR SO GUESTS COMING IN FOR THE GET-TO-GETHER AND I HEARD ANOTHER 5000 OR MORE

—ENDLESS TRACKS ACROSS CENTURIES

EPIC TRAILS—

CAN'T GET TO THE CAMP BECAUSE ROADS IN ARE PLUGGING UP WITH THE TRAFFIC. BIG TENT IS FULL AND RUNNING OVER WITH THE CROWD LISTENING TO THE CONCERT BEING PUT ON BY THE NASHVILLE ENTERTAINERS. LOTS OF GRASS ROOTS PICKIN' AND GRINNIN' GOIN ON OUT BY THE WAGON CIRCLE CAMPFIRES, TOO. NOT TO BE OUTDONE, A BUNCH OF THE LOOSE SADDLE HORSES FROM THE MAIN HERD DROVERS' CAMP GOT AWAY AND CAME OVER TO MINGLE WITH THE WAGON CAMP STOCK AND THE CROWD. WHY SHOULD THEY MISS ALL THE FUN AND STARS JUST BECAUSE THEY'RE HORSES? KEPT SEVERAL WRANGLERS AND COWBOYS FROM BOTH CAMPS BUSY ALL NIGHT ROUNDIN' LOOSE HORSES UP AND SORTIN' 'EM OUT.

A LITTLE SHOWER CAME UP JUST ENOUGH TO SETTLE THE DUST NICELY. THE SETTING FOR TONIGHT'S CAMPS IS BEAUTIFUL. LOTS OF TIMBER AND HILLS TO SOUTH AND WEST. BIG FLAT PLAINS TO NORTH AND EAST. YOU CAN SEE FOR MILES FROM HERE OUT ACROSS THE CHARTER RANCH. OVER THE BUTTE AND RIDGES TO THE SOUTH AND FROM THE MAIN HERD CAMP CAN BE SEEN THE BREAKS OF THE YELLOWSTONE AND BEYOND TO THE SOUTH ARE THE PRYOR MOUNTAINS. IT'S BEEN A BEAUTIFUL DAY.

BESIDES BEING A LITTLE SHORT ON SLEEP AND SEEING OLD FRIENDS ON THE HORIZON I LOOKED UP ON A HIGH BUTTE TO THE WEST AS WE WENT ALONG TODAY AND THERE SAT A BIG BROWN BEAR. BEEN GONE FROM HOME 28 DAYS — 4 FULL WEEKS TODAY — HOPE I'M NOT JUST STARTING TO SEE THINGS?

— ENDLESS TRACKS ACROSS CENTURIES

Chapter 28

LASTING FRIENDSHIPS

As Connie rode along with the wranglers he couldn't help but think about the overall camaraderie with which they did their work. It was really good, being able to see so many old friends and to be able to share this adventure with them. It was also good to make new friends and it seemed this entire trek had been one of excellent opportunity to do both. He was really glad to see Doug Martin and knew it might be another ten years or so before he might cross trails with him again, but that if he were in need, he could call on a friend like Doug and he'd be there to help. That was one of the real dividends about living in this part of the world. People like Ray Hillman and all the others he'd had a chance to reminisce with could go a long time without seeing one another and then pick up and visit at the slightest chance without ever commenting on the interval between visits or without asking any questions. Good friends didn't go about choosing up sides or keeping score. They were themselves and just naturally expected that you would also be, too, without pretense, show or the need any time for explanation.

Connie had already reflected upon the Cattle Drive being a shared event. He really thought about that for a moment as he loped Blue on toward the big red and white Busch® tent set up and marking the location of the next wagon camp. Friends truly shared. They shared common interests, commitment, and appreciation. Your friends were the ones whom you could depend on to see the best in you even when you felt you had done your worst.. When the boot was on the other foot you would hold your friends in the same unquestioned high esteem beacuse of that common bond of commitment. This day, Connie thought especially about friends he knew who were unable to share in this experience, and he wished with all his heart there would be a way that anyone who might have even the slightest bit of cowboy inclination could have the same feeling deep down inside that possessed him. And he felt anyone sharing in this adventure who might not have any cowboy inclinations would surely gain some or at least go away with some appreciation of the cowboy's way.

Friendship, along with kindness, was certainly something this old world could use a lot more of. If more of the world could be experiencing what he was right now, Connie was sure there would be more kindness expressed.

He hoped all the press people he'd seen on the drive would be able in their various media to convey to others some of the kindness, consideration and thoughtfulness he saw being shared along the trail. Everywhere around him he saw people with a more positive and hopeful outlook. They seemed to appreciate themselves and their neighbor for every little thing they were experiencing and were encouraging each other in trying just a bit harder in accomplishing some task which to many may have been a whole new experience.

One of the most encouraging things was to witness the general attitudes of concern and kindness of everyone on the drive for the animals and the environment. People were looking after the comforts of their horses and seeing to their feeding and water needs before doing for themselves. Most everybody was doing their part in caring for the environment by cleaning and picking up after themselves or after their neighbor if he should have a moment of carelessness or forgetfulness. Thinking of the animals, Connie couldn't help being amused at Blue as they topped a rise and the big red and white striped Busch® tent came into full view. The old pony's pace quickened and he nickered and switched his tail in obvious recognition and pleasure. Blue had been very observant of the big tent and other people on the drive had commented that their horses or wagon teams had been quick, too, to zero in on the structure as the "home barn" and place where they seemed quick to learn they'd be unsaddled or unhitched until another day. One teamster had said of his team; "These ol' dead heads jist mope along loafing 'til they see the 'Big-Top' and then they take the bits and I b'lieve'd pull this wagon with the lines alone– could pert near do without the traces hooked up."

One particular act of kindness had almost backfired, though. A kindly rider had offered to share part of an apple with her horse. It was only about half eaten, so was more than just a core, and the horse had greedily grabbed the bite. Instead of chewing it up properly, it had been swallowed as a chunk and the horse choked on it. Owner and steed alike shed a few tears as, fortunately, the attending veterinarians were able to gently dislodge the choke by use of a stomach tube inserted through the horse's nostril, down his esophagus, and then ever so carefully pumping a bit of lubricating mineral oil against the lodged apple while asserting

Free spirited cow country envoy.

Grassroots trail crew from the long trail.

A little 'R' and 'R.'

A good hand to help.

Blue waits for his friend.

Range country 'Reps."

AN OLD TIME CORDIAL

(A Toast To Friendship)

Of all the places in Creation, none has equalled our
American West in practice of hospitality and friendship.
From times of old to the present, it has been a quality
Characterized by generosity and friendliness to guests.

It's like a Cordial; warm, hearty and genuine–as an accord–
An affection shown, a helping hand, good food, shelter
Or drink that stimulates the heart–A Good Medicine. . . .

Once experienced; as with distinctive, warming, aromatic
Spirits–truly, a Cordial–the recipient will travel
Nowhere else in the world without a bit of nostalgic
Longing to know and savor the feeling again and again!

There is something bittersweet which comes back; a sort
Of homesickness, and the longing may be for something
Far away or long ago. Even in faded memories, the good
Feeling which returns is brilliant and very clear, as if
Viewed through fine crystal.

Be it only fleeting, the light that filters for a moment
To warm the heart may have all the hue and color of the
Rainbow . . . . This reflection may give way to a dimming mist
And an instant of poignancy which pierces the heart and soul
With the sharpness and sting of frost!

This sting will as quickly give way to the pleasurable
Stimulation of yet another greeting, another well meant
Handshake–another Cordial–lifted in respect, sincere
Affection and kindest regard–A Toast To Friendship–!

– Endless Tracks Across Centuries

166

– FRIENDS –

"OLDTIMERS"

'Oldtimer', is used with reference to the eras transcended by the lives of men like these. 'Oldtimer', also applied to the person with respect and affection... not only to who he is and has become, but as much to what his life and times have meant in the past, represent now, and will represent as a part of living history to generations yet to come. The Great American Epic that commemorates the winning of the West is marked by the trails carved by earlier generations of such people. Oldtimers truly will have left some of the 'Endless Tracks Across Centuries'. Untold enrichment is the prize of the later day person fortunate enough to turn an attentive ear to the special stories and images experienced and shared by many an 'Oldtimer.'

Photo courtesy of James Henderson.

Hope I'm not starting to 'see' things!

The big red and white 'Busch' tent at each night's wagon camp was a gathering place and center of lots of action on 'The Big Drive of '89.' From the second morning on the trail, many of the animals also knew it was 'the home barn' for the day and they were looking for it.

Beginning' to look and feel like an Oldtimer, myself.

A lotta' snows have blown over the Divide.

Look, Pard', we're headed for the big barn.

Takes a big spoon to stir 'Radar's' Potato Soup!

a bit of pressure downward with the tube. The owner's tears were ones of dismay at the combination of seeing "all that yucky green stuff" coming out her beloved mount's nose, while thinking she had surely "done him in!" The horse's tears were ones of relief at being able to swallow again as the offending morsel was gently eased on down.

Interestingly enough, this was the most serious "emergency" faced on that particular portion of the trek as reported in a press briefing each evening in the big Busch® tent. To be sure, there had been other problems on the trail thus far requiring quick response by the volunteer veterinary staff which were accompanying the drive, and a number of these had been dispatched via the emergency animal ambulance to veterinary hospitals which had kindly offered to keep their doors open on a 24-hour basis in either Billings or Roundup. At the press briefing each evening, there was a severalfold purpose. People were genuinely concerned how everything was going on the drive, and this included the public at large throughout the world, as the press had the focus of media attention world-wide on the cattle drive. The people participating in the drive were very busy with their own particular location on the trail at a given time, or their particular segment of responsibility for the way things were going. With some of the very authentic, and unrehearsed, unplanned "western happenings" taking place, such as overturned stagecoaches or thrown riders, colicky horses, or various other impromptu circumstances resulting in minor injury to a rider or animal, there was need for conveying to the people of the drive, as well as the spectators, near or far, the exact nature of the situation. It was through the briefings that factual information could get related on a timely basis and it appeared all concerned were grateful for this courtesy afforded to them by the Latigo outfit. One thing for certain; in the case of the "big bite of apple," the veterinary doctors spelling the "relief" had two new friends forever.

Connie had to laugh as he thought of some of the questions which had been raised and to which he'd heard the responses as he stood inside the big striped Busch® "barn" and washed a bit of the trail dust from his own throat. One such concern, which it was good to have dispelled, was presented with the query, "What was the cause of all the gunfire someone had thought they heard along the trail?" There was a report being murmured through the crowd gathering in the big tent that some of the wranglers with the loose horse cavvy trailing with the main herd had had to "shoot some horses." Firearms, along with baseball caps, "tenny-runners" and other distasteful trappings or accoutrements for the proper conduct of "The Big Drive of '89," were strictly forbidden. There had been the occasional infraction. Connie knew in one instance where a poor chap had been complaining of a place no longer covered by hair getting cold as it was exposed out the end of his bedroll, so he had unthinkingly covered it with a bright chartreuse baseball cap he'd hidden away in the depths of his duffle. Unfortunately he forgot one early morning as he made his way to and from one of the few "conveniences at the end of a path," which had been an allowed concession to the requirements of modern times. Here he was, in honest to goodness button-fly Levi's®, bright red "long-john" tops, "Festus-style" two weeks growth of scraggly beard and hurriedly donned unlaced lace-up style frontier packer boots making a run for the warmth of his bedroll and hoping for an extra half-hour shut-eye while dawn made its last stand.

And what should happen? Oh, the dam luck of it! He forgot he was wearing also this ghastly brilliant neon-like head gear, and God and a couple of the wranglers, as well as one or two other wagon train people up at the hour to answer the same call he had, all saw him! Worse, they saw the forbidden baseball cap! Connie was pretty sure the man had not been so distraught as to do something so drastic as go shoot himself. He was also sure that God and the wranglers were going to let the matter be, and while there were threats quietly passed around like, " ... ought to be a hanging offense," or, "... out of camp on a rail," the guy was going to get off without more than his own conscience to plague him. Certainly nobody was going to shoot him or horses. In fact, allowing for the proper law enforcement authorities, Connie was confident people had abided by the firearms rules. So what was this question about "gunfire?"

The explanation came simply enough when George Reed and a couple other wranglers demonstrated for a number of people their expertise with long leather bullwhacker's whips, the crack of which sounded like a rifle report. These men did not use the whips to abuse any animal but could deftly direct traffic with them, and the loose horses were trained to pay attention to those directions. However, some of the "clown-type" prankster minded horses made a big game of playing tag with the wranglers, so got constant reminders.

The Old Stetson® Hat

"Old Friends," a cowboy
just doesn't
throw away;

This one protects –
how it's worn's
his stamp.

He tried leaving
it once, to see
if it'd stray,

Did no good –
follered him straight
back to camp!

THE BAR TWO OUTFIT   © 1983

Two of these horses in particular were a matched pair in just about every way. They looked alike, worked together, and when not working actually appeared to go out of their way thinking up games to play together. They were really buddies; great friends. They would constantly run circles around the other horses, as if taunting them to break ranks out of the trail and join in the chase. They'd charge through a gate ahead of everyone else, then turn and charge back through, just as the wranglers were starting to push the bunch through, ducking off to the side and kicking and bucking as they happily scattered everything into confusion at the gate. With their tails in a "9" and their heads shaking from side to side they would split and circle as the wranglers gave chase. The cowboys knew they were getting the horselaugh as if horses could guffaw or say "nyeah-nyeah-nyeah-nyeah-nyeah!" It's no wonder that people would hear the resounding "whack-crack" of those whips as the naughty cayuses got an extra scolding.

It was good fun. What among the finer things in life better conveys an assurance that all is well in our world than a sense of humor? Looking at the humorous side of this situation helped the cowboys dissipate negative energies. They knew the challenges created by these incidents were temporary, and knew a little laughter was good to help them live their lives in a lighthearted manner, so could overlook any inconvenience that may have been caused. While the following incident did not occur on the cattle drive, it serves to illustrate well the innovation with which so called "dumb animals" could think up mischief to do. This happened on a ranch where winter feeding was done with teams and bob-sleds rigged in tandem to carry hay racks. Besides feeding bales or loose hay off these racks the rancher carried sacks of supplement or "cake" which was prepared in a large pellet or cubed form from grain or grain by-products, cotton-seed or soybean meal, probably included some additional Vitamin A and some minerals, and was pressed together with a molasses binding agent. Nowadays, such products, if bagged, are sacked in paper, but in earlier times the good old gunnysack or bag of coarse burlap was used. The hands doing the feeding would make several passes through the snow with team and sled to pack a sort of icy trough, then string the "cake" out of the gunnysacks behind them as they went

– Endless Tracks Across Centuries

Tryin' to size it all up.

Weather worn and trail wise... or they will be if they'll just listen to what they're told!

Lookin' for a friendly face ...

... And what do I see???...

...Strangest sight – but friendly face!

along. The cattle would follow along and would clean up nearly every morsel of this supplement without waste when handled in this manner.

One particular horse which was running loose with others, turned out for winter in an adjacent hilly sagebrush pasture to the meadow in which the cows were being fed hay and cake, would bide his time near the gate and steal or bolt through every time a chance presented itself. This horse loved that molasses cake and not only would delight in swiping some from that already poured on the snow trail, but would also run up to the back of the sled and filch a bite from an opened sack or better yet steal a partial sackful if possible, and run away with it. Once a safe distance from the team and sled, this horse would drop his prize, seize it deftly up again in his teeth, this time by a bottom corner, empty the remaining contents and enjoy the stolen "goodies." Not satisfied with all this, the culprit would then "pour salt in an already open wound" by again taking the empty bag up in his teeth and running around and around the team and sled and through the cows flailing the air with the gunnysack popping like a loose saddle blanket, just to stir up a ruckus! It was a ritual he never seemed to tire of. He seemed to know that it

aggravated the usually stolid old cows or frightened a meadowful of weanling calves, whichever the case might be. But most of all, he appeared to be aware that it sorely vexed the cowboys doing the feeding because they would have to take the team and sled back to the barn and get a saddle horse to come run him off the meadow and get him back where he belonged – until the next time! To make things worse, he was the favorite of the boss man's bride and somehow he knew the cowboys wanted to get even but didn't dare.

As Connie left the increasing hubbub of the big tent to go unsaddle Blue and feed him for the night, he couldn't help noticing the holes in the toes of his old boots were getting a little more raggedy with each day. He'd have to get some more clothes when he got into Billings to replace what he'd lost on the trail but couldn't bear the thought of parting with these boots or of breaking in a new pair. Talk about "old friends," why it was kinda' like the deal with gunnysacks. He'd never liked handling the paper bags of feed and missed the comfortable feeling of things like gunnysacks – and of old boots and his battered old hat. Like other trusted old friends, "they just made do!"

Many a roundup remembered!

– Endless Tracks Across Centuries

Wrangler and Friend – He'll always be remembered when the work's all done in the Fall!

Riding back to see that everything is all right.

174

EPIC TRAILS—

Friday, September 8, 1989. Big Drive Day 5—29 Days on the Trail—

Big night last night. Camp looks like tornado went through. Everybody trying to get little earlier start out of camp this morning. Most ready to leave by 10:30 a.m. Long climb right out of camp to top of Butte for the teams. Some make it easy. Others have a hard time, with a lot depending both on the shape they are in and on how the teamsters know how to drive them and handle their lines. I rode this morning with Roger Brierbach and Bob Black's wagons and visited with them. Both are top hands and know how to handle horses. They are very good teamsters.

Several riders were hitching on to wagon tongues and bolsters with saddle horses and ropes to help those having trouble on the climb. After a while I rode on ahead and had nice visit with Rick and Twila Halmes and their 2 children from Great Falls. Rick is Chairman of the Cascade County cattle drive group and they are trailing with the Yellow Circle of wagons.

Later on as I rode up into the saddle of the ridge that marks the top of the climb over the butte I could see both behind and way out ahead. For 2 and a half miles both directions I wondered at the sight of wagons, teams and riders stretched out and moving all along each way. The slow laboring pull up the

—Endless Tracks Across Centuries

EPIC TRAILS—

NORTH SLOPE AND SWITCHBACK TRAIL AND THE CAREFUL WAY BEING PICKED DOWN THE SOUTH SLOPE AND HAIRPIN TURNS DOWN THE ROAD AHEAD. AND WAY OUT AHEAD WINDING THROUGH THE HILLS AND COULEES, THE MAIN HERD AND DROVERS' CHUCKWAGONS PICKING THEIR WAY TOWARD THEIR LAST CAMP ALONG THE TRAIL. TO A CAMP THAT WILL OVERLOOK THE RIMS OF THE YELLOWSTONE RIVER AND TONIGHT, THE LIGHTS OF BILLINGS.

WHAT A BEAUTIFUL SIGHT! 'BLUE' SEEMS TO SENSE IT, TOO, AS HE STANDS MOTIONLESS AND LETS ME JUST SIT THERE FOR A LONG TIME TO LOOK AND WATCH THIS SPECTACULAR GRAND SIGHT. I DOUBT I WILL EVER GET TO SEE ANYTHING LIKE THIS AGAIN AND I DON'T THINK ANYONE ELSE WILL EITHER. THIS IS AS CLOSE TO HEAVEN ON THIS EARTH AS MAN WILL EVER GET TO. WORDS CAN'T EXPRESS WHAT I FELT AS I SAW ONE OF THE LAST WAGONS MAKING THE CLIMB BEHIND ME AND WATCHED ITS CREW PROUDLY SWINGING THEIR 4 HORSE HITCH OF BIG MATCHED ROANS EASILY AROUND A SHARP TURN AND I COULD SEE THE RIPPLE OF THEIR AMERICAN FLAG AS THE STARS AND STRIPES WAVED OUT FROM ITS PLACE ON THEIR WAGON AS IT HAS THIS ENTIRE DRIVE. GOT REAL HARD TO SWALLOW AGAIN AND LAST NIGHTS LITTLE SHOWER MUST NOT HAVE SETTLED ALL THE DUST. SOMETHING IN MY EYE AGAIN.

CAMP FOR TONIGHT IS ONLY ABOUT 4 MILES OUTSIDE OF BILLINGS. AFTER I UNSADDLED AND TOOK CARE OF 'BLUE', I CAUGHT A RIDE INTO TOWN WITH BRAND INSPECTOR, JIM WEBER. BOUGHT A WHOLE NEW SET OF CLOTHES TO TAKE

ENDLESS TRACKS ACROSS CENTURIES

EPIC TRAILS—

PLACE OF ONES I LOST WITH TRAIL BAG 3 DAYS AGO. AM I EVER GRUBBY AND DIRTY!

WEATHER FEELS LIKE A CHANGE. AIR IS SOFT AS FEATHER. CLOUDY MOST OF DAY BUT BRIGHT —NO WIND, AND LOOKS AND SMELLS LIKE RAIN. MAYBE IT'S WEATHER CHANGE PENDING OR JUST ALL THE INSPIRATION OF THAT SIGHT COMING OVER THE RISE THIS MORNING BUT I KNOW I'M NOT THE ONLY ONE FEELING A TIGHTNESS IN MY MIDDLE AS WE MAKE THIS LAST DAY ON THE OPEN TRAIL. BOB BLACK'S WIFE EVEN COMMENTED ON, "HOW FAR IT GOT BETWEEN TREES," OR, "EVEN A BUSH", BEFORE WE GOT TO THE LAST CAMPSITE! DIXIE'S SENSE OF HUMOR WAS EVEN ABOUT TO 'FLOAT'!

TONIGHT ANOTHER BIG CROWD GATHERED AT THE RED AND WHITE BUSCH TENT FOR AN EVENING OF 'MONTANA' ENTERTAINMENT PERFORMED BY LOCAL MONTANA PEOPLE WHO HAVE BEEN A PART OF THE DRIVE HAPPENINGS THROUGHOUT THIS WEEK. STAN HOWE, OF HELENA AND THIS YEAR'S DIRECTOR OF THE ANNUAL MONTANA COWBOY POETRY GATHERING HELD LAST MONTH IN BIG TIMBER, IS MASTER OF CEREMONIES AND PERFORMED A COUPLE OF ORIGINAL MONTANA SONGS HE HAS WRITTEN. "RIDIN' FOR THE OLD FAMILY BRAND", AND " I STILL LIKE MONTANA BEST OF ALL." GWEN PETERSON WHO HAS BEEN THE FORMER DIRECTOR OF THE MONTANA COWBOY POETRY GATHERING PRIOR YEARS IN BIG TIMBER WAS INTRODUCED AND SHARED HER POETRY AND HUMOR. THEN SHE AND MARILYN PIMPERTON FROM BELT, LED A GROUP OF TEAMSTERS, COWBOYS, COWGIRLS AND JUST FUN ALL 'ROUND CATTLE DRIVE 'HANDS FROM THE YELLOW WAGON CIRCLE, IN A SONG THEY'VE PERFECTED NIGHTS THIS WEEK BY LIGHT OF THE YELLOW WAGON

—ENDLESS TRACKS ACROSS CENTURIES

EPIC TRAILS—

CIRCLE CAMPFIRE. THE SONG JUST NATURALLY IS CALLED "YELLOW CIRCLE" AND IS JUST AS NATURALLY SUNG TO THE TUNE "YELLOW ROSE OF TEXAS". GWEN PETERSON WROTE THE "YELLOW CIRCLE" AND MARILYN DID A FINE JOB TONIGHT LEADING THAT YELLOW WAGON CIRCLE BUNCH UP THERE IN FRONT OF THAT MICROPHONE WITH HER GUITAR. I KNOW IT HAD TO BE A FINE JOB BECAUSE THERE'S NO OTHER POSSIBLE WAY YOU COULD GET A TUNE OUTA' SOME OF THOSE OLD TIMER TWISTERS LIKE PETE CUMMINGS FROM SUN RIVER.

I THINK PETE'S MORE COMFORTABLE FROM THE TEAMSTER'S SEAT OF HIS WAGON WHICH HE'S DRIVEN WITH A NICE TEAM OF BIG ROANS AND CARRIED THE BANNER OF THE MONTANA COWBOYS' ASSOCIATION AND MUSEUM IN GREAT FALLS ON HIS WAGON CANVAS THIS WEEK ON THE DRIVE. BUT I HAVE TO ADMIT PETE AND ALL THE OTHERS IN THE 'YELLOW CIRCLE' MAKE PRETTY GOOD SONG BIRDS TONIGHT.

STAN INTRODUCED A NUMBER OF OTHER SINGERS' AND POETS' WHO SHARED SOME GOOD MONTANA FEELINGS WITH THIS CROWD. HE ALSO CALLED FOR MANY OF THE PEOPLE WHO HAVE WORKED SO HARD TO MAKE THIS 'BIG DRIVE OF '89' A GREAT SUCCESS TO COME UP ON STAGE TO BE RECOGNIZED. THESE FOLKS INCLUDE ARTISTS/CARTOONISTS, STAN LYNDE AND BARRY McWILLIAMS AND RANCHER, JIM WEMPNER, CREDITED WITH FIRST DREAMING UP THE IDEA OF THIS 'GREAT MONTANA CENTENNIAL CATTLE DRIVE' A COUPLE YEARS AGO. WHAT A WONDERFUL MONTANA NIGHT THIS HAS TURNED INTO.

—ENDLESS TRACKS ACROSS CENTURIES

Chapter 29
LIGHTS ALONG THE YELLOWSTONE – BEEN FOUR WEEKS AWAY FROM HOME

The magnitude of last night's gathering would be remembered for a long time by everyone. In order to put the size of the encampment which assembled for the evening's entertainment into perspective in his own mind, Connie reflected that for the one night, there on the expansive Montana plain, the population of the cattle drive wagon camp had grown to a scale which made it temporarily the seventh largest settlement in the state. Montana's population, being less than 800,000 people scattered over 145,392 square miles, might be said to not have any one concentration large enough to really be called a city by some standards. Billings, with about 67,000 inhabitants, led second place, Great Falls, with 56,725 people, as the largest. Helena, the state's capitol, and Bozeman, home of Montana State University, vied for fifth and sixth largest towns with 28,938 and 21,645 people, respectively. Butte and Missoula fit in between with 37,205 and 33,388 residents.

The assembly of enthusiasts for the Nashville entertainment on the Cattle Drive Family Night had exceeded 20,000 ardent Western and Country Music fans. The next half dozen Montana "cities" in order of their respective sizes would be Anaconda, 12,518; Havre, 10,891; Kalispell, 10,618; Miles City, 9,602; Lewistown, 7,104 and Livingston, with 6,994 people. There are only 76 Montana towns with more than 650 citizens each. There are right at 400 other smaller communities scattered throughout the state. Broadview, for instance, David Auer's high school alma mater, boasts 120 citizens. These populations are from 1980 figures and for the most part Montana's census levels have only managed to remain stable during the decade of the '80s. A little gain in some areas was off-set by declines in others.

It is little wonder that Mr. Auer, being Chairman of the Board of the Montana Community Foundation, sees potentially much benefit possible to Montana's rural communities through such an effort as hopefully would be realized from the Rural Montana Endowment Fund. Truly, the aura surrounding the Big Drive of '89 could emanate into a legacy which would make the memory of this great adventure extend into bright and boundless horizons for all Montanans. Pressing among rural community needs, which these smaller communities particularly face, include maintaining what have traditionally been high educational standards, and providing for continuing adequate programs of all types for an increasing senior citizen population. The Rural Montana Endowment Fund will be helpful in addressing not only the needs of such community programs, but will also provide a means by which persons in a given community may be able to directly contribute in an ongoing way to the future of their community and the future of their succeeding generations through their estate plans, trusts, memorials or other means.

As Connie and Blue took in the panorama afforded by their position on the high butte, the "Big Sky" expanse which they could see seemed endless. The camp, which nearly everyone had now departed, had looked as if a tornado had swept through it, and interestingly enough, in the mid-day haze, there were numerous little whirlwinds creating stirs of dust across the shimmering expanse of horizon on the prairie to the East. In the North, the Bull Mountain range was very clear across the range of the Charter Ranch, over which the trail had passed, and from North to South the Western horizon was dominated all along its perimeter with shining mountains from a far distant jumble made up of the Judith and Little and Big Snowy Ranges. Next was the east end of the Little Belt Mountains giving way to the Crazy Mountains off due West and Connie's gaze swept on to the imposing Absaroka Range with the ragged Beartooth Range and Granite Peak looming up in front of the Absarokas near where he knew the picturesque settlement of Red Lodge to be. Way to the South beyond the now visible rims of the Yellowstone, he could see the blue outline of the Pryor Mountains. The vision appeared to undulate and swim for a moment as the entire view of the Great Montana Centennial Cattle Drive just seemed to unroll around this vantage point. As Dr. Jim Curtis's 4-up hitch of big matched roans easily loped with their wagon and two wheeled cart behind it up the trail, the American Stars and Stripes fairly billowed as it waved around the turns. The whole wonderful moment was a sight to behold, and one had the feeling of wishing time could just stand still, allowing this savory emotion to pique the memory forever.

Taking this all in and thinking that it was now four weeks he'd been on the trail away from home, Connie couldn't help but be reminded of the two years of dedicated effort which had been necessary to bring this all about. He couldn't keep from wondering in admiration and amazement at all the details and logistics which had to be dealt with to fit a re-enactment of a matter of fact happening of a 100 years ago into the swirl of today's civilization.

It had taken the grass roots ingredient to pull things together and make this all work out, but Connie was grateful and knew a lot of other people were, too, for the foundation which had been provided by Latigo Corporation on a very continuous basis since being formed nearly two years earlier. At the outset, Latigo had identified three major functional areas with respect to planning and execution of the cattle drive and associated events, of which last night's big gathering was a shining example. These three conspicuous areas identified were the cattle drive proper, ancillary events, and support services. As indicated by their titles, each of these major functional areas would be responsible for a distinct portion of the combined event. However, activities undertaken in any one of these fields necessarily would impact the activities of another and for that reason, the operations of each functional entity had to be closely coordinated with the others.

Coordination and control would be facilitated through a 5 member Executive Committee, which would operate according to the mandate of the previously named 15 member Latigo Board of Directors, supervising day-to-day activities of the corporation. After some growing pains, attrition of certain personnel due to other pressures interfering with the time it became apparent this endeavor was going to take, and some painstaking reorganizational efforts, the following people went to work as the Latigo Executive Committee: Jim Scott, of Billings, Chairman; Dave Auer, of Billings, N.C. (Pete) Hinson, Jr., of Billings; J.K. (Kim) Kuzara, of Roundup; and Cal Winslow, of Billings. This executive Committee would be charged with deriving ideas and making recommendations to the Board of Directors concerning broad planning, organizational and procedural policy. It would also be responsible for ensuring that Board policy was then carried out by corporation committees and subcommittees. To accomplish its responsibilities, the Executive Committee had the authority to temporarily employ or suspend corporation employees pending final Board of Directors action, and to negotiate creating or concluding corporate obligations contingent on Board approval.

A number of additional major, operationally oriented committees were named and charged with implementation of an operational plan pursuant to the establishment of policy by the Executive Committee and Board of Directors. As with the Executive Committee, these committees were given specific responsibilities and powers by the Board of Directors.

From a functional standpoint, five major committees were constituted to handle cattle drive proper planning and execution. Each of these named committees was headed up by a member of the Board of Directors as chairman. Under these five main cattle drive committees, some 22 operational task oriented subcommittees were identified to divide cattle drive activities into manageable proportions. A single major ancillary events committee was tasked with planning and execution of all events associated with the cattle drive other than the cattle drive proper. This committee had three operational committees and some 14 task driven subcommittees. The support services functional area was organized to deal primarily with management issues which were common to both cattle drive proper and ancillary events operations. Support services consisted of six major committees and 9 operational sub-committees.

Latigo Corporation elected the following officers to serve: President, Richard Walker, of Musselshell; Vice President, David Auer, of Billings; and Secretary/Treasurer, N.C. (Pete) Hinson, Jr., of Billings.

The Latigo Board of Directors named a Cattle Drive Advisory Board from a slate of nominees submitted by various businesses and organizations throughout the state. The Cattle Drive Advisory Board selected were: Bud Lake, rancher, from Missoula; Bill Brown, rancher and President, Montana Stock Growers Association, from Sand Springs; Charlie Schwenke, rancher, from Zortman; Donald Bobiney, Vice President/Agricultural Representative, National Bank of Glendive, from Glendive; Bob Barthelmess, rancher, from miles City; Dr. Jim Scott, veterinarian, Bar Two Research and Development, from Great Falls; Dick Hirschy, rancher, from Jackson; Hugh Monroe, rancher, from Browning; Bob Sitz, rancher, from Harrison; and Nancy Espy, rancher and Chairman, Montana Department of Livestock from Boyes. Due to the tragic and untimely death of Bob Sitz from injuries he received in a tractor accident on his ranch, the Latigo Board named Jim Sitz, rancher, from Harrison to succeed his father on the Cattle Drive Advisory Board.

Latigo Corporation retained the following Administrative Staff to perform traditionally accepted administrative activities. These would include record keeping, stenographic, coordination and communicative tasks for both the corporation and its several operational committees. An office was maintained in Billings from which to primarily conduct activities of the Cattle Drive proper and Support Services

The before and after wagons – A place for everything, and everything in place ...

... But some days you just can't keep nothin' nice!

operations while activities mainly associated with support of Ancillary Events operations were conducted out of an office in Roundup. The following personnel made up the Latigo Administrative Staff:

N.C. (Pete) Hinson, Operations Manager; Anne Birac, Assistant to Manager, Accountant, and Volunteer Coordinator; J. Kim Kuzara, Logistics Director; Linda DenBoer, Assistant Logistics Director; Brenda Weeks, Assistant Logistics and Volunteer Coordinator; Bev Hall, Attorney; Jack Dietrich, Attorney; Jim R. Scott, Sponsors Coordinator; Cal Winslow, Media Coordinator; Sherryl Hinson, Scheduler, Statewide County Coordinator; Ginger O'Neil, Assistant to Scheduler, Statewide County Coordinator; Eileen McGee, Computer Operations Manager; Jeanette Mavity, Public Relations/Media Coordinator; Rita Evans, Assistant Public Relations/Press and Office Staff;

Terry Knudson, Assistant Public Relations/Press and Office Staff, and Entertainment Coordinator; Jim Boyde, Products Coordinator, Assistant PR/Press; Cal Winslow and David Auer, Fundraising Co-Directors; Bernice B. Lamey, Assistant to Fundraiser Directors/Products; Bobbie Sullivan, Head Volunteer; Cindy Barr, Secretary to Staff/Receptionist; Jeanie Southworth, Cattle Drive Store; and Dorothy Stephens, Cattle Drive Store.

I. THE CATTLE DRIVE

The five major Cattle Drive Committees had the responsibility of planning, organizing and executing the cattle drive phase of the overall event. These five divisions had, as mentioned, 22 separate task oriented operational subcommittees. The five Cattle Drive Committee Divisions were:

Photo courtesy of Bar Two.

Dust devils doing their whirling dervish dances across the prairie horizon.

– Endless Tracks Across Centuries

HERD CONTROL: Headed up by Alfred Adolph, Board Member. – This Division and its subcommittees would be essentially responsible for managing cattle consigned to the drive from the time they would arrive in Roundup for the assembly phase of the operation until they would be finally disposed of in Billings or returned to consignor after the Drive. Assembly tasks would include receiving the animals in Roundup, verifying suitability for the Drive, verifying cattle ownership, animal identification, weight and owner disposition desires, and preparing the herd for departure. An added pre-drive responsibility of this Division was arranging for custom procurement of cattle by absentee owners or for cattle drive and wagon train participants coming from out of state or from other places afar, who would be desirous of having "their own critter" along on the trail. This is how some of the bidders at the September 2nd auction of Connie's and Larry Klinger's Longhorn cows had known of their pending availability.

Upon conclusion of the Drive the Herd Control Division would be responsible for arranging disposition of the cattle through auctions in Billings or other market avenues. They would also be responsible for making preparations to return animals to owners who desired for whatever reason to take their trail cattle back home.

COUNTY COMMITTEES: Headed up by Jim Wempner, Board Member. – Managing the mechanics by which cattle were to be consigned to the Drive would be the main function of this Division and its subcommittees. It had to maintain communication and liaison with County Chairmen to ensure that livestock producers were informed of cattle drive policies and procedures and to see that ranchers were encouraged to consign cattle to the Drive. Additionally, this Division would coordinate the $^M_{89}$ branding, veterinary clearance, official identification and inspection of consigned cattle, and finally the transportation of cattle to Roundup.

TRAIL ARRANGEMENTS: Headed up by Dick Walker, Board Member. – Securing cattle drive route rights-of-way, planning and executing necessary construction and fencing, preparing cattle bedgrounds and wagon train campsites, and performing re-seeding or clean-up tasks would be the responsibilities of the Trail Arrangements Division. Tasks included identifying routes and sites, negotiating landowner agreements, surveying routes and sites for adequacy, planning site designs, removal and reinstallation of fences, miti-

gating environmental problems, and after-event cleanup and reclamation.

TRAIL BOSS: Headed up by Jay Stovall, Board Member. – Responsibility for the cattle from the time they would leave Roundup until they arrived at their destinations in Billings would be the job of the Trail Boss Division. The actual movement of the trail herd was to be accomplished such that property adjoining the trail routes would not be damaged, the cattle would undergo as little stress as possible, and so that cattle movement time schedules would be met. Work associated with livestock feeding supplemental to limited grazing, work of watering along the trail, veterinary services, drover selection and scheduling, and drover well-being and care would be tasks which were to be performed. A chuckwagon and bedwagon contingency would have to be included with the movement of the main herd to accomplish feeding the drovers and wranglers and transporting their bedrolls and extra tack.

WAGON MASTER: Headed up by Gwen McKittrick, Board Member. – The Wagon Master Division and its subcommittees would have overall responsibilities for ensuring that the cattle drive wagon train would be constituted, moved, and disbanded in an effective, efficient, and safe manner. Work in this Division would consist of all facets of planning for an assembly of some 200 or more horse-drawn wagons and upwards of 5,000 people scheduled to participate in the event.

Major tasks facing this Division included: (a) Scheduling assembly and movement of the wagon train on a day to day basis in a manner which would not interfere with the movement of the main trail herd. (b) Attaining and maintaining a capability to track the location of participants, their belongings, and their horses. This would include a closely coordinated effort with Head Wrangler, Lynne Taylor and his crew of expert wranglers for the management, loose herding or picketing, rounding up, corralling and catching of upwards to 5,000 head of horses on a timely, daily basis to facilitate the wagon train movement from campsite to campsite. (c) Arrange timely and efficient meal periods at each campsite. (d) Arrange entertainment and other amenities of material comforts at each campsite for wagon train participants. (e) Ensuring safety of the participants, their belongings, the wagons, and the wagon train animals. (f) Dealing with emergencies involving participants, their animals, or the surrounding countryside.

Trail herds and drovers of over a century ago suffered many 'Dry Camps' on the way from the Rio Grande to Montana – Sometimes enduring dust choked thirst for several days. Teddy 'Blue' Abbott would have appreciated a site such as this on some of his treks north.

II. SUPPORT SERVICES

The Support Services Committee would be made up of six major subcommittees:

ACCOUNTING AND FINANCE: Headed up by Pete Hinson, Board Member. – This subcommittee would be charged with the management of all funds received throughout the course of the event. Tasks would include receiving, depositing, disbursing, and fully accounting for all corporated and event funds.

ENDOWMENT FUND: Headed up by Dave Auer, Board Member. – Where the primary lasting value of the entire cattle drive operation would be to use the Cattle Drive legacy to help create an endowment for the future benefit of rural Montana and its agricultural communities and families. Considerable thought and planning would have to be devoted to how the endowment would be created, funded, and perpetuated. This would be particularly important in view of the fact that once the cattle drive operations were concluded, Latigo Corporation would have completed its planned purpose and would be most likely dissolved. The ramifications of these issues would be the responsibility of the Endowment Fund Subcommittee.

PROMOTIONS AND PUBLIC RELATIONS: Headed up by Kim Kuzara and Cal Winslow, Board Members. – The ultimate success of the cattle drive would depend on Latigo Corporation's ability to gain widespread public, participant, and sponsor support for the event, and Latigo's ability to attract substantial numbers of people to view the cattle drive and wagon train and attend the ancillary event activities.

Four subcommittees would be identified within the Promotions and Public Relations area: Advertising, Communications, Community Affairs, and Media Relations. Their functions would be as traditionally associated with those classifications.

Photo courtesy of Bar Two.

MVMA immediate past president and his good big 4-up hitch of matched roans have carried "Old Glory" on the Centennial March from Bannack, Montana's First Territorial Capitol to Helena, present-day State Capitol; along the trail of the Milk River Wagon Train 20th Annual Reunion; and now proudly carries her to the banks of the Yellowstone on the "Big Drive of '89!"

– Endless Tracks Across Centuries

PRODUCTS AND ROYALTIES: Headed up by Sherryl Hinson, Latigo Staff. – In its mission role to celebrate Montana's Statehood Centennial, the cattle drive and ancillary event activities would represent a unique commercial opportunity for a wide range of private enterprise efforts. Everything from Cattle Drive Cow Pies and vintage clothing and tack to hand crafted commemorative buckles, spurs and horse gear would likely be offered for sale by enterprising individuals and companies. For that reason Latigo Corporation would need to be prepared to establish standards for products and services, review proposed products and services for harmony with Latigo statement of mission and objectives, contract with producers of goods and services, and ensure some percentage of return to the corporation and endowment fund. These activities would be the responsibilities of the Products and Royalties Subcommittee.

GOVERNMENT LIAISON: Headed up by Jim Scott, State and Federal level; Dick Walker, Local level, Board Members. – Success of the cattle drive would hinge to a large extent on cooperation which would have to be solicited from a variety of government entities. Examples would range from control of aerial activities in the vicinity of the cattle drive to derivation of acceptable traffic flow patterns in and about the drive and ancillary events. Such things as health permits, beverage permits, roadway closings, law enforcement, fire protection, emergency medical transportation, environmental review and a host of others would necessarily involve close coordination with numerous government agencies at the local, county, state and federal levels. Accomplishment of these tasks would be the responsibility of the Government Liaison Subcommittee.

FUND RAISING: Headed up by Cal Winslow, David Auer, Jim Scott, Gay Holliday and Pete Hinson, Board Members. – The sheer magnitude of the cattle drive event would necessitate a significant outlay of money, notwithstanding substantial volunteer and in-kind assistance. Raising of the required funds for the cattle drive, support services, ancillary events and endowment fund would be the responsibility of the Fund Raising Subcommittee. Five subordinate levels would be constituted accordingly to target prospective sponsor groups in the following categories: National Sponsors, Montana Sponsors, Major Foundation Donors, Individual $^M_{89}$ and other Specific Memberships, and Special Events.

In short, the Support Services function would be responsible for performing numerous tasks which would not directly involve the cattle drive or ancillary events operations themselves, but would still be critical to their success.

III. ANCILLARY EVENTS

Depending on the intensity of promotional activities, the cattle drive intrinsically could represent a spectator attraction which might easily result in attendance of many thousands of people per day over a period of about a week. At a very minimum of promotional activity, it would be likely to draw spectator interest in the range of many hundreds to several thousand people per day. As opposed to something like an action-packed sporting event, however, the cattle drive, of itself, would not be expected to hold spectator interest for extended periods of time. In order to ensure financial success of the event and to fully capitalize on its potential to establish a legacy that would lead to perpetuation of the endowment mission, Latigo would have to make sure that a wide range of additional entertaining and interesting activities would be available to spectators who would arrive to see the drive. Moreover, spectators in the numbers anticipated would undoubtedly have a significant impact on the ability of local servicing facilities and governments to provide their temporary needs. Where Latigo would be creating an attraction and its associated impacts, Latigo would also have to bear some, if not all, responsibility for seeing that spectators would be accommodated and that impacts would not become impossible for local services and government to deal with.

All aspects of Ancillary Events, therefore, would have to be driven by anticipated attendance levels.

SPECTATOR ACCOMMODATIONS: – Physically getting spectators into and out of the area, and seeing that they were properly housed, fed, transported and protected would be the responsibility of the Spectator Accommodations Subcommittee. It would be assumed that temporary housing would be required for a majority of the spectators, given the limited facilities available within convenient commuting distance from Roundup and Billings. It would also be assumed that expanded law enforcement, medical, fire protection, transportation and sanitation facilities would be necessary to deal with a possible vast temporary increase in the region's population. All of these items would be issues to be dealt with by this committee.

ACTIVITIES: – Planning, coordination, and execution of a variety of activities for spectators to take part in or attend would be the function of the Activities Subcommittee. These

Winding tracks, stringin' out.

All strung out and trailing' our way.

188

would include such things as concerts, parades, rodeos, western oriented contests, dramas, street dances, and many others.

VENDOR RELATIONS: – A host of food, beverage, souvenirs, and other concession activities would be an essential element of all the spectator activities. It would be the responsibility of the Vendor Relations Subcommittee to ensure that a suitable quantity, quality, and variety of concessions would be available in proper locations throughout the event period, and that Latigo would receive an appropriate percentage of the proceeds to assure physical success of the Drive and ancillary events and to further the contributory mission of the entire effort toward the goal of helping to fund the endowment.

Finally, then, as the cattle drive committees would all begin their detailed operational planning activities, they would need to recognize that certain organizational resources outside Latigo's own framework would be available to assist them with both planning activities and operational efforts. Use of such additional resources would not only simplify the tasks confronting committee personnel by bringing to bear

considerable amounts of expertise, but such use would also help ensure a high quality event.

Widespread knowledge that the Great Montana Centennial Cattle Drive of 1989 was being planned had generated literally hundreds of queries from individuals and organizations who wanted to assist. In a vast majority of cases these contacts had been for volunteered services, equipment, or materials. The State of Montana would itself certainly be one of the most prominent resources available to Latigo. From the Governor's Office down, state officials had almost without exception offered to assist with the Drive in every way possible. Examples included offers from the Department of Livestock with regard to brand inspections, animal health, brand registrations and so forth. Department of Highways personnel indicated a willingness to cooperate in traffic planning, road closures, and other transportation issues. Committee personnel were invited to seek assistance from the Department of Health and Environmental Sciences, the National Guard, the State Extension Service, State Travel and Promotion Bureau, the State Centennial Commission, and many others.

Lights along the Yellowstone will compete with the stars as the drovers turn into their bed rolls the last night on the open trail.

– Endless Tracks Across Centuries

*Fording the
shallows
of the
crossing . . .*

Many other units also expressed interest in helping with the Drive. Officials of the U.S. Bureau of Land Management, Soil Conservation Service, active military and reserve organizations, and the Federal Aviation Administration were examples. The State University System represented a wealth of expertise ranging from environmental impact assessment to promotion and marketing. Local school trustees offered to help in whatever ways they could. The Montana Veterinary Medical Association and service entities such as Emergency Medical Technician groups offered a spirit of cooperation and involvement. Nearly all affected units of local government came forth. City Councils in Billings and Roundup and County Commissioners in Musselshell and Yellowstone Counties expressed a willingness to cooperate. Police and Sheriff Departments did likewise. Others, such as the Montana Stock Growers Association, Guide and Outfitters organizations, local service and civic organizations, youth groups, and countless individuals made contact.

And tomorrow would see the end of the trail. As Connie took one last long look at the trail over which this was all coming to pass and gazed out ahead, Blue's ears seemed to point more intently as they both watched the slow serpentine winding of the main herd and the drovers' chuckwagons moving across the prairie and through coulees far ahead. With a stirring deep inside which was unlike any sensation to which he could put words, Connie proceeded to move Blue easily on down the south face of the butte, reiterating in his mind that the Big Drive had taken a lot of work, but had, in part, really come about by capturing the imagination and support of a society steeped in the romantic traditions and heritage of the legacy of the Old West. Translating that sort of legendary notion and romantic and traditional concept into a working reality had resulted in what was now being experienced, and it could be viewed essentially as an exercise which had bridged a century of time – accomplishing in 1989, in a relatively more complex environment, a feat which was quite routine 100 years ago.

– Endless Tracks Across Centuries

As if to emphasize the time separation and differences between trailing cattle to Montana in the 1860s, '70s, and '80s, and this trek of the past month, Connie was brought back to the present moment by the thought that this cattle drive had indeed been accomplished against the odds of numerous modern day barriers. Bridging the century was a good way to compare it since they were crossing their trail herd of today at places on rivers where bridges hadn't even been thought of, let alone existed, 100 years ago. In the early planning stages he remembered hearing talk that Latigo had hoped to recapture part of the colorful and romantic overtones associated with those early day drives by fording the Yellowstone River just east of Billings as they came into town with this herd. However, as with his own crossing of the Missouri River, this was not going to be the case, because the progress and advancement of civilization had placed too many obstacles in the way. Not all these barriers were actually physical impediments. Regulations, ordinances and other

restrictions of a bureaucratic nature could be just as formidable as urban sprawl in serving to barricade the re-enactment of an old time river crossing so certain concessions were inevitable. While, as has already been indicated and acknowledged, there had been great cooperation and help from all corners, Latigo had still encountered some interesting focal points which required that extra ounce of patience and reasoning.

One such instance had to do with convincing a given particular officious individual that the city of Billings would probably NOT have to mobilize the municipality's entire fleet and arsenal of snow removal equipment to clean the parade route after the cattle drive and wagon train had passed by! It had taken more than a little extra effort to assure this worrywart that monumental mountains of effluent, which had originally been grass, were not going to completely inundate the area. This was serious business – It wasn't all "jist buffaler chips 'n meader muffins" to him!

. . . and swimming the deep.

– Endless Tracks Across Centuries

Preservation of the heritage and history of the cowboys who rode the open range is the purpose of the Museum of the Montana Cowboys' Association located in Great Falls. The visitor to the MCA Museum will find a variety of cowboy memorabilia including some lore of the cinch ring and long-rope!

The rims overlooking Billings were silhouetted by the lights along the Yellowstone as the people of the Cattle Drive pitched their last camp just a few miles north of the edge of town. The only way to describe the sentiment which prevailed was that it was a "Montana feeling" through and through. Even with this proximity to town, there was still a sense of openness at this campsite and the feeling was one of needing to savor that special "something" which had grown throughout the trek. There were a lot of tired, bone-weary souls in camp but the predominant emotion shared by most was one of wishing there might be some way for this adventure to go on and for the "feeling" to never end. The experiences relived as old friends had chanced upon one another, and had ridden stirrup to stirrup for a ways, or the tales swapped as new acquaintances joined them, got told and retold around the campfires at the wagon circles. That this last night close to the open trail, yet so close to the trail's end, should culminate with these experiences willingly shared in a "Montana night" under the big tent just seemed the right thing to do.

Another aspect in the bridging of a century of time one could associate with this "Big Drive of '89," was the number of two and three and perhaps, even a few, four generation families which partaicipated in this happening together. The memories these families would take home and relate again and again would be part of the fabric of what life in Montana was all about. If some member of each of those families could or would attempt to preserve or record some of those tales and experiences along with the personal pictures they had taken along the trail and in camp, there would be special stories and images to share about Montana life with descendants of these families for generations and centuries to come! Cases in point, besides his own family, came to Connie's mind as the Yellow Wagon Circle "chorus" group, including some "old twisters," like Pete Cummings, did their song for everyone to enjoy. Pete, along with a number of other people in the group, was on the Board of Directors of the Montana Cowboys' Association and Museum. Preservation of the heritage and history of the cowboys who had ridden Montana's open ranges was the purpose of the MCA and their museum, located in Great Falls. Pete was an excellent twinkly eyed old yarn spinner, and he and other MCA Board Members along on the Drive, such as Gary Anderson, Dr. Jim Scott, and Bud Mortag, Cascade County's official Drover' invited all they saw to visit the MCA Museum when passing through Great Falls, Montana's "Electric City," along the banks of the Missouri River!

– Endless Tracks Across Centuries

EPIC TRAILS —

SATURDAY, SEPTEMBER 9, 1989. 'DAY SIX — THIRTY DAYS' TRAILING —

EVERYBODY UP EARLY. BREAKFAST AT 4:00 AM. DON'T THINK SOME OF THE CHUCKWAGON COOKS NOR LOTS OF THE HANDS AND RIDERS WITH THE WAGON CIRCLES EVEN CRAWLED INTO BEDROLLS LAST NIGHT. ED "RADAR" KIRBY, WHO TOOK OVER COOKING FOR THE CANADIAN LK RANCH WAGON WHEN BUCK DRAPER GOT HURT LAST MONDAY SAID HE, "SERVED MY CREW THE LAST OF FRIDAY NIGHT'S 'POTATO SOUP' AT 2:30 A.M. AND GENE JOHNSON OF SAND COULEE AND DON BOYER FROM MOUNT VERNON, OREGON, BOTH WITH JOHNSON'S O/J RANCH WAGON, WERE AT MY COOK FIRE AT 3:00 A.M COMPLAINING THE 'POTATO SOUP' GAVE THEM HEADACHES AND HOLLERIN' FOR COFFEE." GUESS THAT CAN HAPPEN IF YOU GET INTO A BAD BATCH OF 'POTATO SOUP' OR IF YOU DRINK 'ER EAT TOO MUCH OF IT ??

WITH BREAKFAST AT 4:00 A.M. EVERYBODY HURRYING, EATING — LOOKING FOR HORSES IN DARK — SADDLING HORSES, HARNESSING HORSES AND HITCHING WAGONS UP. NO TIME TO HARDLY EVEN LET OLD WOOD COOK STOVE COOL OFF BEFORE TYING IT TO SIDE OF WAGON. GETTIN' READY FOR THE BIGGEST PARADE WITH CATTLE, HORSES, WAGONS, RIDERS, MAYBE THAT HISTORY HAS KNOWN AND IT'S ABOUT TO GRACE WITH DIGNITY AND HONOR MONTANA'S 100TH YEAR AS A STATE AS IT TRAILS THROUGH THE STREETS OF BILLINGS.

AT 6:30 A.M. THE CATTLE ARE ON THE MOVE AND THE WAGONS ARE ROLLING. AT 6:40 A.M. I LOPE 'BLUE' OUT TO CATCH THE WRANGLERS AS THEY ARE HEADING THE LOOSE HORSE HERD FOR

— ENDLESS TRACKS ACROSS CENTURIES

EPIC TRAILS—

DOWNTOWN BILLINGS. LYNN TAYLOR AND SONNY LINGER, TWO
GREAT MONTANA COWBOYS — IN AND OUT OF THE RODEO ARENA —
POINT THE LEAD AHEAD OF THE HORSES WITH 35 OR 40 WRANGLERS
FLANKING ALONG EACH SIDE AND PUG JORGENSON, DON SPANG
AND MYSELF AT THE BACK OF THE HERD OF HORSES. TWENTY-FIVE
OR THIRTY THOUSAND PEOPLE IT LOOKS LIKE ARE LINING BOTH
SIDES OF THE PARADE ROUTE WAITING TO CHEER AND WELCOME
THE DRIVE INTO BILLINGS.

AT 9:02 A.M. THE LOOSE HORSE HERD IS IN THE CORRALS
AT B. L. S. (BILLINGS LIVESTOCK COMMISSION CO.) ON THE SOUTH
SIDE ACROSS THE YELLOWSTONE RIVER EAST OF TOWN. IT HAS
BEEN 8.4 MILES FROM WHERE WE BROKE CAMP TO THESE YARDS
OR CORRALS. ONE HOUR LATER HALF THE CATTLE ARE ALSO IN
THE CORRALS AT BILLINGS LIVE — AND THE OTHER NEARLY 1500
HEAD ARE IN THE CORRALS AT P.A.Y.S. (PUBLIC AUCTION YARDS)
AND THE 'BIG DRIVE OF '89' IS DONE. THE MAIN HERD CHUCK WAGONS
AND BED WAGONS ARE CIRCLED ON THE GROUNDS AT METRA PARK
WHERE THEY'LL PREPARE A BIG FEED FOR A FINAL REUNION OF
OLD TIME COWBOYS THAT LATIGO IS INVITING TO JOIN IN THIS
OCCASION WITH THE DROVERS, WRANGLERS AND SUPPORT CREWS
WHO'VE HELPED BRING THIS 'BIG DRIVE' ALONG. THE WEATHER WAS
PERFECT FOR THE PARADE INTO BILLINGS — NOT TOO HOT — NOT TOO
COLD AND I DON'T KNOW OF A MISHAP ALL ALONG WITH THOSE
THOUSANDS OF WONDERFUL PEOPLE WELCOMING US ALONG THE
WAY.

I UNSADDLED 'BLUE' AND TOOK CARE OF HIM AT BILLINGS LIVE —

ENDLESS TRACKS ACROSS CENTURIES

EPIC TRAILS—

WHERE HE'LL GET A CHANCE TO REST UP A LITTLE ON GOOD FEED AND WATER BEFORE HEADING NORTH TOWARD HOME. CAUGHT A RIDE TO WESTERN RANCH SUPPLY WHERE I HAD A DRIVER LEAVE MY PICKUP TRUCK AND CAMPER. BY MID-DAY I WAS HEADED FOR A SHOWER AND SOME REST FOR MYSELF.

DURING THE AFTERNOON THERE WAS A LOT OF ACTIVITY GOING ON AT THE METRA PARK. THE CHUCKWAGON FEED FOR TRAIL HANDS AND COWBOYS; ENTERTAINMENT AND RECEPTIONS IN THE BIG TENTS; A TRAIL'S END SALE AUCTIONING OFF SOME OF THE LEAD HERD LONGHORNS, WESTERN ART AND COWBOY ANTIQUES; AND EVEN SOME TRICK AND FANCY ROPING BY LOU UDALL OF GREAT FALLS.

EVENING SEEMED TO COME IN ONLY A MATTER OF MOMENTS. JOINED THE CROWD AT THE METRA TO SEE THE SORTA GRAND FINALE, THE TRAIL'S END CONCERT FEATURING LEE GREENWOOD PRESENTED BY BUDWEISER. THE CONCERT ALSO INCLUDED ENTERTAINMENT BY HOYT AXTON, SHEB WOOLEY, ED HUNNICUTT, BRENDA WILLIAMS, THE GAIRRETT BROS. AND SUZI MAKI AND THE CATTLE DRIVE BAND. IT WAS A GOOD SHOW. LATIGO BOARD OF DIRECTORS GOT INTRODUCED AND I THINK EVERYBODY REALLY APPRECIATES, NOW THAT IT IS THE HARD REALIZATION THIS CELEBRATION IS SIGNALING THE END OF THE TRAIL DRIVE, HOW HARD THEY AND ALL THE ADVISORS, VOLUNTEERS AND SPONSORS WORKED MAKE THIS THE EPIC HISTORIC EVENT IT HAS BEEN. DR. JIM SCOTT, WHO HAS DIRECTED AND COORDINATED THE VETERINARY SERVICES FOR THIS ENTIRE DRIVE, SHARED A COUPLE ANIMAL INTEREST STORIES WITH THE AUDIENCE AND CLOSED THE CONCERT WITH HIS "NIGHT WATCH PRAYER". THE DRIVE IS OVER.

—ENDLESS TRACKS ACROSS CENTURIES

Chapter 30

TRAIL'S END
"THE GREAT MONTANA CENTENNIAL CATTLE DRIVE" PARADES INTO BILLINGS TOWN

Friday night was a night with a mixture of excitement. The Montana night entertainment by Montana people in the big tent had been a great gathering. Officials of Latigo, in charge of coordinating the Grand Finale, the parade into Billings and all the events to take place on this Saturday, the last day of "The Big Drive of '89," had a real dilemma facing them in trying to make a choice of wagons that would be selected to participate in the parade from all those which had made the trek to this point. Traffic and crowd control concerns in Billings wanted to dictate a very limited number of the wagon train participants to make up the actual parade in view of time constraints and other imagined problems. All the thousands of people who were gathering to observe the entry of the drive into town were not going to be happy about this and Latigo knew it was an impossible task to decide which few wagons should qualify for the parade while leaving hundreds, which had all made equal effort to make the drive a success, stuck in camp to just now pack up and go home. The concession had already been made to have the parade at a very, very early hour indeed to satisfy some of the "worrycratic" traffic concerns. With all due respect to these concerns, it seemed hardly a fair "Prime Time" finale befitting what was unanimously being hailed as the Centennial's premier event.

The grass roots spirit, which had proven time and again throughout the week capable of "making-do" when a need arose, came through again. It was not a matter of a decision which wagons would parade and which would not – it was a "given" that the entire wagon train would parade – much to the pleasure of everyone who participated and who gathered to watch, and much to the credit of Montana's Centennial and all her people for a splendid finale to an already spectacular happening!

One particular moment of excitement which occurred also on Friday night was one which everyone could have just as well done without. Tyler Stovall, one of the main herd drovers, and son of Trail Boss, Jay Stovall and Trail Secretary, Juanita Stovall, was hit and injured by a passing pickup on U.S. 87 as he stepped from behind a truck loaded with hay for the evening feeding of the herd. He was rushed to St. Vincent Hospital in Billings where it was determined he

had a fractured jaw and knee, and he lost several teeth and had general contusions and bruising. It turned out Tyler would be sharing the same floor but different wards with Dr. Draper, who had been first injured on the trail last Monday. While it was unfortunate that these men were hurt seriously on the Drive, and that there had been some other injuries, though not as severe, it was at the same time a gratifying thing that the Drive would end with no other serious mishaps. It was also gratifying that certain negative thinking "Las Vegas type" odds makers would be seriously mistaken regarding specific dire predictions which they had made and which had appeared in the press about the Drive.

For those who might wonder at the magnitude of the undertaking which the cattle drive parade into Billings would involve, some comments regarding Latigo's planning for this portion of the event are in order. The movement of the trail herd from the Thursday night bedground to their Friday night bedground would be a short one. In preparation for Saturday's parade, the trail herd would be bedded some two miles to the north of the Friday night wagon campsite on the Billings Shrine Black Horse Patrol property adjacent to U.S. Highway 87. While it did not prove so for Tyler Stovall, selection of this last night's bedground location was by design as a parade safety consideration. First, the property being situated a relatively short distance from the previous Thursday night bedground would allow the cattle an extended rest after their arrival there on Friday. Secondly, the site offered lighted corrals and sheds which would enable herd cowboys additional advantage in readying their horses and beginning Saturday's cattle gathering operation well before daylight. Further, the cattle would be moved along U.S. Highway 87 at a rapid pace and in a more compact unit very early Saturday. This movement would have the triple purpose of reaching the Roundup Road/Billings/ Shepherd Road intersection at or before 7:00 a.m., exercising and somewhat tiring the cattle to make them more manageable, and acclimating the cattle to tight, rapid movement on a pavement surface.

In order to appreciate the parameters within which movement of the cattle herd during the parade through Billings would take place, it would be appropriate to discuss

– Endless Tracks Across Centuries

One more beautiful dawn and bright horizon and an Epic Trek will fade into history.

The end of the trail and Billings town is just over the rise a day ahead.

197

the cattle themselves so that Latigo's cattle containment strategy might be more meaningful. Typically, cattle are both social and usually docile animals, which means that they prefer a familiar group and generally prefer to avoid group conflict. Within their groups, they develop a social order. New animals in such an order create conflict until the new animals become integrated into the existing herd social order.

Where the cattle making up the herd for the cattle drive would not have been, for the most part, of a previously common group, a period of adjustment would be required for the social order to form. This had been a major reason for the timing and duration of the assembly phase in Roundup. The herd had been built up over a period of several days and an added few days had been made available to hopefully help complete this needed social adjustment for the newly formed herd. At the same time, the herd drovers would have ample opportunity to observe the behavior of the herd and new animals as they arrived.

The assembly phase would be utilized to identify the obvious cattle which could cause trouble on the Drive.

Furthermore, this period would enable the cattle to become accustomed to being worked with highly trained and aggressive horses. It was a given that a good percentage of the cattle making up the herd might never have been exposed to manipulation by mounted riders. Animals that appeared at the outset easily excitable, exhibited a volatile disposition, or those which were unacceptably aggressive or disruptive would not be included in the Drive.

During the five day trailing phase, cowboys would have the herd under constant observation under conditions that at times would be relatively stressful for the cattle. This, then, would be a period providing considerable opportunity to identify animals which might not be temperamentally suitable for the parade through Billings. With a short move on Friday, cowboys would be able to sort through the herd after they arrived at the Black Horse Patrol bedground to remove those cattle they had observed throughout the Drive as being unsuitable for safe passage through populated and vehicle intensive areas.

This last rise and the roll into Billings town makes it pretty close to a round trip!

– Endless Tracks Across Centuries

Another important aspect of the Black Horse Patrol marshalling area was that of the feeding schedule for the cattle herd. Early arrival at that bedground on Friday would facilitate feeding and watering of the cattle earlier in the day. This would have the affect of considerably altering the digestive routine of the animals in the herd and greatly reducing the quantity of manure and urine to be contended with during the parade through the Billings streets on the following day. Feeding and watering schedules would then be returned to normal at the final disposition sites of Billings Livestock Sales and Public Auction Yards facilities on Saturday evening.

The composition of the parade through Billings would consist of the entire cattle herd remaining after any unmanageable animals had been removed, together with, as already mentioned, the entire wagon train. Unfortunately the lead herd of Longhorn steers would not be included since it had been deemed necessary to move them into the Metra grounds by truck early Friday morning to facilitate preparation for the Trail's End Auction which was scheduled for midday Saturday in the Metra. The plan had been for the composition of the parade to be adjusted in numbers to fit as well as possible a combination time span window allowable for the parade as recommended by Latigo's engineering consultant firm, HKM Associates.

The drovers' camp chuckwagon and bedwagon contingency would be detached from the parade as it passed the Metra Complex and would be moved into the Metra grounds in preparation for the events involving the chuckwagons there later in the day Saturday. The remaining parade would stay intact to its division point at First Avenue and U.S. 87 East where approximately one-half of the cattle and drovers would split off to the east on U.S. 87 for final disposition at the Billings Livestock Commission Company Sales Yards (BLS) . Wagons, wagon train riders and the remaining half of the herd and its drovers would turn right at First Avenue and proceed into town along First Avenue to its intersection with North 13th Street and Montana Avenue. Turning left at that point this assembly would pass beneath the Montana Rail Link overpass and continue along the whole of Minnesota Avenue to the Public Auction Yards Sales Company (PAYS).

The purpose of pulling the drovers' camp chuckwagons and bedwagons into the Metra Complex was to circle them up and have them prepare a big chuckwagon bill of fare to feed all the drovers, wranglers, volunteers and support crew, along with a reunion of old time cowboys which had been invited to be guests of Latigo and the Trail Drive. Each of the six chuckwagons would take responsibility for preparation of one particular dish (or should it be said, kettle or cauldron-full) for the menu. One would do the meat entrée, one, the spuds, another, the salad, and so on, with the sixth preparing pies, or cobbler. "Radar II" of the LK wagon drew the potato detail. He said, "You never heard such a bunch of fussin' as when I put that whole outfit of old twisters to peelin' spuds – shucks, if I hadn't had a good refill of "potato soup" for them to work on while they were doin' it, we'd never've got those spuds done!" When asked to give out his "potato soup" recipe, Radar would only say, "That's an international trade secret an' it's classified."

With the roll into Billings, the LK chuckwagon was coming very close to completing a long-time roundabout round trip. This old wagon had originally been a roundup wagon in the Powder River country down by Broadus, Montana. In 1926 it had been taken to a ranch between the Bow River range and north to the Red Deer River range in Alberta. It had seen many seasons as a roundup wagon in the years that followed and had even been raced in chuckwagon races prior to the streamlining of those rigs to the modern day version seen today in chuckwagon racing competition so popular in the Canadian prairie provinces. As an ambassador of range country roundup trail days this old wagon and its crew had made a wonderfully authentic and good fun addition to "The Big Drive of '89." The crew was made up of Neil McKinnon, owner, teamster, Ken Greenway, who'd provided part of the 4-horse hitch, Bob Hale, Dick Havens, Frank Gatty, Tom Butterfield, Jim Arthur, and octogenarian, Burt Shepard. Neil McKinnon had said, "We'll come but none of us is a cook so see if you can find us a cook!" That is how Buck Draper came about cooking for the LK wagon until his accident with the horse. Ed "Radar II" Kirby was with Gene Johnson's O/J wagon assigned to Dr. Scott for carrying veterinary supplies, and Ed just sort of got "volunteered" to fill in as cook when Buck got hurt. He did a very good job.

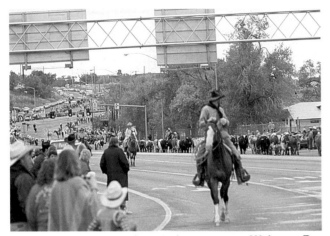

Crowd lined the route from before sunup to Welcome Drive...

Never could find that durn'd ol' burr!

... And they were treated to a Parade of Parades...

Early Ursuline Mission Schools remembered.

...with dress from the past to the work-a-day!

'Buddies', we started together an' we're stickin' together.

Pack trains, as well as wagons, hauled freight.

Oh, this'n was lots bigger when we started!

We had green lights all the way.

By now 'The Big Drive of '89' had already had 'Prime Time'!

The end's in sight!

Returning to considerations for a successful and safe parade through the city streets of Billings it is interesting to note how Latigo planned for their herd containment strategy to work. As was mentioned, the distance between the Black Horse Patrol campsite and the Roundup Road turnoff at Main Street in Billings Heights would be used to exercise the cattle after an extended period of rest the previous day. In addition the rapid pace at which the herd would be moved during the very early hours of Saturday morning would be aimed at both somewhat tiring the cattle, and at getting them prepared to move faster than they had been moved the previous few days. Moreover, the herd would be compacted into a somewhat shorter tighter unit during that period of movement to reduce it from being strung out as far as usual.

Central to the containment strategy was the fact that around the clock manipulation of the cattle by riders on horses would have been now experienced for a period of from some seven to ten days. In that period of time, the cattle remaining in the herd would have learned an extremely healthy respect for horses, mixed with shouting, noisy people, and the loud, sharp cracking sounds emitted by popping lariat ropes, bullwhacker whips and quirts as cowboys slapped their leather chaps. Being then exposed to crowd-lined streets and vehicular traffic should have hopefully little, if any, effect on the manageability of the herd.

It should be pointed out that herds the size contemplated here had been moved on paved surfaces many times in rural areas of Montana. More importantly, these herds were typically moved by drovers numbering less than twenty men or women. To illustrate, a herd of some 3500 head of range cattle had been moved through unfenced residential and business sections of Roundup by six men. This was accomplished without any damage to yards and without significant disruption of traffic. In that case, of course, the herd was stretched out over a fairly lengthy distance and the population/vehicular density was nowhere near what would be contemplated here. However, in this case there would be a great deal more manpower devoted to the effort. Throughout this Cattle Drive, some 125 highly skilled drovers would have been working the herd. As a function of the ordinary, that number represented more than five times what was actually deemed necessary.

For the duration of the parade, the 125 drovers would be increased by at least 75 more cowboys. These cowboys would also be highly experienced people who had been selected to manage the wrangling of all the wagon train horses throughout the Drive. A cadre of at least 200 professional cowboys, then, would form the core of the parade herd management team. That number of hands represented something like ten times the number ordinarily needed to move such a herd. If it would appear from observation of the crowd and vehicle conditions existing along the parade route on Saturday morning that additional manpower would be needed, Latigo would have it readily available. An additional cadre of experienced horsemen drawn from the mounted wagon train riders would be held in reserve at all times to augment the initial 200 cowboys and cowgirls. With the sophisticated communications systems being dedicated to the Trail Drive, this decision and the movement of these augmentees could be quickly accomplished concurrently with the cattle herd's entry into town at Billings Heights. Flexibility in this regard would be maintained because as the number of cowboys increased, the space available for compacting the cattle herd might be reduced and duration required for movement would likely be increased. Moreover, it was Latigo's position that the hazard level might increase with too much of an increase in the number of working cowboys and horses where rapid mounted response to cattle movements might become overly congested.

In summary of Latigo's staging, sequencing, cattle handling, parade composition, parade routing and herd containment strategy, by the time the cattle reached the parade route, they would be well trail broken. They would have been culled to remove any animals which might represent a threat to easy herd management. They would have been sufficiently fatigued to help eliminate, as much as possible, any remaining animal propensity for bolting toward people or vehicles.

Crowd control would be another major concern which Latigo would try to pre-plan in order to, as best possible, head off problems before they might occur. Latigo anticipated large numbers of people to be lining Main Street on the morning of the parade. The greatest danger to spectators might be the spectators themselves, as opposed to danger from the cattle. It would be assumed that people would have a tendency to crowd closer and closer to the curb line of Main Street or maybe onto the street itself. This could reduce the amount of space available for the cattle, and especially the horse-mounted drovers, to maneuver. Opportunity for injury would stem not so likely from cattle/people contact, but more likely from horse/people contact where a drover's trained cow horse might be concentrating on controlling cattle and be oblivious to an innocent bystander. Youngsters, of course, did not possess the stature where a horse could easily see them, especially when a child might dart or move behind a moving working horse.

Paramount then in Latigo's plan would be the creation of an enforceable crowd line. Latigo would intend to address this issue through the creation of a dynamic crowd line which would actually move along with the cattle herd. In concept, riders dispersed in a line along the length of the cattle herd would move along the route some few feet inward from the curb line to move and hold the crowd away. At the lead end of this moving line a vehicle (preferably a marked squad car) would essentially usher people off the street and funnel them back a distance. The rider line would be manned at intervals by previously briefed riders drawn from the wagon train participant pool. Latigo would be prepared to dedicate between 200 and 300 riders for this purpose, depending upon how the cattle were strung out as they trailed into town.

In instances where emergency traffic might have to penetrate the cattle herd, such as the emergency animal ambulance trailer having to load an injured or lame animal, the rider line would be parted momentarily at the affected location or intersection. In addition, mounted riders previously briefed on the procedure would enter the herd on point and the emergency vehicle could follow immediately behind as the cattle separated before the horses.

Latigo appreciated the concern over emergency services access to areas which would be effectively isolated by the parade, particularly east of Main Street. Latigo would be prepared to provide a prepositioned ambulance in that area manned by qualified emergency medical technicians, again drawn from the Cattle Drive participant pool. In addition, Latigo would have either orbiting or stationary helicopter support dedicated to emergency medical service.

Haven't spooked at anything all week – this may be my last chance!

– Endless Tracks Across Centuries

Infinite Patience, Practice and trust

Partners in gracefulness, dexterity and execution with perfection.

204

Two initial response firetrucks were to accompany the wagon train throughout its trek from Roundup to Billings, in case of fire along the trail or out of hand in camp. These vehicles would be available for prepositioning at the trail's end in the district east of Main Street. As previously mentioned, penetration of the cattle herd could be accomplished when necessary. In addition to the cattle herd, the wagon train and riders could be stopped to allow passage of emergency vehicles. Again, a complete communications system would be utilized to communicate these needs to parade leadership and participants.

Fire and emergency medical service to the west end of Main Street could be accommodated in a similar fashion, though this area had existing fire protection facilities and medical services in the form of clinic branches. Latigo would endeavor to augment these services as necessary. As with medical services, Latigo would be prepared to dedicate a helicopter for law enforcement and fire protection emergency use.

The routing of the cattle would involve two rail crossings—one overpass just east of the Lockwood Bridge, and another near the intersection of Montana Avenue and 13th Street. Close coordination with Montana Rail Link officials had already been initiated in anticipation of this project. Scheduling of trains would be closely monitored so as to preclude a threat to the parade animals and spectators from this factor.

With regard to the previously mentioned "worry-cratic" concern for cleanup of the city streets after the parade had passed, Latigo also preplanned for this need. Given the positioning of the cattle herd on the day before the parade and the already explained rationale therefore, undue impact from herd effluent on Main Street and beyond was not anticipated. As a precaution, however, the trucks Latigo employed to haul water to the livestock while they were enroute out on the trail would carry spreader bars which could be used for street flushing purposes.

Finally, Latigo would not intend to engage in, encourage or sponsor vending activities of any sort along the parade route.

This then, was some of the behind-the-scenes effort which Latigo had undertaken in order to have the loose horses in the corrals at BLS by 9:02 a.m., according to

Connie's time calculation, and have the trail herd divided and in the pens at BLS and PAYS about an hour later on parade morning. The feeling which prevailed as the waiting crowd welcomed the wagon train and riders and trail herd, and were greeted back in response as the parade passed by, was overwhelming. People were tired, to be sure, but suspense, anticipation and excitement had sustained them. With the parade over, there was still a great deal going on the rest of the day. The Trail's End Auction would be getting underway inside the Metra. Lead herd coordinator and Chairman, Jim Leachman, and his committee had an exciting offering of western art, cowboy memorabilia and antiques, as well as some of the magnificent lead herd Longhorn steers, ready to go before the auctioneer's hammer. Much of the sale proceeds would be planned to go toward the cattle drive's endowment fund mission.

There were receptions in several big tents on the Metra Complex Grounds, the chuckwagon feed for trail hands and old time cowboy guests would be getting under way and there was music, trick and fancy roping exhibitions and all sorts of entertainment happening during the afternoon. It would be no time until evening when the crowd would gather again at the Metra to see the planned Grand Finale, The Trail's End Concert, sponsored by Anhauser-Busch and featuring Lee Greenwood.

Some general notes of interest are offered here in response to many questions that arose from genuinely curious people who wondered at all that had transpired during the week before this most spectacular of parades had passed by, thrilling them beyond expectations.

There had been right at 3000 cattle on the drive. In round figures, the crowd watched over 3500 horses and a good many mules go by with 200 wooden wheeled, iron tired wagons and more than 3500 riders and wagon support people dressed in every imaginable kind of period clothes, Native American Ceremonial finery, beautifully preserved, and rough and tumble work-a-day garb typical of a century before. A lady from Great Falls even rode in the Habit of the Ursuline Order, which started some of the earliest Mission Schools in frontier Montana. This lady was Dana Ball and she with her husband, John, had worked very hard at the county level to help Cascade County Co-Chairmen, Rick Halmes and Al Eli, coordinate their group for their part in the Yellow Wagon Circle. The Ursuline Sisters in Great Falls had been most happy to help Dana with the authenticity she wished to represent.

Over 1400 volunteers on 67 task oriented committees had been involved to bring this parade to a culmination before the happy Saturday morning crowd. Seventy tons of hay had been fed to the cattle and horses per day (about five semi-trailer loads per day). Water for the animals was hauled over distances of from a mile to about 12 miles, and totaled about 60 tank truck loads, equalling about 200,000 gallons each day. Some 250 stock watering tanks were moved each day along with 150 "porta-potties." The camps generated 80 cubic yards of garbage per day. Around 200 dusty souls per hour welcomed portable showers each evening.

Five to six tons of food were served per day and 14,000 gallons of drinking water were used daily. Between 10,000 and 12,000 cans of beer and about 5,000 cans of pop were served each day.

There were 12 doctors and 60 EMT's and upwards to three dozen veterinarians with the Drive at all times. Communications were enhanced by the use of 140 portable hand-held radios, 30 cellular phones, 5 repeater sites, 6 frequencies, 2 complete command centers, and 3 computer centers. Well over 400 press and media people were in and out of the wagon train and with the main herd at times, including representatives of Soviet Tass. One Montana citizen, Arthur Renander, with the World Trade Center Office in Great Falls, unable to be in Montana for the time of the Cattle Drive because of prior scheduling commitments, reported that the newspaper headlines he saw in hotel lobbies and businesses in Geneva, Switzerland, that week, featured "The Great Montana Centennial Cattle Drive."

In order to divert, delay or re-route traffic and accomplish over-all traffic control, 397 traffic control devices—signs, cone systems, lights, and barricades—were engineered and used at a cost combined for the devices and the engineering of $88,500.

Timing and coordination of the entire event had been a large concern. Latigo Logistics director Kim Kuzara's records showed that from the minute the Cattle Drive and Wagon Train started out of Roundup on Monday morning, September 4, until the last animal was in the stockyards in Billings, on Saturday morning, September 9, they were 50 minutes ahead of planned arrival time at Billings Livestock

Commission Company and they were 35 minutes behind schedule closing the gate after the last animal at Public Auction Yards.

Recognition of key Latigo people responsible for the undertaking and completion of the "Big Drive of '89" has been attempted herein, but logging of this tally record would be remiss if it failed to include additional deserving people who helped to cement the grass roots accomplishments into the reality which made it all happen. Besides other Committee Chairmen already named, it is hoped the reader will bear with our effort to give credit where due, and be forgiving when repetition occurs, or, worse case, when someone deserving of credit may be inadvertently omitted. As the open trail gave way to the final parade into Billings, the hard work and heartfelt dedicated effort of a number of people would come to mind.

Coordinating Chairman over all County Chairmen, Bob Sivertsen, of Hill County, had been one of the hardest working individuals observed on the trail, and for weeks prior to the start of the Drive. He seemed to be just about everywhere. Livestock Feed and Livestock Water, taken for granted by many, didn't just happen to be there. Mike Mullowney and Jim and Bob Sindelar made sure it was there! Dr. David Drill, of Billings, coordinated plans for the establishment of emergency medical services prior to the Drive and provided a daily update of happenings at press briefings all along the Drive. The Communications Committee was co-chaired by Mark Cantor, Rod Hutt and Cory Wolcott. Catering and Concessions Committee Chairman was Bonny Milligan. Solid Waste & Portelettes Committee Chairman was Ziggy Ziegler. Potable Water Committee Chairman was Loren Herlyn. The Drive could not have happened without these people.

Additionally, to make all the facets of the Cattle Drive and ancillary events mesh together, much extra work and coordination was included from already very busy people. Entertainment at various assemblies and at the camps was the responsibility of a committee headed up by Terry Knudsen. Co-Chairmen of a committee to deal with all the details of the Grand Finale, its Parade, Trail's End Auction, Concert and other events, were Denny Eubanks, Terry Knudsen, Jim Scott, Cal Winslow and Jim Leachman. The important Sponsors Committee was a Co-Chaired responsibility of Jim Scott and Gay Holliday. Continuous help and coordination to the press was accorded by the Media Committee, headed up by Cal Winslow, Jeanette Mavity and Mike Murphy. The Family Night Committee was led by Suzi Steffanich, Denny Eubanks, Cal Winslow and Terry Knudsen. Cash Management was the responsibility of a committee headed up by Packy Walker. Participant Transport Committee head was Jim Boyde. Mike Mullowney got off the hay trucks in time each day to make sure power and generators would be working at each night's camp. Parking and Security Committee work was coordinated by Mike Mullowney and Kim Kuzara, and Kim Kuzara, like Bob Sivertsen, seemed to be everywhere at once as Logistics Director and Coordinator of Command Post activities.

County Chairmen, co-chairmen or committee persons had worked for the better part of two years with Latigo to make this the Epic Event people were enjoying today. Without the efforts of each and every one of these people

something would have been missing from this Centennial celebration. County, by county, these people did their part: BEAVERHEAD–Buzz Kirkpatrick, of Wisdom, and Jay Nelson, of Jackson; BIG HORN–John McCleary, of Hardin, and John Small, of Busby; BLAINE–W. Strauser Drugge, of Zurich, and Ralph Snider, of Turner; BROADWATER–Bill Higgins, of Townsend; CARBON–Jack Hash, of Roscoe; CASCADE–Al Eli, of Sun River, Rick Halmes, of Great Falls, John and Dana Ball, of Vaughn, and Dr. Jim Scott, of Great Falls; CARTER–Corky Harkins, of Ekalaka, and Keith Larson, of Ekalaka; CHOUTEAU–Aaron (Duke) Pursley, of Big Sandy, and Frank Mayo, of Geraldine; CUSTER–Bill Damm, of Miles City, and Robert J. Gray, Sr., of Ismay; DANIELS–I.H. Halverson, of Peerless, Bill Tryan, of Flaxville, and Mary Harrington, of Scobey; DAWSON–Don Walker, of Glendive, and Eldon Evans, of Glendive; DEER LODGE & POWELL–Phil Murphy, of Deer Lodge, and Pete

Hey, dress it up you critters – you in the middle, get back in step and close up these flanks – 'er ranks!

– Endless Tracks Across Centuries

Cartwright, of Deer Lodge; FALLON–Leland Gundlach, of Baker; FERGUS–Joe Delaney, of Grass Range, and Marvin French, of Judith Gap; FLATHEAD–Leo Hargrave, of Marion, and Mel Riley, of Marion; GALLATIN–Bill Myers, of Bozeman; GARFIELD–Lester Guptill, of Jordan, and Kenneth Fogle, of Jordan; GLACIER–Cliff Guith, of Cut Bank, and Valerie Wadman, of Cut Bank; GOLDEN VALLEY & MUSSELSHELL–Richard Walker, of Musselshell, Tootsie Bartow, of Roundup, and Dot Youngblood, of Roundup; GRANITE–Paul Greany, of Drummond; HILL–Bob Sivertsen, of Havre, and Melvin Billy, of Box Elder; JEFFERSON & MADISON–LeRoy Fadness, of Boulder; JUDITH BASIN–Dan Holzer, of Stanford; LAKE–Walt and Pat Vermedahl, of Polson; LEWIS & CLARK–Dave Baum, of Helena, and Harold Adams, of Helena.

The additional counties of Montana were represented as follows: LIBERTY–Suni Lou Thompson, of Whitlash, and Fern Wolery, of Joplin; LINCOLN–Robert Boothman, of Libby, and Debbie Doble, of Eureka; McCONE–Bud Braaten, of Wolf Point, and Marvin Doornek, of Wolf Point; MEAGHER–Jamie Doggett, of White Sulphur Springs; MINERAL–Shirley Hollenback, of Superior, and Gordon Hendrick, of Superior; MISSOULA–Ed and Kalli Deschamps, of Missoula; PARK–Cliff Olson, of Wilsall, Edwin Nelson, of Livingston, and Henry Valgamore, of Springdale; PETROLEUM–Dick Delaney, of Grass Range, and Carroll Manuel, of Grass Range; PHILLIPS–Cindy Olsen, of Malta, and Larry Simpson, of Saco; PONDERA–Bob Boucher, of Conrad; POWDER RIVER–Jack (Slug) Mills, of Boyes; PRAIRIE–Bruce Kalfell, of Terry, and Gary Larsen, of Terry; RAVALLI–Wayne Eby, of Victor, and Tom Bryant, of Corvallis; RICHLAND–Jim Steinbeisser, of Sidney, Tim Bouchard, of Sidney, and Robert Traeger, of Brockton; ROOSEVELT–Nick Nichols, of Culbertson, and Lloyd Aspenlieder, of Culbertson; ROSEBUD & TREASURE–Earl Bonine, of Hysham; SANDERS–Jeff Priddy, of Dixon; SHERIDAN–Ron Nelson, of Westby, and Tom Cheetham, of Redstone; SILVER BOW–Linda Rogers, of Butte, and Dan Harrington, of Butte; STILLWATER–Ed Miller, of Absorokee, and Ted Hill, of Columbus; SWEET GRASS–Bill Pruitt, of Big Timber, and Sonny Todd, of Big Timber; TETON–Ray VanDeRiet, of Augusta, and Jack Salmond, of Choteau; TOOLE–Jerry Murray, of Shelby; VALLEY–Bill Blankenship, of Nashua, and Jack McCuin, of Saco; WHEATLAND–Jane Glennie, of Two Dot; WIBAUX–Albert Rojic, of Wibaux, and Robert Petermann,

of Wibaux; and YELLOWSTONE–Jack Asay, of Billings.

The formation of the county efforts had come about following local response to scattered meetings around the state in late 1987 and early 1988. Jim Wempner, Stan Lynde, or Barry McWilliams were speaking to a few groups about the "Cattle Drive" idea. At the Heritage Inn, in Great Falls, early in January, 1988, all three were there. The thought presented was to tie it in with the various Montana Statehood Centennial celebration plans being developed. As with Latigo, the separate county groups which had started up in response to the exuberant proposal had people with great vigor at first, who then lost interest or became involved for a short while, only to find they couldn't commit time to the effort. The local groups went through periods of attrition, readjustment, and priority reconsideration, just as Latigo was. But from the start made, an enthused and cohesive exertion began to take shape.

The trails, finally converging in Roundup, came from every corner of Montana, and some from far outside the state's borders. And, as Connie Cox had experienced when he started his own Longhorns from his Saskatchewan/Montana north fenceline, many of these down to earth individuals and local committees had listened to lots of "naysaying" that "the Cattle Drive will never happen." These folks had left home for the trail head at Roundup with the faith that it was going to happen. It had been the coming together of this grass roots cohesiveness which, as mentioned previously, no one could predict, that was now bringing "The Big Drive of '89" to a focal point the whole world was being made aware of.

One official drover, it had been said, was traveling a different range early in the week the Cattle Drive was getting under way. He had been asked, in effect, by U.K. Prime Minister, Margaret Thatcher, "What in the world are you doing here when you should be in Montana carrying on with the Great Cattle Drive?" This drover, needless to say, got back to his home range to ride with the trail herd! With all the planning and all the work, Latigo officials "knew" the event should come off as expected. However, because of all the changes, major and insidious, in the 100 years since such an effort had been commonplace, and with the ups and downs their own efforts had experienced during the past two years, each and everyone breathed a sigh of relief when that indefinable constituent – the grass roots element – revealed itself. The Drive was over!

– Endless Tracks Across Centuries

EPIC TRAILS—

Sunday, September 10, 1989. 'And on the Seventh Day —

It turned colder and rained a good shower in the night. There's even some snow showing on the high hills around and a little slush on the ground early. It's not quite ready to stick yet but sure feels like Fall for certain this morning. It'll be muddy for people waiting for today or Monday to break camp and get wagons out. It was truly a lucky week for the weather. Some of that ground is pure gumbo for mud.

Went to Billings Livestock to work our cows and sort the rest of them up about 8:00 A.M. Then just spent most of the rest of the day laying around and doing some more visiting. Sale of Drive cattle will be tomorrow at B.L.S. and on Tuesday at P.A.Y.S.

Chapter 31

... REST? ... NO – BETTER SORT THEM UP

The Trail's End had been reached yesterday, and the "Big Drive of '89" was over, but if the Legacy of the Cattle Drive were to be realized, a lot of hard work lay ahead. Some of that work would have to be addressed as early as this morning. The trail herd cattle at BLS and PAYS must be sorted and shaped into sale lots in preparation for Monday and Tuesday's auctions. It might be the Trail's End but a lot of tracks were yet necessary in order to establish a perpetual endowment for the benefit of Montana ranch families and rural Montana Communities, as one of the three stated objectives in the overall mission of the Cattle Drive. It appeared from the enthusiasm of all concerned yesterday, participants and spectators alike, that the other two objectives were being accomplished. There was no question there had been a celebration of Montana's Statehood Centennial through recognition of the State's Western Heritage and commemoration of the 19th Century livestock industry in Montana. The promotion of the modern day beef industry in Montana would be necessarily an ongoing endeavor. However, Montana's livestock industry and the nutritional value of beef in the diet had received excellent attention these past several days through the media/spectator opportunity and participation provided by the Drive, and much of this had been conveyed in a positive manner to the public awareness by the media.

That the Drive and Saturday's Grand Finale Celebration had provided an excellent regional social opportunity for ranch-oriented people, their guests, and a wide array of visitors, local, national and international, had become a wonderful reality. Back to the work at hand, there would be busy moments today as ranch people and Drive participants alike made ready for the coming auction sales. New marketing opportunities might come about as a result of the limelight garnered by the efforts of the Drive. This would remain to be seen and constant work, imagination, enthusiasm, innovation and informed activism would be required to accomplish this portion of the mission. In the meantime these immediate auction sales would be a start toward realization of the Cattle Drive Legacy.

There would also be some sorting up in the last camp of the wagon circles. The camp had been left estab-lished at the Friday night site as an accommodation to anyone needing extra time in packing up to head back home. Latigo's assignment of the color codes for each wagon circle according to region had worked very well. The wagon camp was now beginning to look pretty darn lonesome, but the efficiency with which it had been possible to form up the train, dispatch it onto the trail each day and re-establish a given color coded circle of the same wagons at each night's campsite was still being discussed by some of the out-of-state participants and dignitaries among the "hangers-on." Some of these people had marveled at how they had managed to keep from getting lost, or more appropriately, how Latigo had managed to keep from "losing them" in the vast Montana landscape!

Actually, Latigo's wagon train color code plan served two important purposes. Tack, tents, bedrolls, and tags on horses assigned to a given wagon circle, along with the people who would be riding and camping with that segment of the wagon train, could be readily identified by support personnel, wranglers, wagon captains, and the participants themselves by the assigned color. From that point on, familiarity within the wagon circle unit itself prevailed and a proper sort seemed to usually result. Besides establishing a point of location of wagons from each region in the train itself and giving each rig a designated position at each campsite, the plan had the added purpose of providing a point of orientation for the out-of-area or out-of-state visitors who would participate in the Drive.

As each circle had been formed up, the counties in that region, and for that designated circle or unit within the train, were asked to select their wagon circle captains. These people would take charge under the direction of overall Wagonmaster, Gwen McKittrick, and serve as wagonmaster for their given group of circle-member rigs comprised of some 20 to 30 wagons. In addition to the rigs, each circle wagonmaster would be responsible for keeping track of his group of teamsters, their teams, swampers, outriders, families, and an assigned list of up to 200 or 300 wagon train riders signed up to participate on the Drive. The only thing this circle wagonmaster didn't have to keep track of was the "critter" or critters" of the bovine type which his wagon train riders had consigned to the Drive. Jay Stovall and his drovers would look after that chore! Jay could say to McKittrick, "this herd is 'rainbow' colored but it's not color coded!"

It is appropriate to herein list the respective designated color coded wagon circles, their assigned counties, any additionally assigned out-of-state areas from which riders may have been attached to those circles, and the wagon circle captain or wagonmaster and town of origin for each. As with other Committee Heads in the Latigo organizational plan, the Drive and Wagon Train could not have happened in the fine manner it did without the dedicated work and enthusiasm of these local area people. Besides acknowledging their services to the Cattle Drive and the participants in their respective segments of the Wagon Train, it is hoped this listing will provide a source of reference for future reunion purposes as the participants may wish to look up some "old Rawhider" to re-live some of these memories and experiences.

THE WHITE WAGON CIRCLE:
Yellowstone and Musselshell Counties–Joe Feist, of Ballantine, Montana, Wagonmaster;

THE BLACK WAGON CIRCLE:
Custer, Rosebud, Treasure, and Carbon Counties, plus Wyoming, North Dakota and South Dakota–Donald Cain, of Volberg, Montana, Wagonmaster;

THE RED WAGON CIRCLE:
Fallon, Powder River, and Carter Counties–Jack (Slug) Mills, of Boyes, Montana, Wagonmaster;

THE YELLOW WAGON CIRCLE:
Teton, Cascade, Meagher, Judith Basin, Fergus, Sweet Grass, and Stillwater Counties–Al Eli, of Sun River, Montana, Wagonmaster; additionally, wagon transportation was made available with this circle as an extended courtesy to Media personnel. Walt Johnson, of Raynesford, Montana, and Bill Strobbe, of Cascade, Montana, were with this wagon to help with needs of media personnel;

THE ORANGE WAGON CIRCLE:
Phillips, Valley, Daniels, Sheridan, and Petroleum Counties, plus Texas and Kansas–Cindy Olsen, of Malta, Montana, Wagonmaster (the Drive's only lady Wagonmaster, and a heckuva good hand);

THE PURPLE WAGON CIRCLE:
Roosevelt, and Richland Counties, plus Minnesota, Wisconsin, Illinois, and Pennsylvania–Nick Nichols, of Culbertson, Montana, Wagonmaster;

THE GREEN WAGON CIRCLE:
McCone, Prairie, Dawson, and Garfield Counties, plus Colorado and Nebraska–Don Walker, of Glendive, Montana, Wagonmaster;

THE BROWN WAGON CIRCLE:
Liberty, Hill, Chouteau, and Blaine Counties, plus Canada–John Hebbleman, Jr., of Chinook, Montana, Wagonmaster;

THE BLUE WAGON CIRCLE:
Lincoln, Flathead, Sanders, Lake, Glacier, and Lewis and Clark Counties–Leo Hargrave, of Marion, Montana, Wagonmaster, and Darryl Cozad, of Kalispell, Montana, Co-Wagonmaster;

THE PINK WAGON CIRCLE:
Granite, Ravalli, Beaverhead, Madison, Park, Missoula, and Gallatin Counties–Wayne Brewer, of Bozeman, Montana, Wagonmaster.

Head Wrangler Lynne Taylor's hand-selected cadre of cowboys, especially picked to handle all aspects of wrangling the 3,500 head of horses with the Wagon Train, had a very busy and varied schedule throughout the Drive. A chuckwagon and bedwagon contingency was assigned directly to the wranglers, to hopefully be able to keep up with this hectic schedule, and keep wranglers' bodies and souls at least somewhat together with grub, coffee and a bedroll ready if those hands could find time to find it.

The wranglers did not have to handle all these horses, but they dealt with a very large percentage of them in the course of the week on the trail. Many of the teamsters kept their teams at their wagons when in camp. These horses would be led to water and then fed by the wagon and tied at the wagon wheels to rest. A good many saddle horses were picketed on long lines secured at both ends to buried "deadman" anchor chains and supported at a uniform height with standards spaced evenly along the picket-line. Many horses could be safely tied and fed along these picket-lines after being led to water.

Jack Gist of Hill County is credited with the particular picket-line design approved for use on this occasion and it is a good one. Jack was with the Brown Wagon Circle and personally helped anyone interested with the picket-lines.

It was the preference of many people to let their horses range loose when not in use so these horses were loose herded in a remuda or cavvy at night. The wranglers kept watch in turns, moved these horses out from camp, gathered them up again in the early mornings, corralled groups at a time in old-time rope corrals, and roped individual mounts, which were then led out to where a waiting rider could halter the animal and lead it to where his saddle and tack were waiting. If the rider was a novice, a wrangler usually took the extra time and care to help with saddling, and seeing that everything was in order for this rider to be off safely on the day's ride.

With all this, there were times, usually between about 2:30 a.m. and 3:15 a.m. some mornings, when some of these wrangler cowboys actually got to complaining "there's jist not a durn thing to do!" Some said these times were when "Ol' Taylor'd see to it a bunch of loose horses would git away, or git mixed 'th some've Stovall's bunch jist to cut down on th' gripin' 'bout all th' spare time!"

George Miller, of Columbus, Montana, headed up the chuckwagon contingency for Lynne Taylor's Wranglers and Support Staff.

The Billings Gazette Wagons with Terry Weaver and Staff were handled by Glen, Jim, and Susan Sorenson and Ted Nelson, Roxanne Haughey, and Carl Anderson.

Leachman's Lead Herd had their own wagon contingency for Jim Leachman's Drovers and Support Staff, including the beautiful shiny bright red and brass lamped Concord stagecoach for V.I.P. and dignitary accommodation which had been the subject of a bit of excitement referred to on the third day, trailing between Roundup and Billings.

The Staging Area Support Staff, Headed up by Jack McGuinness, of Billings Livestock Commission Co., and also on the Drover Committee, had been very busy getting animals processed into the Roundup trailhead readying them for the Drive. Now they would be again quite involved in the sort-up, preparing sale lots of the trail herd cattle for tomorrow and Tuesday's auctions. In addition to McGuinness, the Staging Area Support Staff Crew consisted of the following hands: Mark Bertolino, of Billings; Gary Davis, of Shepherd; Jim Oja, of Billings; Brian Okragly, of Billings; Jack Hedrick, of Billings; Bart Meged, of Roundup; Dan Catlin, of Billings; Jim Barringer, of Billings; Burton Farley, of Huntley; Greg Halvorson, of Billings; Tom Drennen, of Billings; Jeff Halvorson, of Billings; Lori Trafford, of Ballantine; and Tim Trafford, of Ballantine.

These people were just some of the many behind-the-scenes volunteers whose coordinated efforts helped make the "Big Drive of '89" pleasurable for everyone.

One other group which had a great deal to do with "sorting them up" all week long and which was able to sort themselves out and begin to disband, following the Parade and Grand Finale yesterday, included Dr. David Drill's Emergency Medical Services force. Some 12 of these doctors had been on hand at all times throughout the Drive, many of them traveling with wagons and a number of them riding horseback from Roundup to Billings. Along with five dozen qualified EMT's these doctors maintained regular clinic shifts in a medical field services tent at each camp, accompanied field and helicopter ambulances, rendered emergency medical stabilization right on the trail and dispatched cases needing additional care to area hospitals and clinics.

The volunteer doctors with the Drive were, besides Dr. Drill: Chris F. Dennis, M.D., of Billings; Isabelle T. Dennis, M.D., of Billings; R. Byron, M.D., of Crow Agency; L. Byron, M.D., of Crow Agency; Ron Peterson, M.D., of Great Falls; Debbie Drovdal, M.D., of Great Falls; Jeff Stone, M.D., of Red Lodge; Amy Hachigian, M.D., of Great Falls; Sheri Rolf, M.D., of Billings; James R. Scott, M.D., of Billings; David Earl, M.D., of Bozeman; Fred Deigert, M.D., of Billings; Jack Halseth, M.D., of Great Falls; Donald R. Huard, M.D., of Billings; Norman Silverman, M.D., of Lewistown; David Anderson, M.D., of Great Falls; Robert N. Hurd, M.D., of Billings; and Gladys Young, M.D., of Malmstrom Air Force Base, Great Falls.

When the "sort-up" is completed, all the volunteers of the "Big Drive of '89" belong in the "Top-Cut!"

Appreciating the simple things in life.

Skiff of snow – time to think about fall roundup and shipping work.

He'll remember his first spurs.

EPIC TRAILS—

MONDAY, SEPTEMBER 11, 1989. THIRTY-TWO DAYS —

WENT TO B. L. S. AT 8:00 A.M. TO BE THERE WHEN THEY START AUCTION. WATCHED SEVERAL LOTS SELL INCLUDING SOME OF OURS. MOSTLY PRETTY GLAD WE AUCTIONED THE ONES WE DID A WEEK AGO SATURDAY IN ROUNDUP. VISITED A FEW BRIEF MOMENTS WITH DR. SCOTT ABOUT THE PHOTOGRAPHS WE WILL BE LOOKING FOR FROM CAL SORENSON AND ABOUT MEETING AT THE RANCH IN NEXT FEW WEEKS TO REVIEW JOURNAL AND PHOTOGRAPHS. HE IS LEAVING TO DRIVE TO SEATTLE AND HOPES TO BRING HIS WIFE AND DAUGHTER HOME FOR THE FIRST TIME SINCE DAPHNE WAS INJURED LAST SPRING IN A LIGHT PLANE CRASH.

AFTER WATCHING CATTLE SELL I DROVE OUT TO PARK CITY WITH BOB ANDERSON TO LOOK AT CHAROLAIS CROSS CALVES WEANED OFF OUR LONGHORN COWS BEFORE WE STARTED DOWN THIS LONG TRAIL. WE'D HAULED THE CALVES TO FEEDLOT AT PARK CITY WHERE WARD FENTON HAS BEEN TAKING CARE OF THEM. CALVES ARE DOING GOOD AND ARE THRIFTY AND IN TIP-TOP HEALTH. THE LONGHORN - CHAROLAIS CROSSBRED HAS WORKED WELL FROM OUR FRENCHMAN CREEK BREAKS JUST AS OUR BLACK AND RED BALDIES HAVE.

CAME BACK INTO BILLINGS AND MET MY BROTHER-IN-LAW BOB SIVERTSEN AND HIS FRIEND JUDY. BOB IS 52 YEARS OLD TODAY SO WE WENT OUT TO THE SPUR FOR HIS BIRTHDAY DINNER. HE DID A GREAT JOB OF COORDINATING ALL THE COUNTY CHAIRMEN FROM ACROSS MONTANA TO MAKE THE BIG DRIVE COME TOGETHER

ENDLESS TRACKS ACROSS CENTURIES

EPIC TRAILS—

THE WAY IT DID. MOST FOLKS THINK THE TRAIL FROM ROUNDUP INTO BILLINGS WAS THE 60 MILES LIKE THE MAP SHOWS OR AS THEY SAY 'THE CROW FLIES'. BOB KNOWS IT WAS A LOT FARTHER. HE COVERED A LOT OF EXTRA MILES EACH DAY TROUBLESHOOTIN' ONE BOLLIX OR ANOTHER BEFORE THEY GOT TO BE MAJOR MIX-UPS OR BIG PROBLEMS. IT WAS THIS KIND OF EFFORT THAT THE GRASSROOTS PEOPLE OF LATIGO PUT FORTH WHICH MADE IT ALL WORK. I EXPECT ON A GIVEN DAY ANY TIME LAST WEEK BOB AND HIS HORSE WOULD COVER 40 OR 50 MILES WHILE MOST OF THE DRIVE WOULD BE DOIN' 8 OR 10 OF TRAILIN' MILES.

—ENDLESS TRACKS ACROSS CENTURIES

A story of Montana ranching and cowboy life in itself.

216

God knew there was going to be a Great Cattle Drive as He made the weather perfect for 34 days.

217

Chapter 32

IF IT WORKS – DON'T FIX IT!

"If it works – don't fix it!" is a favorite "Connieism" people visiting with the man may hear repeated. Connie says he does not know where the phrase may have originated, but he credits our good friend and neighbor, Sherm Ewing, with using the brief expression when discussing the proposal of The Planned Cattle Breeding program, developed by BEEFBOOSTER™ Cattle, Ltd., of Alberta and Montana, with Connie a number of years back. Connie was interested in possibly using the strains of genetically proven seedstock which BEEFBOOSTER™ had been years in developing to improve the beef production efficiency of his own herd. A concern he had expressed to Sherm Ewing was, "What do I do with my present cow herd, which is now accustomed to these breaks and sparse, rugged conditions under which they have to earn their living, and mine and my family's?" Deep down, Connie knew there had to be ways to make more progress than it seemed at times he was, but he was worried that he might lose a lot of ground if he had to "start from scratch and educate a whole new bunch of cows to this harsh range."

"If it works – don't fix it!" was Sherm's response to the concerns Connie raised. Sherm had continued in answer to additional questions Connie had posed, and that visit, like so many other things Connie had pondered over this past month on the trail, was reflecting through Connie's mind as he watched the sale lots going through the BLS auction ring. He thought to himself "all a rancher has is the little bit of grass he can grow, and he'll use those cows which he'd worked so hard to get started in this tough old piece of country to try and make that grass into something he could utilize." The market place would tell the story.

Some discussion of the BEEFBOOSTER™ Genetic Improvement Strategy is in order here. The purpose of beef production is to raise cattle to convert grasses or other forages into high quality protein for human consumption. Production can be increased in three ways.

First, the land base used to grow grass and forage can be expanded; thus more cattle can be raised.

Second, Husbandry practices can be improved to make the most of the land and cattle available.

Third, the genetic ability of cattle to reproduce and grow and furnish a food staple of high nutrient density can be enhanced. Healthful and delicious beef that is genetically trimmed is the result.

The first option is becoming less and less feasible. The continued growth of human population increases urban sprawl, recreational needs, and demand for other agricultural products, minerals and energy. These requirements limit the area of land that can be used for beef production. The second option will be under-utilized because a high percentage of beef cattle are produced by secondary or part-time enterprises. Increased productivity is not essential in such operations, but it is a must for one such as Connie's.

Thus, the third option, to increase beef production and productivity through genetic improvement, is the most promising, especially for commercial operations for whom efficiency is vital. Very little extra cost is incurred by going this route.

BEEFBOOSTER'S™ main pursuit is with this third option, Genetic Improvement Strategy.

In the early 1950s, certain ranchers in the foothills of Southern Alberta abandoned the traditional pedigree system of cattle breeding and began to use scientific methods to improve their cattle. By the early 1960s, there was a sharing of mutual ideas and concerns by a number of these individual cattlemen. They were beginning to retain the assistance of various technical advisors, such as Dr. Roy Berg, geneticist; Dr. Jim Scott, a veterinarian with special tracking interests versed in beef cattle reproductive efficiency and breeding soundness, in later years to become defined as the science of Theriogenology; Dr. Bill Garrett, nutritionist; and others.

In 1970, BEEFBOOSTER™ Cattle, Ltd., was incorporated by four of these innovative and progressive Alberta cattlemen to utilize the genetic potential in cattle by coordinating their individual ranch management operations and cattle breeding programs in a controlled and systematic manner of planning. Three of these cattlemen were from the foothills area west of Calgary, near Cochrane. They were Marshall Copithorne, of CL Ranches, Neil Harvie, of Glenbow Ranching, and John Stewart-Smith, of Horse Creek Ranching. The fourth was Tom Gilchrist, of Deer Creek Ranching, in the Sweet Grass Hills area near Milk River, Alberta.

A review of the scientific literature showed them that the most effective strategy for genetic improvement must:

— Exploit Heterosis (hybrid vigor) in the cow via crossbreeding, to improve reproductive traits which are of low heritability;

— Utilize Selection to improve traits with higher heritability, such as, rate of gain, feed efficiency and carcass merit;

— Accelerate the Process by "synthesizing" specific seedstock strains.

Further, an examination of the fundamental crossbreeding systems revealed that a minimum of five strains are needed to implement these systems. No one type or strain of animal would be all things to all requirements. The criteria for each strain would be based upon fundamental functional efficiency with economic merit as a basis.

The strains required are:

— Four maternal strains to provide the basis for crossbred cows. Two of these strains each have another function as well.

— One terminal strain to mate to these crossbred cows.

The group thus incorporated set about setting standards for the synthetic strain development of their seedstock. BEEFBOOSTER™ seedstock is produced by licensed breeders according to criteria determined by the BEEFBOOSTER™ Seedstock Committee, aided by distinguished Technical Advisors. These are the guidelines and specifications for BEEFBOOSTER™ Seedstock Production:

ALL STRAINS —

A live calf is the essence of beef production, so fertility and calving ease are vital. Thus BEEFBOOSTER™ Seedstock must be born unassisted, females must calve every year, and the breeding period is limited to 50 days. These three prerequisites are met by all five BEEFBOOSTER™ Strains.

MATERNAL STRAINS, (M_1 & M_2) —

Their function is to produce cows that will raise a large calf every year with the least amount of winter feeding. Weaning weight is the chief measurement used for selection in these strains.

HEIFER STRAIN, (M_3) —

The role of this strain is to produce sires suitable for mating to yearling heifers of any breed or crossbred combination, so that their first calves are born with minimal difficulties. Hence the aim is to produce lightweight calves at birth in this strain. Thereafter, yearling weight is used for selection.

ALL-PURPOSE STRAIN, (M_4) —

As the name implies, this strain must perform well in all traits. It has been designated for crossbreeding systems where the use of the more specialized terminal or heifer strains is inappropriate, yet another strain is required to sustain hybrid vigor. Yearling weight was chosen as the best single measurement to use for selection of this strain because it combines both maternal and terminal characteristics.

TERMINAL STRAIN, (T_x)—

The purpose of these cattle is to produce sires that when mated to crossbred cows will result in progeny that excel in rate and efficiency of growth and yield a desirable carcass. The prime measure for these terminal cattle is the rate of growth of lean meat after weaning.

GENERAL POLICY —

Home-raised BEEFBOOSTER™ bulls provide the principal bull-power for improving the strains. Nevertheless, BEEFBOOSTER™ has an ongoing policy of never completely closing any of its strains. Artificial insemination can be used from any bull of any breed which can intensify the traits sought in a given strain, but henceforth any 'traditional breed' will not be introduced into more than one of the BEEFBOOSTER™ Strains. Thus each for seedstock purposes will be kept genetically separated so retaining the potential for hybrid vigor when used for commercial crossbreeding.

Multiple sire breeding is used in all seedstock herds to put indirect pressure on the "mating ability" of the bulls.

An explanation of how the BEEFBOOSTER™

Montana – Land of Challenge, Grandeur, Contrast and Inspired Reflections As Events and Highlights of 'The Great Montana Centennial Cattle Drive of 1989' Pass Through The Mind.

Genetic Improvement Program is implemented is in order here.

Performance and progeny testing are indispensable components of a genetic improvement program. BEEFBOOSTER™ has facilities for performance testing several hundred bull calves from each of the strains. In addition, a commercial crossbred herd representative of the F_1 females produced from BEEFBOOSTER™ Maternal Strain bulls is maintained. These cows are used to progeny test terminal sires. The performance of the resultant progeny is recorded from "breeding to the rail and cutting room" and is analyzed.

The progeny test serves another important purpose. It monitors the whole BEEFBOOSTER™ program. The progeny test herd is fully performance-recorded, which enables the overall progress of the project to be assessed. This herd is the epitome of the crossbred commercial herds in the BEEFBOOSTER™ Genetic Improvement Program.

Electronic data processing is an integral part of seedstock production. It enables the breeder to identify the superior individuals in his herd faster and more accurately. BEEFBOOSTER™ has developed a comprehensive computerized system for storing and analyzing data as an aid to selection and to measure progress.

Increasing the efficiency of beef production by genetic manipulation of cattle populations is a slow process. It takes 2-4 years before the first calves are ready to evaluate for desirable lean meat quality. It takes 6-8 years to change the genetic makeup of a cow herd, speaking of those 1,000 or 2,000 days which has been discussed elsewhere in this book. And it takes 12-15 years for the effects of selection to become significant. Still, selective cattle breeding is worthwhile, and although genetic improvement in beef cattle is slow, it is permanent, cumulative from year to year, and transmitted to future generations.

What are some of the advantages and benefits which may be seen?

The specific strains of cattle bred by BEEF-BOOSTER™ are performing well for the originator ranching operations. The initial core group of Founding BEEF-BOOSTER™ ranchers had now grown to a group of well over two dozen. As a result, since 1979 increasing numbers

of seedstock have been sold to other commercial beef producers throughout Canada. BEEFBOOSTER™ Montana was started in 1981 or 1982, and a number of commercial Montana ranches are using the bull power from the expanding seedstock base available.

Commercial cattlemen participating in the BEEF-BOOSTER™ Planned Breeding Program get many benefits and advantages.

First and foremost, they have a definitive breeding plan which has been custom designed by BEEFBOOSTER™ Field Staff and Advisors to match their given resources and particular operations.

Second, the commercial rancher is guaranteed a supply of functionally efficient seedstock with which to carry out his breeding plans. The BEEFBOOSTER™ Seedstock is priced to reflect the improvement that can be made in a commercial cow herd, as well as being related to the current market value of feeder calves. And, lastly, participating beef producers have access to the knowledge and experience of the associated ranches, BEEFBOOSTER™ Field Services and Technical Advisory Group, and to BEEFBOOSTER's™ computerized data processing and economic analysis capabilities.

This then is an overview of a master plan for modern cattle breeding which can be designed to fit your operation. It is a prototype which will be replicated to produce beef more efficiently in other places besides Alberta and Montana. In countries with a temperate climate, existing BEEFBOOSTER™ seedstock strains can be infused and transplanted into local herds. In countries with a tropical climate, new strains can be designed and developed using indigenous cattle as a foundation, and using the application of the BEEFBOOSTER™ Planned Breeding Program.

Furthermore, this prototype gains added significance in that it can be effectively adapted to other ruminant species such as sheep and goats. Naturally the "gene pools" will differ but the organizational structure, the techniques, and the procedures developed by BEEFBOOSTER™ are nevertheless applicable.

The role of livestock in food production is being questioned because animals sometimes consume feed grains which could otherwise be consumed directly by humans. Yet is must be emphasized that feed grains are only a small element of the total feed consumed in the beef production chain. Unlike poultry and hogs, the main element for beef production is grass or other forage. And it is, of course, grass which anchors and indeed nourishes man's most basic resource; the soil. Moreover, being ruminants, beef cattle utilize many other materials which are not digestible by simple-stomached animals, including man himself.

We foresee that cattle will continue to garner forage from tillable and non-tillable lands, thereby providing such essential products to man as high quality protein, leather, and a natural source of bio-chemicals. In addition, cattle form a highly flexible food reserve for the world's population. In order to compete viably with other meat-producing species and with vegetable proteins, the beef industry must utilize the genetic potential of cattle fully. The future development and extent of beef production will depend on the rate and efficiency with which cattle can be made to reproduce and grow. BEEFBOOSTER ™ is leading the way towards meeting this challenge. "If it works – don't fix it," seemed to fit much of what was going through Connie's mind.

Chairman of the Montana Statehood Centennial Commission, Lieutenant Governor Allen Kolstad of Montana, dedicates the Lyle Johnson sculpture as the official monument of "The Great Montana Centennial Cattle Drive of 1989."

– Endless Tracks Across Centuries

EPIC TRAILS—

TUESDAY, SEPTEMBER 12, 1989. 'THIRTY-THREE DAYS' —

NOT GETTING AROUND TOO FAST TODAY. TOOK CARE OF 'BLUE' FIRST THING. HE'S PICKING UP, LOOKS GOOD AND FIT. LOOKS LIKE HE'S READY FOR ANOTHER 300 MILES BUT NOT SURE I AM. AT 9:25 A.M. I WENT TO THE 'HAIR STATION' RUN BY JOYCE RINGWELSKI. HAD HAIRCUT AND FIRST SHAVE SINCE START ON DRIVE. LOOK 20 YEARS YOUNGER AND FEEL 20 YEARS OLDER THAN I DID 33 DAYS AGO.

WENT TO PUBLIC AUCTION YARDS TO WATCH DRIVE CATTLE SELL. APPEARS THE 'BIG DRIVE OF '89' WILL NOT ONLY BE ACTUAL PHYSICAL SUCCESS IN THE 'DOING' OF IT, BUT SHOULD ALSO REALIZE THE GOAL SET OF CONTRIBUTING A CENTENNIAL REMEMBRANCE TO THE RURAL ENDOWMENT FUND OF THE MONTANA COMMUNITY FOUNDATION.

AFTER SEEING CATTLE SELL AT P.A.Y.S., I TOOK BOB ANDERSON TO HIS MOTEL AND DECIDED TO CALL IT A DAY.

—ENDLESS TRACKS ACROSS CENTURIES

If it works – don't fix it!

Chapter 33

HIGHLIGHTS

Monday had been quite a day. Connie thought to himself it was a good thing Sivertsen's birthday only came once a year. They'd had a good visit and Connie felt a bit as if he'd put the whole 300 miles on the trail under his belt all over again while celebrating Bob's birthday last night. Thinking again of his meditations of yesterday and his reconsideration of that advice Sherm Ewing had given him those years back, he decided there was one thing for sure that "wasn't working" this morning. He had kept running his hand over the stubble on his jaw and suddenly realized he wasn't merely running his hand over it. He could run his fingers through it! It was definitely time to go do something about "fixing" that situation.

That was only the half of it. Seems like Blue was looking sort of oddly at him now since the old horse had had a couple days of "R" and "R" and the reaction wasn't unlike the one he'd registered last week when they saw the bear. If Blue was going to go acting snorty with only this short a rest, Connie figured he'd better shine up a bit. One thing for certain he couldn't afford the way he felt this morning to have Blue begin thinking himself some darn old bronc. Why, at this stage, some of what was just "creakin'" would prob'ly start cracklin'" and Connie'd had just about all the time off the boss would tolerate. Wait a minute, he was the boss – guess that's why he was so cognizant of the limits allowable! Well, there was one way to "fix" the problem Blue had of having trouble recognizing him. Connie headed for Joyce Ringwelski's "Hair Station" to get his hair cut and the much needed shave.

The wind-down from the Drive wasn't letting loose of lots of people. A couple of the participants had been overheard discussing the matter of getting back to the "real world" and one had been quoted to say, "I really hate to see this come to an end. Wouldn't it be great if we could just do this full time and make a livin' doin' it?"

No doubt about it; there were many highlights from this adventure and they ranged from some of the simpler things like the steaming hot towel that it'd taken to soften up a month's growth of beard, or like heating up a can of soup over a noon camp fire, to the realization as he sat in at the cattle sale now at PAYS, that the Drive might well have the hoped for Legacy for rural Montana off to the desired start.

Among the highlights was the inclusion today of the dedication ceremony for the Lyle Johnson sculpture cast in heroic dimension bronze. Lieutenant Governor Allen Kolstad, who has served as Chairman of the Montana Statehood Centennial Commission, officiated at the dedication of this permanent Monument to the Cattle Drive. The sculpture of Longhorn steers bearing the $^M_{89}$ Cattle Drive Brand being pursued by an 1880s Commemorative Cowboy is being located in front of the Billings Chamber of Commerce offices, and will be viewed by many for years to come as they enter Billings along their travels off Interstate 90. Lieutenant Governor Kolstad and the Centennial Commission people in Helena had been a great help with many details in bringing the Cattle Drive to a successful realization.

Another highlight which Connie knew many people shared with him, participants and spectators alike, including viewers from a distance, of the television coverage, and of the newspaper accounts, was the electrifying feeling experienced as the Drovers and Wranglers had done their work throughout the Drive. These people were truly professionals and to have been able to see, especially, first hand, all their activity as they handled the cattle and horses, was unforgettable. Moreover to have been chosen as an official Drover or Wrangler by one's home county or by Jay Stovall or Lynne Taylor, was an experience that would illuminate many memories for the balance of lifetimes. Their participation and service to the Drive and its Legacy is no less deserving of recording and preservation for the knowledge and benefit of future generations than has been the accounting of the efforts of all the other Latigo and grass roots people who shared in accomplishing this endeavor. To have had the good fortune to ride along for a spell and visit with one of the seasoned old timers or to exchange aspirations with a very capable younger hand was the pinnacle of the highest level for many.

The times at night around the camp fires and the chuckwagons just listening to stories or singing some of the old ballads would evoke poignant remembrances no matter what walk of life the person so privileged would return to. It was no wonder people didn't want the adventure to end. Any number of people would gladly have turned vagabond by the

– Endless Tracks Across Centuries

end of the trek. They had experienced free spirited cowboy life and it suited them. It had been a chance for those who sometimes felt they were born 100 years too late to put a dash of yesteryear fascination into their lives and at the same time to be a part of a moment in history. The Cattle Drive Drovers and Horse Wranglers are listed here partly because they deserve the recognition, but as much because somewhere down the trail ahead that spellbound feeling so many people experienced one way or another, whether as a Drive participant or spectator, will return and perhaps a ready reference as to Who, Where or What might be welcome.

Following is first a listing of the Official Drovers for the Great Montana Centennial Cattle Drive, and then a listing of the Horse Wranglers. If there is on occasion a name duplicated or a crossover between Drover and Wrangler names it is most likely due to an occasional need for crossover or interchange of duties between the Main Trail Herd and the Wagon Train.

TALLY OF OFFICIAL DROVERS
Drover's name, town and county are listed:

JAY STOVALL–Trail Boss, Billings, Yellowstone;
BILL BROWN–Segundo (Assistant Trail Boss), Sand Springs, Garfield;
SAM REDDING–Segundo, Hardin, Big Horn;
TOM BONKO–Main Herd Head Horse Wrangler, Garryowen, Big Horn;
JUANITA STOVALL–Trail Herd Secretary, Billings, Yellowstone;
BUZZ KIRKPATRICK–Wisdom, Beaverhead;
JOHN SMALL–Busby, Big Horn;
CHARLIE SECREST–Hardin, Big Horn;
HANK ESP–Hardin, Big Horn;
HALE JEFFERS–Lodge Grass, Big Horn;
TORREY JOHNSON–Busby, Big Horn;
RICHARD REAL BIRD–Garryowen, Big Horn;
GEORGE REED–c/o Little Horn Ranch, Wyola, Big Horn;
DAVID STEVENS–Lodge Grass, Big Horn;
ORRAL BLOCK–Lloyd, Blaine;
BOB MASALO–Townsend, Broadwater;
JIM DeSAVEAU–Roberts, Carbon;
BILL STOVALL–Red Lodge, Carbon;
MIKE O'SHEA–Red Lodge, Carbon;
BILLY GREENOUGH–Fromberg, Carbon;
BUD MORTAG–Cascade, Cascade;
JIM WILSON–Ridge, Carter;
ROCKY J. HIGHFILL–Geraldine, Chouteau;
PAT PHALEN–Ismay, Custer;
BOB NUNN–Miles City, Custer;
WESLEY TIBBETS–Miles City, Custer;
I.H. HALVORSON–Peerless, Daniels;
ROBERT KINNEY–Glendive, Dawson;
LEE JACOBSON–Glendive, Dawson;
C.L. ASKINS–Baker, Fallon;
HANK OLSON–Grass Range, Fergus;
MARCUS MATOVICH–Lewistown, Fergus;
LEO HARGRAVE–Marion, Flathead;
ARTHUR (BUD) SANDQUIST–Belgrade, Gallatin;
GEORGE T. WILSON–Brusett, Garfield;
HUGH MONROE–Browning, Glacier;

FRED HARPSTEAD–Lavina, Golden Valley;
DOUG MARTIN–Hall, Granite;
MELVIN BILLY–Havre, Hill;
ORVILLE WORTMAN–Boulder, Jefferson;
LANNIE PROCTER–Stanford, Judith Basin;
WALT VEREDAHL–Polson, Lake;
HAROLD ADAMS–Helena, Lewis & Clark;
SUNI LOU THOMPSON–Whitlash, Liberty;
ROBERT BOOTHMAN–Libby, Lincoln;
JIM SITZ–Harrison, Madison;
BRUCE WRIGHT–Wolf Point, McCone;
JIM LIND–White Sulpher Springs, Meagher;
ALAN BROCKWAY–Superior, Mineral;
DAVE HEIBERGER–Lolo, Missoula;
FRANK HOLLIDAY–Roundup, Musselshell;
ALFRED ADOLPH–Roundup, Musselshell;
DICK WALKER–Musselshell, Musselshell;
DON TOMLIN–Roundup, Musselshell;
GEORGE GRIENSMAN–Roundup, Musselshell;
JIM SARRAZIN–Clyde Park, Park;
CARROL MANUEL–Winnett, Petroleum;
PHIL MATOVICH–Mosby, Petroleum;
RICK OLSON–Malta, Phillips;
BETTY STEELE–Malta, Phillips;
CHARLIE SCHWENKE–Zortman, Phillips;
BOB BOUCHAN–Conrad, Pondera;
CHARLES PATTEN–Broadus, Powder River;
DOUG TAMCKE–Deer Lodge, Powell;
HAROLD COLE–Terry, Prairie;
MARK BOONE–Darby, Ravalli;
AL FRANZEN–Sidney, Richland;
RANDY WOLFF–Culbertson, Roosevelt;
MERLE BALLARD–Forsyth, Rosebud;
ED PRIDDY–Dixon, Sanders;
RON NELSON–Westby, Sheridan;
DAN HARRINGTON–Butte, Silver Bow;
ED MILLER–Absarokee, Stillwater;
CAROLYN FRASIER–Reedpoint, Stillwater;
SAM SMEDING–Reedpoint, Stillwater;
TED HILL–Columbus, Stillwater;
DAVE LEITHEOD–McCleod, Sweet Grass;
BRUCE LEE–Choteau, Teton;
JERRY MURRAY–Shelby, Toole;
WAYNE KUHL–Hysham, Treasure;
LESLIE Best–Bighorn, Treasure;
JOE FOX–Hysham, Treasure;
DON NELSON–Glasgow, Valley;
BILL BLANKENSHIP–Nashua, Valley;
JANE GLENNIE–Two Dot, Wheatland;
STANTON BRANNIN–Two Dot, Wheatland;
CURT CALE–Wibaux,Wibaux;
DICK WELDON–Billings, Yellowstone;
SCORP KORBER–Billings; Yellowstone
EARL ROSELL–Billings, Yellowstone;
JACK KUKOWSKI–Billings, Yellowstone;
DALE CAMP–Billings, Yellowstone;
HARRY CROFT–Billings, Yellowstone;
GENE MESSER–Billings, Yellowstone;
TYLER STOVALL–Billings, Yellowstone;
TURK STOVALL–Billings, Yellowstone;
MANNY STOVALL–Billings, Yellowstone;
ADRIAN WILSON–Shepherd, Yellowstone;
BURTON FARLEY–Huntley, Yellowstone;
J.B. FARLEY–Billings, Yellowstone;
ERNIE VERMANDEL–Pompeys Pillar, Yellowstone;
PETE HINSON–Billings, Yellowstone;

The list of Cattle Drovers continues:
JACK McGUINNESS–Billings, Yellowstone;
BOBBY KRAMER–Billings, Yellowstone;
STEVE CHARTER–Shepherd, Yellowstone;
SHORTY ROBINSON–Custer, Yellowstone;
JIM BODE SCOTT–Shepherd, Yellowstone;
BEV HALL–Billings, Yellowstone;
JIM TETERS–Huntley, Yellowstone;
CARLA CAMP–Billings, Yellowstone;
DWIGHT McKAY–Billings, Yellowstone;
CONRAD BURNS–Billings, Yellowstone;
MAX BAUCUS–Billings, Yellowstone.

The Main Herd Drovers' Camp had six chuckwagons and six bedwagons trailing with the main herd. These chuckwagons served a combined total of nearly 550 meals per day. Each wagon had an average of about 30 Drovers each taking three meals per day. Some Drovers developed a favorite cook or settled on the menu preparation of a certain cook so these averages tended to vary. There were also a fluctuating number of press and media people traveling with the Main Herd plus a veterinary contingency and the intermittent visits of dignitaries, and V.I.P.'s. At a given meal, one chuckwagon cook might get 60 or 70 people to feed at his stove.

The following wagons trailed with the Main Herd:

PADLOCK RANCH CHUCKWAGON–Dan Scott, Teamster, with a crew of Gill and Jack Harris, Jack Walls and Tom Mattingly;

GERALD RAAUM CHUCKWAGON–Gerald Raaum, Teamster, with a crew of Chris Schatz, Terry Traeger, Merle Olson, Swen Hauge, Terril Raaum, Loren Schledewitz, and Lois Raaum;

BOB TRAEGER CHUCKWAGON–Bob Traeger, Teamster, with a crew of Ron and Tracy Hauso, Ron Schmierer, Fred Eberly, Don Labor, Larrie Smith and Patsy Quillico;

ROLAND HEBEL CHUCKWAGON–Roland Hebel, Teamster, with a crew of Erma Evans, Tracey Pool, Kathy Teters, and Sherry Farley;

CLAUDE SAYLOR CHUCKWAGON–Claude Saylor, Teamster, with a crew of Nathan Saylor, Lester Guptil, Calvin Thomas, Edwin Clark, Dave Roderick, and Jack McCuin;

LK RANCH CHUCKWAGON–Neil McKinnon and Ken Greenway, Teamsters, with a crew of Bob Hale, Tom Butterfield, Dick Havens, Frank Gatty, Jim Arthur, Burt

Shepard and Dr. Buck Draper. This crew consisted, as mentioned elsewhere, of all Albertans with the exception of Dr. Draper, who is from Washington State.

In addition to the Chuckwagons traveling with the Main Herd each crew also manned an accompanying bedwagon with their chuckwagon. Because of the large number of Drovers it was necessary to haul part of the bedrolls for this large crew in a separate support vehicle consisting of a pickup and gooseneck trailer. This was one concession made to the modern day drive as opposed to a drive of 100 years ago. But then the drive of a century ago had a crew usually of 10 to 20 men for a herd of corresponding size to this one headed up by Trail Boss Jay Stovall. The wagon crews would get ready to break camp and would load as many bedrolls as possible in the bedwagons. The extra bedrolls were stacked neatly and the support vehicle crew would unobtrusively pick their load up as the wagons were pulling away from each previous camp and just as unobtrusively deposit the load of extra bedrolls at the next camp in a pre-designated location before the Main herd and the Drovers' Chuckwagons pulled into the next camp.

In addition to the Chuckwagons and bedwagons, two other wagons traveled with the Main Herd. One was a Press Wagon. The other was assigned to Dr. Jim Scott's veterinary services group for carrying veterinary supplies on the trail.

MAIN HERD PRESS WAGON–Hugh Cummings, Teamster, with a Press Crew of R.D. Lewis, Buford Madsen, Alice Madsen, Cindy Strecker and John Games;

MAIN HERD VETERINARY SERVICES SUPPLY WAGON–O.E. (Gene) Johnson, Teamster, with a Veterinary Assistant Crew of Ed (Radar II) Kirby, Don Boyer, Lou Udall and Dwight LeMay. With exception of Don Boyer, who was from Mount Vernon, Oregon, this crew was all from the Great Falls, Sand Coulee area of Montana. The flexibility of this crew made it possible to "volunteer" Ed Kirby's talents as a roundup cook to Neil McKinnon's Chuckwagon when Dr. Draper was injured by the horse rolling over backwards on him the first morning out of Roundup. They also were able to carry part of the bedrolls.

Dr. Brent Thompson, Veterinarian from

Roundup, rode as Veterinarian in Charge full time with the Main Herd as it trailed from Roundup to Billings and led a pack horse so that he had supplies with him at a moments notice if he were any distance from the Veterinary Services Supply Wagon. Dr. Thompson was able to be in position to continuously monitor the cattle in the herd and put lame or otherwise stressed animals off the trail so they could be picked up by the support vehicle trailer making rounds during each day's trailing. This worked very well and kept the herd in tip-top trailing condition.

Following is a tally of the Official Horse Wranglers which traveled with the Wagon Train along with the home locality of each. All but two were Montanans. One was from Wyoming and one from Wisconsin.

TALLY OF OFFICIAL WRANGLERS

LYNNE TAYLOR–Head Wrangler, Shepherd, Montana;
DARYL NEWMAN–Ingomar;
DONALD JOHN CAMERON–Ingomar;
ROD BROSZ–Shepherd;
DALE FELDMAN–Wibaux;
CHARLES HAHNKAMP–Dillon;
ROD LEE–Miles City;
SPUD CREMER–Big Timber;
GARY CROWDER–Billings;
MARION TAYLOR–Shepherd
WAYNE EDWARDS–Joliet;
ED GREBE–Melstone;
JASON GREBE–Melstone;
AUBREY SMITH–Hardin;
JOHN BENSON–Melstone;
WALLY NEWMAN–Ingomar;
ALBERT NEWMAN–Ingomar;
MORRIS WARE–Ingomar;
MAY WARE–Ingomar;
JUSTIN HAWKS–Ingomar;
TOBY HAWKS–Ingomar;
RAY (Rainbow) HILLMAN–Roundup;
TOM HOPE–Bighorn;
J.T.HOPE–Bighorn;
JERRY JACK–Helena;
JACK LAURIE–Miles City;
DOUG MOTHERSHEAD–Big Timber;
MARVIN LEY–Glendive;
PAT HOWEY–Bridger;
SAM McDOWELL–Bridger;
JUNE REDDING–Hardin;
STEVE TAYLOR–Jordan;
ROD VENN–Miles City;
MIKE PIERSON–Jordan;
BUD NELSON–Jordan;
TERRY BUCKINGHAM–Miles City;
JIM STEVENSON–Dillon;
MATT WOODS–Dillon;
GLEN HUTCHINSON–Glendive;
SAM SELMAN–Glendive;
CASPER SHAFER–Miles City;
EARL BONINE–Hysham;
BOB HAUGLAND–Belgrade;
RAY HAUGLAND–Belgrade;
TERRY KNUTH–Ismay;
JOHN MOORE–Miles City;
VERN TAYLOR–Miles City;
PUG JORGENSON–Lewistown;
CRAIG TAYLOR–Miles City;
DAN HARRINGTON–Butte;
KEITH NORBY–Fairview;
MARGE MESSER–Billings;
RES KLUTE–Musselshell;
DON SPANG–Colestrip;
C.T. RIPLEY–Billings;
SONNY LINGER–Miles City;
BRIAN O. KRAGLY–Billings;
MARY HELEN SONGER–Wyola;
ROWDY BURNS–Melstone;
BUSTER JOHNSON–Shepherd;
GEORGE SMITH–Hardin;
TIM SMITH–Lodge Grass;
MATT YELLOWISER–Lodge Grass;
TRACY GROW–Glendive;
KELLY GROW–Glendiive;
PETE HARMES–Big Timber;
SHANE TAYLOR–Miles City;
PAT SANFORD–Bridger;
CLEVE REDDING–Hardin;
JACK BLANKENSHIP–Hardin;
GEORGE MILLER–Absarokee;
JO ANN GEE–Stanford;
ANNA LEA REDDING–Bighorn;
ROGER ST. CLAIR–Birney;
AUDREY STEVENSON–Brusett;
KARI BURNS–Melstone;
JOY FORTIER–Laramie, Wyoming;
HERB NAPIER–Saco;
LINDA SMITH–Billings;
PAM BENSON–Melstone;
BILLY BOB BENSON–Melstone;
J.B. BENSON–Melstone;
ALICE CAMERON–Ingomar;
SWEDE UPHAUS–Glasgow;
CHERYL REESE–Havre;
CINDY OLSON–Malta;
DICK WALKER–Musselshell;
BRIAN WALKER–Musselshell;
DENNIS STORK–Fort Atkinson, Wisonsin;
PAT PERRY–Billings;
CHUCK PERRY–Billings;
CONNIE COX–Whitewater;
JEFF STRAW–Shepherd.

To try picking out one highlight from another put Connie to thinking that in all reality he would be hard pressed to make such a sort. He'd "sleep on that one for a bit," he commented to himself after he had taken Bob Anderson to his motel. The cattle were sold and in all truthfulness he guessed the real highlights of the trek numbered just about 33! Each day had been its own adventure and he was plain too tuckered out to make a choice right now. Tomorrow would be another day.

Homeward Bound.

229

EPIC TRAILS—

WEDNESDAY, SEPTEMBER 13, 1989. 'THIRTY-FOUR DAYS —

MET WALT COLLINS AT 8:00 A.M. AT P.A.Y.S. TO STRAIGHTEN UP ON COWS, THEN HEAD FOR BILLINGS LIVESTOCK TO PICK 'BLUE' UP. IT IS NOW 9:20 A.M. AND I AM HEADED NORTH FOR HOME FOR THE FIRST TIME IN 34 DAYS. I DO HAVE MIXED EMOTIONS AS I DRIVE NORTH ON HIGHWAY 87. GLAD I'M GOING HOME AND SORRY IT IS ALL OVER.

I KNOW IT WILL NEVER HAPPEN JUST THIS WAY AGAIN, ESPECIALLY THIS BIG OR IN THE MANNER IT CAME ABOUT. SOME OF THE GREAT PEOPLE I MET AND VISITED WITH I'LL LIKELY NOT EVER SEE AGAIN. OTHERS, I KNOW I WILL. I FEEL 'SPECIALLY SORRY FOR THE PEOPLE ON 'SKID ROW' WHO COULDN'T HAVE A PART OF THIS. PARTICULARLY IF THEY MIGHT HAVE AT ONE TIME KNOWN THE FREEDOM OF RIDING A SNAPPIN' GOOD HORSE UP TOP 'A RIDGE AND FEELING THE BREEZE IN THEIR FACE AND SEEING FAR AS THEIR EYES COULD TELL. OR IF MAYBE THEIR ANCESTORS KNEW THESE PLAINS AND RIVERS WHEN BUFFALO SEEMED TO PROVIDE FOR MOST ALL NEEDS AND TRUE OR NOT, OTHER CARES WERE FEW.

WITH THE END OF THIS EXPERIENCE, I WANT TO THANK LARRY SIMPSON WITH HIS WAGON AND GOOD GRAY TEAM, 'KING' AND 'MAGGIE'. IT'D BEEN A LOT TOUGHER TIME MAKING THIS DRIVE WITHOUT LARRY. THANKS, TOO, TO THE MANY OTHERS, ANDY AND ALL, WHO TRAILED WITH US, HOWEVER FAR OR BRIEFLY. I ESPECIALLY WANT TO THANK MY FAMILY. THEY NEVER TRIED TO

ENDLESS TRACKS ACROSS CENTURIES

DISCOURAGE ME. THEY WERE THERE WHEN I NEEDED THEM AND DIDN'T COME AROUND WHEN I DIDN'T NEED THEM.

THERE ARE FOUR THINGS THAT STAND OUT TO AMAZE ME ON THIS TRIP.

ONE, THE FRIENDLINESS OF THE PEOPLE. THEY WILL HELP YOU ANYWAY THEY CAN. SECOND, THE WIDE OPEN SPACES OF OUR BEAUTIFUL COUNTRY WHERE YOU COULD GO FOR MILES AND NOT SEE A BUILDING OR ANOTHER PERSON. THIRD, GOD KNEW THERE WAS GOING TO BE A GREAT CATTLE DRIVE, AS HE MADE THE WEATHER PERFECT FOR 34 DAYS. FOURTH, AND LAST, BUT NOT LEAST, HOW SO MANY PEOPLE...NOT USED TO RIDING HORSEBACK, WENT THE LAST FULL 6 DAYS... I TAKE MY HAT OFF TO THEM!

I HOPE YOU ENJOY SHARING THIS EXPERIENCE AS MUCH AS I HAVE IN TRYING TO NOTE IT AND RELATE IT.

Connie Cox

ENDLESS TRACKS ACROSS CENTURIES

"EPIC TRAILS –
ENDLESS TRACKS
ACROSS CENTURIES –

From those etched
in the prairies and
hillsides and along
river banks from
aeons past to
those that go
fleeting beyond
far horizons."

Chapter 34

TURNING BLUE HOMEWARD BOUND

As Connie led Blue from the pen at BLS to his trailer he couldn't help but sense an eagerness in the old horse's step and his eye as he saw the familiar open trailer door and waiting rig. People who thought animals were "dumb" in the perception that they were "brutish" or didn't know anything were just plain "low rent" in the district where they wore their hat, as far as Connie was concerned. They just didn't know much about "nothing" he figured. Blue had been very pleasant to him last night when he'd gone to feed him and to check on his water. Connie didn't know whether it was the haircut and shave. Even giving the old pony all the credit he could for good common "horse sense" Connie doubted Blue could tell the difference between English Leather®, or Mennen Skin Bracer®, or one of his own favorite essences, the smell of fresh soaped saddle leather, for that matter.

Whatever it was, Blue seemed to have forgiven him and he was glad he wasn't getting the same reproachful look of yesterday morning. Blue didn't change or break his lead as they approached the rear of the trailer. He just stepped in as Connie tossed the halter shank over his withers and gave him a gentle slap on the hip. Blue looked around as if to say, "Well, close the end-gate and let's go home!"

Connie thought about his reflections yesterday on all the highlights of the Cattle Drive and of the entire past month; what was this, the 34th day? The look Blue had given him as he had tucked his head to peer back from the narrow trailer stall, and his own feelings inside as he double-checked to make sure the trailer end-gate was secure and safely fastened so there'd be absolutely no danger of it accidentally opening, all mixed together in a dimming swirl. He knew he was eager to see home and to get at all the things he had planned for the Fall work. It was obvious Blue knew they were headed homeward, but there was a bit of sadness, too, that this adventure and all the undertaking it had required now had to be put to rest. A rush of many emotions passed over Connie. He shivered for an instant as he swung the pickup north. He could feel a tug, as if by a magnet, when he topped the first rise north of Billings and could see the blue horizon marking the distant expanse that lay ahead.

Though it was morning so he couldn't see the stars Connie leaned forward over the steering wheel to look up into the sky as if drawn by that feeling inside him just now. He could imagine the position of the North Star and even envision the Dippers around it, and the Dragon his Indian friends claimed stood in between the "Big Bear" and "The Little Bear." Connie wished he could remember the Dragon's name? He guessed he'd seen the "Dipper" constellations in every possible position, like spokes of a giant ghost-like wagon wheel rotating in the heavens between dusk and dawn the many different nights on the trail. He knew there was a Force out there but at this daylight moment it seemed to be a mix of the celestial bodies, the galaxies he knew he was feeling but now could not see, and the mythical, and most specifically, a feeling of the spiritual graces of faith, hope and charity which were deemed to draw souls to the Theological.

All these emotions flooded by in a flash. The only thing Connie actually saw when he looked up into the big morning sky brought him back to the reality of the moment and of the times. The contrails of a high flying jet caught his eye and he thought, "What a contrast – one instant, concerned with the mystical and century old scenes of the memory, and the next – a jerk back to now, or through it. This was a fleeting glimpse of something suggesting an extension or separation of time and the possibility of passage beyond the horizon and even into infinity." Better keep his eyes on the road. That moment had been "quite a trip," from ancient trails under starlit nights that had been worn into the land between the Rio Grande and the Red Deer, to fan-tailing across the heavens and space on wings which modern thinking would have you believe might not have any limits!

Concentrating on the road ahead and looking off to the left, trying to see if he could notice any scarring of the landscape from the Big Drive, Connie really came back to the actual fact of the moment. Steve Charter, whose range they'd crossed last week and camped on for two nights, was a student of a practice now being called holistic range management; "HRM," for short, and the Charter Ranch grasslands were some of the best Connie thought he'd seen. Connie wished some of the environmentalists lurking in the canyons of tall buildings on metropolitan avenues would have been with them on the trail these entire past several weeks

– Endless Tracks Across Centuries

Thanks, too, to the many others who trailed with us – however far . . .

and could see the serenity of this land as he was seeing it this morning. There would be a lot less time for some of the negative obtuse thinking and unintelligent acts which some of these "movements" could seem to dream or conjure up. There would be less of the torpid contrivances they ballyhooed to the often all too gullible consumer with titles and slogans which seemed to make a lot of trashy headlines.

He wondered if some of these do-gooders had actually ever done an honest day's work, or got a blister on their lily-white hands from digging a post-hole, let alone any real calluses from truly laboring to provide for themselves or their family. That would be assuming they had family. More, it appeared, rather than having been conceived and family reared, seemed to have been, "stump hatched and sunbaked" as to both origin and the lame brained effect resultant mentality displayed. He felt sure many hadn't a clue where real replenishable resources came from or what it

really took to assure they would be replenishable. Many apparently didn't know about or chose to ignore the fact that it took a very complex pipeline starting with the producer to keep their supermarket shelves supplied! A cattle drive or wagon train surely could be a ripe seminar ground for giving a bit of insight to minds that at present appeared impenetrable and incapable of being pierced with the slightest bit of common sense. It could be a real "vision quest!"

Brought back, thus, to the moment, Connie's thoughts turned to one little side jaunt he'd made downtown, off the main drag, as he'd taken a swing by St. Vincent Hospital to visit Buck and Tyler. The guys were doing as well and as comfortably as modern medical care and nursing could make them and both were beginning to mend. When it came to "cowboying-up" and getting a job done these men seemed to epitomize to Connie what true western capability really was. He was relieved that both

– Endless Tracks Across Centuries

235

When the work's all done this fall...

... It'll be wintertime.

236

. . . . or how briefly. It was all the people and the shared experiences that will be memories to look back on for years to come.

would be up and going, albeit with some "hitches in their getalong" as soon as they could harass their doctors and nurses into knowing their own lives would return to normal faster, the quicker these cowboys were out of the hospital! Connie had then gone by that other part of town along "skid row," where the rescue mission was and it made him sad to think how some of those folks would have responded to the stimulation of his adventures over the past month. Maybe there could be a way to do these things which were running through his mind right now. It seemed possibly this "Legacy" that could result from the Cattle Drive efforts would work best if a way might be found to combine the lasting effects of a perpetual endowment with the ongoing energies that grass roots involvement could envision and innovate.

Now he and Blue were headed back north toward home together. Larry Simpson and Bruce, Andy, Amos and Red Knudson, and all the others who'd trailed with them were much on Connie's mind. What a wonderful time they had all had together. They were all going their separate ways

now, and Connie hoped each and everyone realized how much he appreciated their various efforts to have made the Drive happen. It must have been tough back 100 years ago when those cowboys parted company with their trail partners after months trailing northward. Some had stayed on to make Montana into the ranching country he now knew. Others had ridden to what few railheads had existed then, such as Butte, and had ridden the train back South to get ready to bring another herd North up the trail. Some had had to part with their trusted and beloved horse or string of horses because the boss had sold the mounts along with the herd to help stock these ranches and provide working cowponies for the hands that stayed behind. But they'd gone back and they'd "cowboyed-up" and started a new string of green horses, from which they'd claim another "favorite best cowpony that ever cut the track of a cow," or "onliest horse to trust my life with, swimming the North Platte or Missouri," And "cowboy-up" was what he and all the rest of Montana would need to do when they got back home now and started trying to put this all in perspective!

– Endless Tracks Across Centuries

A BEEFBOOSTER™
M₁ Seedstock
Mother and Calf

When the production of the M₁ Maternal Family is crossed in a planned commercial crossbreeding program with the production of the M₂ Maternal Family; and has an infusion of . . . . >

A BEEFBOOSTER™
M₂ Seedstock
Mother and Calf

A BEEFBOOSTER™ M₃ Seedstock Mother and Son whose main objective in life is helping first calf heifers deliver their first calf with a minimum of difficulty.

> . . . . .*The additional hybrid vigor available from either or both of these two specialized Maternal Seedstock Strains, the result produces an exceptionally ideal . . . . >*

A BEEFBOOSTER™ M₄ Seedstock Mother and Son which when crossed commercially with production of the M₁ and M₂ Strains results in a highly complimentary triad.

A group of
BEEFBOOSTER
T_x Seedstock
Beef Sires

> . . . . F_1 type functional Commercial Broodcow whose main characteristics are maternal ability and hybrid vigor. Cow herds with this breeding are fertile, hardy and productive. They are the backbone of the commercial herds using BEEFBOOSTER™ Bulls in their planned cross breeding systems. When F_1 type Maternal Females are mated to T_x Seedstock Sires a highly productive beef market animal is the resulting offspring.

A typical
BEEFBOOSTER™
F_1 type Broodcow
with her T_x Sired
Beef Calf.

240

EPILOGUE
ENDLESS TRACKS – Home Fires, Happy Trails and Bright Horizons

As Connie drove homeward a lot of things were going through his mind. It was interesting to look again at the vast landscape as he retraced the general route over which they had trailed the past month. Via the highway, the trek was a bit shorter than the meandering path of the cattle trail. Connie reflected upon landmarks he knew he had seen many times over the years he had driven between the ranch on Frenchman Creek and Billings, but he was filled with wonder at how much more detailed things appeared after the time he had had to really see what he was looking at from the perspective of the saddle. He had known the wide open spaces were there but he knew he had a much greater appreciation of the beauty of this great land by having made the effort to trail the Longhorns. It would be wonderful to be able to share a portion of the distant vistas it had been his opportunity to really survey with an entirely new regard.

The friendliness of the people was another thing he would hold in his memory. He had never questioned the openness and hospitable reputation of his Montana neighbors before, but the time on the trail had sharpened his awareness of those wonderful qualities. He wondered if he would ever be able to show his gratitude for all the helpful ways and kindnesses everyone had shown. He was especially thankful he had the family he did. They had been so supportive in every way and there is no way he could have undertaken the trek without all their help at home and at all the needed intervals along the way. All the people whose ranches he'd obtained permission to trail across had entered into the spirit of the adventure as his trail crew had and this had combined for an experience of a kind that would go a long way toward improving understanding the world over if only it could be shared. These Montanans, like the weather which had been bestowed upon them during the entire drive, Connie felt, were an example of a generosity which could only come from a much Higher Order than man.

As Connie wended his way down the narrow ridge and switchbacks into the ranch he thought of the span of time the Cattle Drive had commemorated and he knew he'd miss those old Longhorn cows. But he was happy that it had been possible to have them show their mettle as a part of this occasion. This thought brought his attention to the remaining cow herd here on Frenchman Creek. He was anxious to see how they were looking, particularly after seeing how well the Charolais cross calves off of the Longhorn mamas were doing at Ward Fenton's lot along the Yellowstone. Another six weeks or so and it would be time to wean the calves from the main bunch and get ready to ship. After that visit with Sherm Ewing of a few years ago, Connie was using some BEEFBOOSTER™ M_4 bulls with his black and black baldie cows, along with continuing with some Charolais bulls and trying some Brangus. It was going to be interesting to dig into this matter of genetics improvement some more as he looked forward to comparing the various offspring of these crosses. Here, the past month's adventure on the Cattle Drive made him pause as he made a mental note of some time frame comparisons.

He was placing a different perspective on the time it took to make serious tracks in this cow business. While it was a one step at a time world, Connie couldn't help but wonder what the nature of progress in this beef cattle ranching business would be in the next 100 years. The varied interests in the genetics of the Longhorn breed was just one case in point. How was it that a gene pool which had been in the Americas since, he guessed, sometime in the 16th Century, was still mostly being sampled on a trial and error basis? A look at the 100 years which had just been commemorated maybe provided part of the answer. It was going on 40 years, nearly half a century, that the people who had begun the BEEFBOOSTER™ Genetics Improvement program had started seriously thinking about working together for some answers. To be sure, purebred cattle breed organizations had been around a lot longer than that, but it was pretty hard to get any two cowmen even working in the same breed of cattle to agree on details of what they were looking for from that breed. It kept a commercial producer, such as himself, plenty confused.

Whether he went into it as a full time program for his ranch yet or not, it was refreshing to know that a group of ranchers with similar economic concerns to his were willing to sit down with him and outline a common sense proposal, which took into consideration the unique conditions these rough breaks required him and his herd to adapt to. He really liked the looks of the BEEFBOOSTER™ cattle he'd seen and if the offspring of the M_4 bulls he was using proved to work well into his ranch program, he would be more than interested in pursuing a more in-depth involvement. He liked the fact that BEEFBOOSTER™ offered a commercial cattle operation such as his a complete genetic improvement service; from assistance in breeding plan design to advice on marketing options. Coupled with this, they provide a reliable source of "performance selected" seedstock from 5 distinct strains of efficient beef producing cattle.

He'd checked into the details further before going ahead with the M_4 bulls as the optional starting point of a program for the cow herd he was developing. This included learning about and comparing the genetics available from the 5 different strains. This is what he learned in addition to Sherm's earlier admonition of, "if it works – don't fix it."

The main functional characteristic of the M_1 strain is maternal ability, hence cow herds with this breeding will raise big calves and be easy to winter. Using BEEFBOOSTER™ Planned Crossbreeding Program, the M_1 is an integral part of the cow herds that are developed. The primary functional attribute of the M_2 strain is also maternal competence, the same requirement as for the M_1.

The prime objective measurement for both the M_1 and M_2 strains is weaning weight, the best indicator of cow productivity. All M_1 and M_2 sires are from superior dams and are heavy calves when weaned. These strains impart milking ability to "F_1" type hybrid cows in commercial herds. The M_1 and M_2 cows have great mothering instinct and they will protect their babies. Once weaned from these good mamas, potential M_1 and M_2 breeding bulls are performance tested on a low energy ration in mid-winter to test their susceptibility to cold. Only those that perform well under this regime qualify to be herd sires. This results in much less costly winter maintenance in herds which have M_1 and M_2 offspring. Replacement females sired by these bulls have adaptability. Selected under range conditions, M_1 and M_2 seedstock are foragers and "fit" the commercial environment under which they must perform.

The genetic base of M_1 seedstock is predominantly Angus with an infusion of North Devon and Welsh Black. Salers and Tarentaise have been sampled in this strain. All contribute to solid pigmentation as well as enhancing maternal traits. It remains to be seen whether these two latter breeds will surface with a positive effect in the established M_1 genetic make-up.

The M_2 is predominantly Hereford, dating back to one of the oldest and earliest performance selected herds in the industry. This strain has an infusion of Simmental and Brown Swiss in its genetic compositon. This assigned genetic make-up offers good maternal qualities and darker pigment which helps reduce the incidence of cancer eye and sunburnt udders.

The M_3 seedstock strain has a genetic base which started from a variety of small cows which had no record of calving difficulty. Breeds assigned to this original make-up of the M_3 include the Red Poll, Jersey, Longhorn and Shorthorn. The main purpose of the M_3 strain is to produce sires whose progeny have light birth weights and are born easily. Heifers bred to M_3 sires experience little calving difficulty as two year olds. Since the aim of the M_3 is to produce light weight calves at birth, the prime objective measurement is a limited birth weight, following which M_3 bull prospects which meet the low birth weight requirement are selected for yearling performance. The extra growth which results produces a respectable market animal, allowing some compromise for the advantage of freedom from serious calving difficulty.

Cattle of the M_4 seedstock strain combine maternal ability with growth. The male calves with highest weaning weights are placed on performance test. The prime objective measurement for the M_4 strain is the 365 day weight, which is a measure of many economically desirable traits. The M_4 used as a third cross with crossbreds of M_1 and M_2 background, provides an excellent contribution to the F_1 type brood cow in commercial herds. Started from Hereford, Red Angus, Beefmaster base, the M_4 strain has a primarily Limousin background with a strong infusion of Gelbvieh. They are cattle with a predominantly solid red-brown pigmentation, though some are brockle-faced. The South Devon breed is assigned also to the M_4 but has not been sufficiently sampled to have contributed any significant data to the strain.

The T_x strain of BEEFBOOSTER™ seedstock has as the prime objective measurement, the rate of growth of lean beef after weaning. This transforms into economical gains with excellent feed conversion and more efficient beef production for cattle feeders. Performance tested for weight gain in a commercial feedlot environment on high energy, the T_x must grow fast and not fatten too quickly while keeping on growing. The main function of the T_x strain is to produce sires that when mated to F_1 type maternal brood cows will produce progeny which also excel in rate and efficiency of gain and yield a desirable carcass. Started from a predominantly Charolais base, the T_x has an infusion of other large framed, well muscled breeds, specifically Chianina, Holstein and Maine Anjou.

In the performance testing of all strains, home ranch performance is necessary to get weaned bull calves to the BEEFBOOSTER™ Central Test Station. Detailed results of test are provided to commercial bull buyer clients. All bulls are thoroughly evaluated for breeding soundness by qualified veterinarians. All BEEF-BOOSTER™ seedstock are continually screened for structural soundness. This includes good feet and legs in all cattle and selection for good udder and teat conformation in females of all strains. The strains are selected and managed for disposition. Only bulls which meet rigid standards throughout the selection process are classified as 'BEEFBOOSTER™ Bulls" and offered for sale as breeding prospects.

BEEFBOOSTER™'s Progeny Test Criteria require a herd of crossbred females which are obtained from various clients using BEEFBOOSTER™ bulls. Thus, these brood cows are a representative sample of the type of crossbred cows that are in production in commercial herds. The F_1 yearling heifers are bred to M_3 bulls to calve as two year olds. Thereafter, they are bred to T_x bulls for the rest of their life-time in the herd. Single sire mating is used in the progeny test herd and several T_x bulls are progeny tested annually, breeding each to a randomly selected group of 25-30 head of F_1 type cows. Full performance records are kept on all progeny from birth to end product. All animals are individually identified so that carcass appraisal data may be obtained.

Analysis of all the recorded data enables an evaluation to be made of all the bulls and cows, as well as, their progeny. Thus it is possible to monitor all aspects of the BEEFBOOSTER™ program to see how well it is serving the needs of commercial beef ranchers, beef processors and consumers.

Measuring the performance and progress of the seedstock herds alone is not enough. The superiority striven for of the seedstock has to be translated into efficient commercial production and then be appraised for the economic merit resulting to the commercial producer. BEEFBOOSTER™ is unique in this respect.

As Connie pulled into the yard at home, the shadows were getting long on this mid-September evening and he was glad to be back. He pulled down by the barn and unloaded Blue. As Blue backed carefully out of the trailer he exhaled a great big sigh, stood and just looked around for a long moment, then shook himself so vigorously he nearly lost his balance. Connie had to step aside to keep from losing his own equilibrium. It had been a long drive home today and he felt glad to be standing on his own ground again, and knew Blue was happy about it too, the way he had looked around. The old pony sort of nickered as Connie turned him loose through the gate. It seemed he was almost chuckling inwardly to himself as he continued this little almost inaudible half-whinny-nickering sound and picked a dusty spot to have a good roll.

Connie had to laugh a little himself at the sight of this almost ritualistic series of antics Blue was going through. There was no doubt he was aware he was home and glad of it. Yep, this was one day at a time country. One of the things cowboy life teaches is that life can be lived simply – a day at a time – get through the moment; tomorrow will not be here 'til tomorrow! It made Connie think of the Night Watch Prayer he'd heard a few nights ago. As he ambled toward the house, the first "star" of the evening twinkled over the western horizon and the breaks were hanging on to the last vestige of deep purple shadows before darkness claimed the landscape below the far ridges. He automatically glanced up to the flag and beyond to see if any sign of the North Star shone yet, but it was still too light. Oh, well, it was surely still there, but he'd be sound asleep in his own bed tonight before it was fully dark. There's no place like home!

A NIGHT WATCH PRAYER

Oh, Lord, the range is ever changing–
                And time moves fast along,
Yet our Night Watch steadfastly keeps,
                This rose and sage scented eve–
As it has kept in fiery storm or lonesome quiet,
                Wherever hope and faith are strong.
Give us, please, bright stars to light our trail–
                Long as we believe.

Our Night Watch responsibility is this snuffy herd,
                Of beef–hide–hooves and horn;
And our Prayer to You–our Maker–
                Great 'Rep' over yonder Divide,
Is for a song to sing to this restless sea of critters–
                A calm on the evening breezes borne.
And that You'll count us in Your Circle of Grace–
                Wherever we may ride.

May our reward for this lonely solitude–
                Find all hands richly blessed,
With gifts that mean the most–Free Spirit–
                Kindness–love–laughter and a smile.
May the dawn that on the 'morrow breaks,
                Be every bit our very best;
Full of blue sky Glory and the quest for hapiness,
                After we keep this Night Watch the while.
Amen.

–Endless Tracks Across Centuries

Drawn constantly by the beckoning of Polaris as it beckons ever toward the North.

Connie had considered at length regarding endless tracks. A century ago Montana had been a net importer of beef by virtue of the great numbers of cattle which had trailed into the territory. Today, with a sparse number of people and the productivity of the cow-calf business in the state, it could essentially be said Montana is a net exporter of its cattle production. Likewise, it is basically a net exporter of a majority of the rest of its agricultural production. Hay was probably the notable exception, although some years considerable tonnage of hay was also shipped out of state. With the extended periods of drought experienced at different times, Connie surmised there might be years when Montana was a big hay customer for neighboring places like Alberta, Saskatchewan, Idaho, Nebraska, or even longer hauls. He knew, too, that there were years when it worked the other way.

The main difference in the tracks was that the mode of movement of cattle to market and out of state now was almost exclusively by truck, taking the place of the trail drives of 100 years ago. Interesting enough, it seemed to him that major shifts in trends related to the marketing of cattle had followed the changes in styles of wheels you could load them onto after the first method of mass shipment had followed the trail herds into town on endless tracks of iron. Places like Dodge City, Abilene, Denver, Cheyenne, and Kansas City had grown into major market areas and some like Denver, Chicago, Omaha, Kansas City and Dallas-Fort Worth had become great central markets with many big Commission Companies and Packing Operations.

Shipment by rail was then the way for a number of decades, and many a cowboy off the Montana ranges got his first taste of life and excitement under the Big City Lights, when the boss had him stash his cowpony and tack at the livery barn in Miles Town, Havre, Glasgow, or Augusta, and accompany a train-load of big three and four year old steers to Chicago or Omaha or Sioux City. The hand from the PN, the Antler, the Matador, Soap Creek, N Bar or E–Y had swapped his chaps, slicker, dusty old black neck scarf of the trail, and saddle, temporarily for a "high necked" shirt and some more colorful dry goods in the way of neckerchief and vest, and had taken his first jolting ride in a railway caboose.

He had in his pocket the "draw" the boss had given him for expenses, and he walked tall as he was "in charge" to see that the cattle were properly delivered. He should have taken the slicker with him, because it rained the entire time he was in the "Windy City" and he couldn't remember a norther sweeping down out of the Bears Paw Mountains much colder than that blamed wind off Lake Michigan. But, "Windy City?" Shucks he'd like 'em to spend some time around Great Falls, Shelby or Livingston, if they wanted to know 'bout wind!

When done with the cattle delivery, the payment having been wired to his boss's bank, he spent a few dollars on a gewgaw or two for his little sisters and brother. He bought a new hat, some good gloves, a harmonica for himself, and a lacy shawl to send to his mother and a meerschaum pipe for his dad. The rest of his "draw" went to "do th' town!" And he was stone broke as he headed back for the train station.

He'd walked right into a lamp-post once while gawking at something back down the other side of the street. It'd caused him to spill all his "makin's" as he was just working on a "roll yer own," and he got a black eye from smacking into the post. Anyway, that's what he told the boys back at the ranch – how he'd come by the shiner – when he had returned to the outfit and dropped his trail bag at the home bunkhouse.

Rail shipment and the great central terminals began to give way to movement of cattle to market by trucks and after World War II, country auction barns sprouted up, it seemed, in very nearly every little wide spot on the road. By the early 1960s, the big "18 wheelers" were becoming the rig to haul cattle to market points. The big city stockyards were closing down and the packing plants which had been numerous around them were, one-by-one, becoming vacant, as meat processing operations started to consolidate away from the big metropolitan areas. The 18 wheel tractor-trailer trucks became more sophisticated and today most are "look-alikes" of shiny diesel powered, sleepered, chromed, pin-striped, clearance-lighted, aluminum "potted" double decked efficiency. Like the great central markets, a railroad "cattle car" can't be found hardly anywhere in Montana, or anywhere else in cattle country.

Oh, the railroads still haul country freight, all right. In place of cattle cars and cabooses, 56, 100, or 110 car "unit-trains" will carry Montana wheat or barley to the Clarkson-Lewiston inland sea-port docks or "Mr. Peabody's" coal to distant power generating plants. Instead of endless tracks of iron the rails are now massive snake-like ribbons of continuous welded steel and there aren't any country "whistle-stops" anymore. Talk about lonesome. To be able to hear again the distant steam whistle and pistons "chugga-chugga-chugga" of an old fashioned steam locomotive coming, seemingly, from forever away, then rushing by, fading, just as forever, the other direction. All during this a Western Meadowlark cheerfully tried to outsing the train whistle, while you sat on your horse waiting to open the gate. No hurry, the boys were holding the cattle back aways, and you didn't try to hurry spooky cows over a crossing ahead of an oncoming train. The Meadowlark was claiming the top of the gatepost anyway!

"That would be livin' – no – that would prob'ly mean you'd died an' gone to Heaven, since that combination of sounds would likely never grace a cowboy's ear again," Connie thought to himself. And like he had said before, when he did take that last jog over the horizon, he hoped his "Home would be in Heaven, but I'm not homesick yet!"

Nowadays, when Fall roundup and shipping time came, you usually either loaded the weaned calves or yearlings up and hauled them to one of the remaining local livestock auction rings, of which approximately a dozen and a half still provide a market service in the state of Montana. Or you dealt with one of a number of "order buyers" who'd buy cattle at your ranch in the country, usually, on behalf of a third party, possibly a mid-western feeder.

Conditions of such a sale often include, besides delivery date, an agreed price per pound (often with a weight-break, which translates into a discount against heavy calves over a certain weaning weight), weighing conditions stipulated (such as, overnight stand, off feed and water to "shrink" them, or a 2% or 3% "pencil-shrink" subtracted from actual off-the-scale weight), and shipping arrangements (who orders trucks and pays freight). If you are not careful, any investment you have made in improved genetics or improved management, to get bigger, better weighing calves, can end up as a benefit only to the buyer or commission man. If there is a little profit to be made or an improved margin, it seems the guys who lived with that coupon since the old cow delivered it at calving time should get first crack at it!

More and more, Connie knew some ranchers were looking at the option of some means which would allow retained ownership of that calf further down the pipeline chain.

This was not without its moments of excitement, either. One rancher he knew in another area of the state had gone the route of partnering his calves into a custom feedlot, and the arrangement this man had made had worked out well to keep him, the custom feeder, and both their bankers happy. In another situation, things hadn't gone so well and everybody was unhappy! This rancher had said, "I couldn't have gone broke quicker if I'da rehearsed it!" It all took planning. It is interesting to consider, when talking to honest, bona fide businessmen at extreme ends of the beef marketing chain, how much difference there may be in a similarly sounding statement made by each.

The rancher will say, with all honesty, "We made a little headway this year – realized a profit which our accountant tells us translates into a whole half of one percent on our investment in ranch, cow herd, equipment, feed for winter, overhead and operating costs – we did okay." The retailer, equally candid, quotes a similar percentage figure. He's selling T-bones and hamburger, and chuck roasts. The rancher was selling weaned calves. The rancher rolled his dollars one time in 12 months. The store operator rolled his on the average of one time every 5 to 6 days. Some difference in the handling of the details of the given opposite ends of the pipeline. Connie equated the pipeline to being more funnel-shaped, with the small end pointing up, and being the end lots of ranchers were attempting to pour their operation through. The profits were what dribbled through the center and the losses were what so easily shed down the outside. "About time to take a new hold on the contraption," he figured. "Don't pay to pound sand down the same 'rat hole' for very long!"

Refreshed, after a good sleep under his own roof, Connie was up next morning at his usual early hour. After a couple cups of coffee and a telephone call or two to visit with cattle buyers, checking on the market situation, and a call in response to a neighboring rancher's inquiry about laying in the winter's supply of cow "cake" supplement, he walked out to find Blue soon as it was light enough to see. He saddled up and rode out to have a look at things. Going up the trail on the ridge leading past the flag, he paused on that little pinnacle for a moment to watch the sunlight spill across the meadows below. His eye caught the flit of a whitetail doe and her fawns as they faded into the willows with the shadows retreating from the morning sun.

The Connie Cox Family – Casey Cox, holding Cassidy, Diane, Connie with Tia Coleman, Margie,

Tip Coleman, Charlene Cox Coleman with Cash Coleman, Clinton and Denise Cox.

The warmth of the sun felt good as the first rays touched his old battered hat and his shoulders. The September early morning air had the definite chill of impending Fall about it, but the day would be warm. Connie never tired of seeing the deer, nor of seeing the funny little patterns that swished through the now yellow and reddish leaves of the willow thicket as a faint zephyr stirred through the branches, trying but failing to become a whirl-wind. It wanted to do a fancy whirling dervish dance across the creek bottom, but at this early hour could only muster enough action to do the slightest curtsy to the bobbing willow twigs as it scurried away.

The early morning breeze was really just a little bustle as it made a light flurry against the flag above his head. There was the faintest "fop-fop--fop" noise rustling against the beauty of it in the morning light, but the wind could not create sufficient ado to get the banner unfurled. Connie sat for a little while longer, heedful of a number of sentiments which the flag stirred in him even if there were not enough breeze to stir the flag. He thought about his family and the serenity of the homestead below, still in the shadow of the ridge upon which he and Blue were soaking in the sun. Maybe one of the benefits to look forward to out of the Legacy of the Cattle Drive would be added opportunity for Montana's young people to find more meaningful livelihoods of their choosing here in the state, if this rural endowment effort worked the way he believed it was being envisioned. Montana certainly needed to take a back seat to no one when it came to the quality of education generally available at all the various levels in the state to date, but as the sparse rural communities appeared to be getting even farther off the beaten path, he knew the ability to maintain this quality was a concern. Of equal, or actually, greater concern to all people of Connie and Margie's generation was what the generations of Casey, Clinton, and Charlene's ages and of their children and beyond were NOT finding in the way of favorable, or affordable, vocational circumstances to enable many of them to build their lives and futures here in Montana.

Indeed, this concern translated into a fact that one of Montana's greatest exports had to be her young people. Montana could educate them, but many then had to go elsewhere to find productive employment, or obtain business or professional endeavors of merit. If ways could be generated to add value to Montana's many resources which were of a primary nature, including all her agricultural productivity, and to be able to do this by innovative means here within the state, Connie knew many of Montana's young people would prefer to live and work and rear their families here. Lots of home fires would glow a great deal more brightly if such were the prospect which they could look forward to. Connie wondered how many of Montana's financial leaders would get behind the Legacy effort as envisioned by the Cattle Drive and Community Foundation leaders, or how many of them were status quo complacent in their self-satisfaction with things as they existed for them because of gains which had been placed to their advantages by the generations which had preceded them.

He knew there were many resources in the state that aggressive and imaginative economic development endeavor had not been applied to, and there were those which, conversely, had received such attention only to have failed to produce the desired results. He guessed he needed to know more about the "whys" and "hows" and hoped the rural development endowment might be a serious determined effort resulting in some answers to these questions for himself and others like him. With the talk of free trade and expanding export markets, the formation of economic development authorities, and foreign trade missions coming to visit Montana, it seemed that more effort should be expended to "act locally" along with, and maybe as a prerequisite to, "thinking globally."

This was one of the things which influenced his thinking in a very positive way about his involvement with the genetics improvement program outlined for a cow herd such as his by BEEFBOOSTER™ Cattle, Ltd. Even though Connie knew he was just scratching the surface with these first M_4 bulls he was using in his commercial beef breeding program, he felt enough homework had been done to make this group and their seedstock a combined entity that he could depend on being there for a long time in the future. He could see the trail ahead as one offering him some options in value added opportunities for his operation. Expanding or broadening his marketing options was just one possibility. As he and enough other commercial ranchers expanded the utilization of these proven bulls and the pool of performance predictable calves could be traced back to this genetics improvement source, he could see some real benefit to mutually coordinated numbers, if not a downright safety net.

As Connie loped Blue in an easy gait off down the other side of the ridge, his reflections of the moment were very happy ones. It was good to be home and the bends in the trail as he viewed it this morning represented challenges which excited his free spirited nature. If he could draw a similarity between the accomplishment of this great fun adventure he had just experienced for better than the past month, "The Big Drive," and the challenges he felt were out there on the horizon ahead, that likeness would be that most anything could be possible and made to work, if planning and coordinated efforts were approached with a similar dedication and enthusiasm. There would be unknowns around some of the bends, but working in concert with other like-minded hands had some distinct advantages. One, somebody else may have already rounded the bend or traversed a rough crossing and could signal back a better or safer approach. Another, "many hands make light work," had always been a favorite expression among Connie's sayings, and a shared task of dealing with problems could render those problems more tractable, giving you more capability of solving them beneficially.

Blue carried Connie quickly and effortlessly through the hours and their day's circle brought them in a clockwise swing, which had them go in just a little while from their initial vantage point topped with the American Stars and Stripes to a northerly by northeasterly direction, and then east a ways along the ranch north fenceline. This was the U.S. – Canadian border, the friendliest fenceline in the world. Connie had neighbors closer in Saskatchewan than he did in Phillips County, and closer than several of his Valley County neighbors. After riding a little ways along the 49th Parallel, Connie swung Blue towards the south through the breaks and back towards the west where the breaks descended into the meadows through which Frenchman Creek meandered its way below the ranch headquarters on its way to the southeast.

He was always fascinated by what he saw along the banks and bluffs that rimmed the breaks into these bottoms. They came by the old weathered shack and tumbledown corrals which some of Connie's hunter friends used as a focal point each October and November. It wouldn't be long before it'd be that time again. There was an old relic of some type of wagon running gear with the remains of a weathered wooden wheel sporting the ostentatious display of a brightly fuchsia colored and fresh scent saturated wild primrose nestled in a sensual love affair against the iron clad symmetry of the gray grained old hub and splay of broken spokes. The rusty rim which had once upon a time held the wheel tightly together as it bumped over ruts and rocks or stumps and took the jolts from, perhaps, thoroughbrace cradled carriage suspended above, now lay bent and twisted askew and half buried by the sands of time. Connie wondered whether the wheel relic and its mates had carried travelers or mail or maybe just some needed supplies, and which direction it might have been going, up or down, as it followed Frenchman Creek along. The sweet smell of the primrosebuds and panicles of ivory yucca blossoms in Spring, along with blooming sage, were Connie's favorites. Some called the yucca spires "The Lord's Candles," and the term fit. Now the rose petals were giving way to hips, laden with pungent rose-oil which would hold that aroma of Spring and Summer, through now and right on into wintertime.

Riding by the petrified remains of what had obviously been some type of enormous tree, Connie wondered what had been the dominant animal and plant life forms making up the biographic zone of this area. It would have had to have been, relatively, a much moister era than it usually was now or apparently had been for centuries, since what now lay as fragmented giant stony logs once had stretched tall as a magnificent tree.

Maybe Dr. Draper was correct and some sort of aquatic crustacean life had been able to ply along in deeps in some ancient time where now the whitetails and pheasants enjoyed a flourishing life in the protection of the willow thickets along Frenchman Creek. Perhaps the apocalyptic expectations of some early century Montanists could prophetically forecast some sort of schismatic disharmony which would ultimately dictate the destiny of the world. Montanism was supposedly an early Indo-European Christian sect which stressed the continuing prophetic gifts of the Spirit and strict ascetic discipline. Decisive climactic changes had, without a doubt, taken place between the time of the tree life which had preceded these petrified logs and the time of the dusty tracks rutted by the now brittle, and who knew, maybe also petrifying carriage remains and broken spokes of the wagon wheel. Perhaps there was more meaning to Montana's name than just "Mountainous Regions!"

I'm Proud To Be An American and Thankful to Be A Free Spirit In This Montana Land!

As Connie and Blue moseyed happily along the trail up the creek toward home, the only clouds visible in the sky were the criss-crossing of several jet contrails as they caught the light of the sun now declining toward the bright westerly horizon. The breaks and rims ahead in the direction of the setting sun were already taking on the blue-purple colors of deepening shadows as the day was passing. Tomorrow they'd have to go over west by Turner in Blaine County and check on the pairs over there. As he watched the contrails fanning out and evaporating into the azure blue of the afternoon sky, Connie wondered at the prospects of being able to load selected replacement heifers pregnant with selected genetically superior embryos on those jets in Great Falls and being able to send them over those contrail tracks to places that needed them the rest of the world over. Better yet, why not ship fresh or frozen beef already processed to feed the hungry? Lots to ponder; still if he had a preference of the kind of star to hitch his wagon to, he'd most likely think longingly of a 4- or 6-up constellation that could pull a rocking-rolling shiny coach of the Concord variety. Yep, there were plenty of happy trails and bright horizons for tomorrow. Right now the home fireside beckoned!

. . . . Looking for a "4- or 6-up" galaxy of stars to hitch his wagon to.

– Endless Tracks Across Centuries

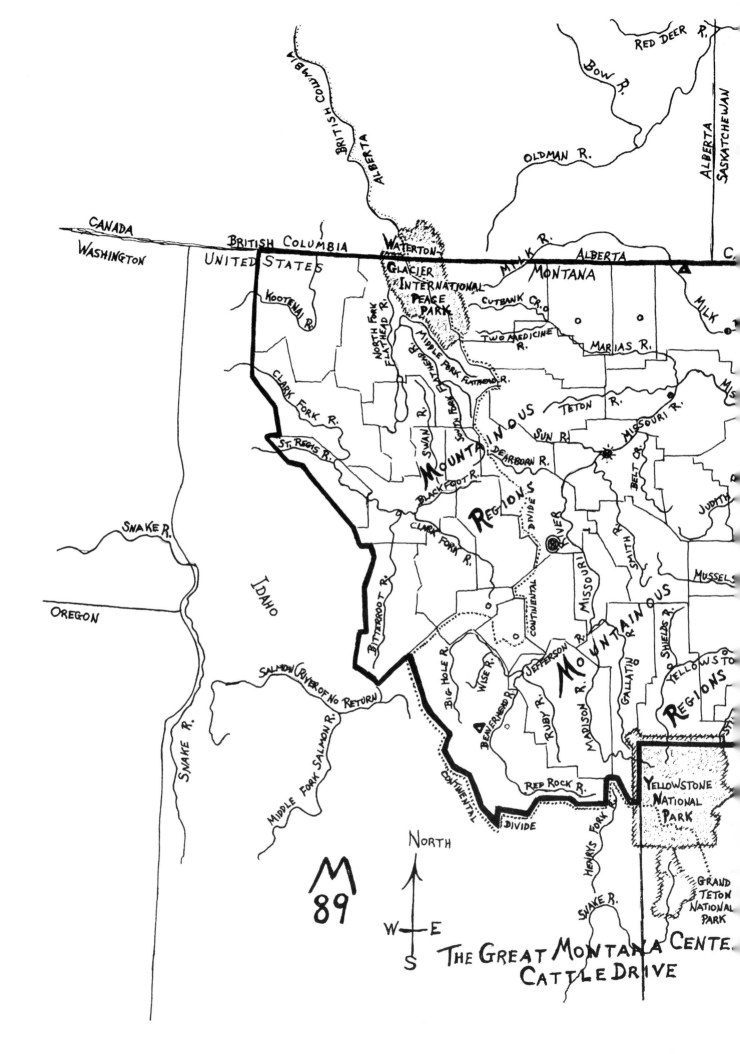

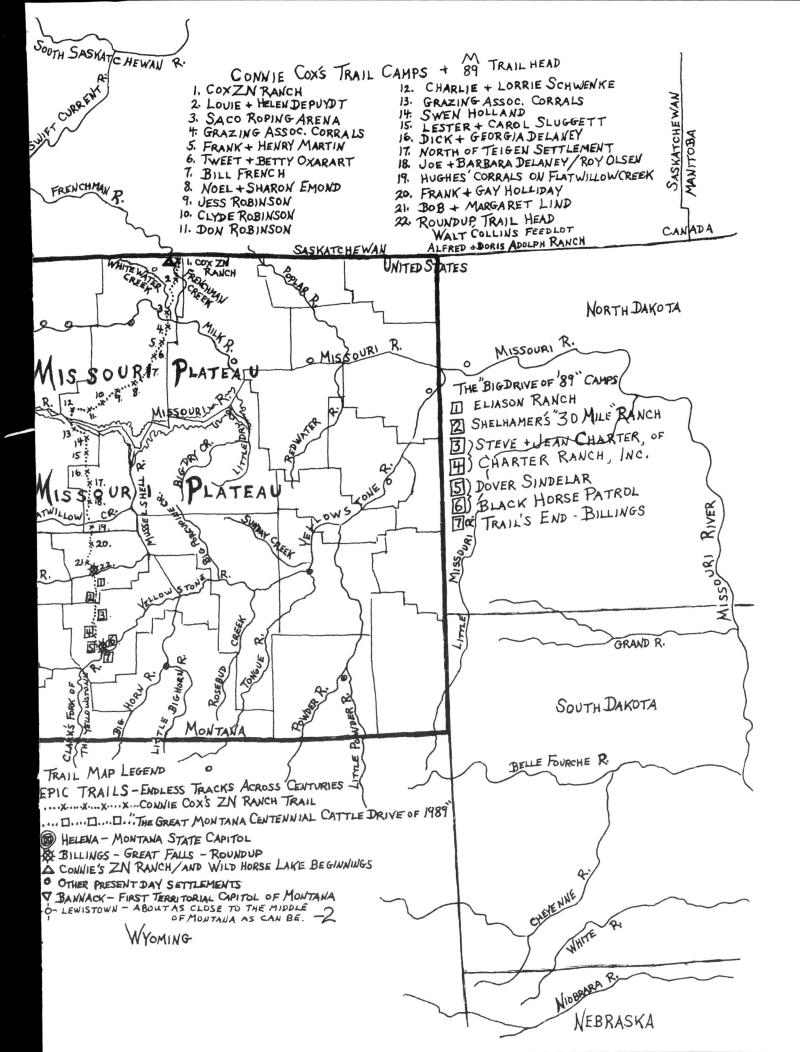

CONNIE COX'S TRAIL CAMPS + $\overset{M}{89}$ TRAIL HEAD

1. COX ZN RANCH
2. LOUIE + HELEN DEPUYDT
3. SACO ROPING ARENA
4. GRAZING ASSOC. CORRALS
5. FRANK + HENRY MARTIN
6. TWEET + BETTY OXARART
7. BILL FRENCH
8. NOEL + SHARON EMOND
9. JESS ROBINSON
10. CLYDE ROBINSON
11. DON ROBINSON
12. CHARLIE + LORRIE SCHWENKE
13. GRAZING ASSOC. CORRALS
14. SWEN HOLLAND
15. LESTER + CAROL SLUGGETT
16. DICK + GEORGIA DELANEY
17. NORTH OF TEIGEN SETTLEMENT
18. JOE + BARBARA DELANEY / ROY OLSEN
19. HUGHES' CORRALS ON FLATWILLOW CREEK
20. FRANK + GAY HOLLIDAY
21. BOB + MARGARET LIND
22. ROUNDUP TRAIL HEAD
    WALT COLLINS FEEDLOT
    ALFRED + DORIS ADOLPH RANCH

THE "BIG DRIVE OF '89" CAMPS

1. ELIASON RANCH
2. SHELHAMER'S "30 MILE" RANCH
3. STEVE + JEAN CHARTER, OF CHARTER RANCH, INC.
4.
5. DOVER SINDELAR
6. BLACK HORSE PATROL
7. TRAIL'S END - BILLINGS

TRAIL MAP LEGEND
EPIC TRAILS - ENDLESS TRACKS ACROSS CENTURIES -
....x....x....x....x.... CONNIE COX'S ZN RANCH TRAIL
....□....□....□.... "THE GREAT MONTANA CENTENNIAL CATTLE DRIVE OF 1989"
HELENA - MONTANA STATE CAPITOL
BILLINGS - GREAT FALLS - ROUNDUP
CONNIE'S ZN RANCH / AND WILD HORSE LAKE BEGINNINGS
OTHER PRESENT DAY SETTLEMENTS
BANNACK - FIRST TERRITORIAL CAPITOL OF MONTANA
LEWISTOWN - ABOUT AS CLOSE TO THE MIDDLE OF MONTANA AS CAN BE. −2

THE BADLANDS

Have you ever seen the badlands?
Where the Frenchman River flows?
The mighty beef herds wander . . . .
And the diamond willow grows?

The waving flats of blue joint
Are a sight for any eye . . .
The hills that guard forever
Standup, rugged, next the sky.

They have not the painted beauty
Of our Nation's mountain parks,
For the stumps are old and petrified,
Withered, grey and dark.

There's something strange about their beauty
The blue haze and the tan.
It roots itself forever
In the heart of every man.

For they've shunned the brunt of ages,
Through generations, they have stood,
And a tale of many pages
They would tell you if they could.

They've seen the redskins fading . . .
They've seen the buffalo fall
They've seen death in the river,
And stood and watched it all.

They've bedded down the Longhorn,
When his time came to pass,
The draft horse and the hot bloods,
Munch the upland grass.

Then the Angus and the Hereford,
In their joy and their pride,
Like kings of a mighty empire . . .
Roam up and down their sides.

When the Angus and the Hereford,
Give away to something new,
I'm sure they'll still be standing
With their heads high in the blue.

For often in my travels,
Before the door of time does close,
I'll think of that wild country
where the Frenchman River flows.

Poem written by John D. Munn
Courtesy of Ed Ostlund, and
reprinted in EPIC TRAILS with
the author's permission